Michele ~
Love and blessings
always ~

Stronger

KATHY CRABB HANNAH

HANNAH HOUSE
PUBLISHING

DEDICATION

This book is dedicated to Steve Hannah, the most loyal man I know.

CONTENTS

ACKNOWLEDGMENTS

For many years I have known that I would one day write a book. The Lord confirmed this several times, and I knew it would happen; I just didn't know when. I knew I wanted to put on paper my vivid memories. I wanted to write it myself, be it right or wrong. I wanted to own the story with my words and my voice. After all, it was *my* story.

During the first week of November 2014, the Lord instructed me in specifics. He said, "Go to a mountain, I will meet you there." I know this sounds a bit super-spiritual. However, this is exactly what happened. I went to the mountain. I poured my heart out to Him for days upon days. I talked. He listened. I cried a river of tears during those days on that mountain with God, and I wrote 90,000 words. Some of these were gut-wrenching chapters, but together, WE did it.

I pray that as you walk through my life, my journey, you will be encouraged and realize that you too will make it through this thing called life. This literary journey is candid, a bit raw, and packed full of "God" moments. I pray you will read it, be encouraged, and understand that what doesn't kill US truly makes us stronger.

I want to thank my husband and my entire family for walking this road with me. Thanks for your gentle patience and undying support. Thanks for reading and rereading. I am blessed to know you, and more blessed to call you mine, each of you.

I want to thank my friends, who have loved me when times were good and loved me when times were bad. You know who you are and you know how much I love you. Some of you have been around for 50 years. Some of you have seen the good, the bad, and the ugly, yet you loved me. Thank you. This book happened because you kept telling me I could do this!

Teresa Schweinsberg has stunned me with her tireless effort. She worked around the clock and poured her love into these pages. Thanks to Brian Hudson for your rich 20-year friendship, your honest advice, and your ability to keep me sane when the world unhinged. Thanks to Micah Schweinsberg for your photography and cover design. I always stand amazed at the depth of your talent, and you didn't disappoint. Hair and make-up was done by the talented Eden Nicole; this girl works magic. Linda Warren, you have been an amazing friend and proofreader. You are *all* special to me. Thank you for sharing your gifts.

STRONGER

FOREWORD

"Let each of you look out not only for his own interests, but also for the interests of others."
—Philippians 2:4

I first met Kathy (Crabb) Hannah about 20 years ago at a Christian music function in Nashville, Tennessee. Her young family group was hot and gaining steam faster than anything I had seen in a long time. However, something was different about them. Yes, they had incredible talent, contagious charisma, and stirring songs, but they also had questions. They wanted to learn how to be more effective. They were like sponges when given advice—they soaked it up. They were confident, yet humble. They knew where they wanted to go and they were willing to ask for help to get there. I knew this was special and I was anxious to learn more about this family from Kentucky.

My observation is that success can best be described as a random concoction of talent, ambition, work ethic, communication savvy, negotiation prowess, a healthy appetite for risk, and an intentional focus on your goals. Now, add to this the gifts and calling of God that are without repentance, a Spirit-led anointing, the faith to be obedient when God tells you to take a chance, a praying mother, and a powerful song, and you have what the world came to know as the Crabb Family.

It can be said, with all sincerity, that a force of nature rarely comes along that uses its tireless energy and enthusiasm to further the careers of others like Kathy does. She has cheated death more than once—both emotionally and literally—and continues to flourish as the ultimate picture of strength and resilience. Somehow in His wisdom and as a part of His bigger story, God allowed our paths to intersect at pivotal times— for both of us. To be in the inner circle of this ministry was to be welcomed into their family. They made me feel like family, like one of them. We encouraged each other. We coached each other. We prayed for one another. We spoke truth into each other's lives, and as iron sharpens iron, we have become better ambassadors of the goodness and faithfulness of God as a result. Kathy taught me that hard work, persistence, professionalism, patience, and prayer still play a role in the life God wants me to lead, regardless of my calling. She taught me about self-sacrifice and that if I worry less about who gets the credit as long as God gets the glory, we unzip Heaven and blessings begin to fall from above. She taught me to live a life of generosity toward my family, my friends, and my cause.

So I now encourage you, the reader, with these lessons from Kathy. It's cliché, but Kathy is going to tell you that you are indeed blessed to be a blessing to others. Go live that life. Find others to encourage, coach, pray for, and speak truth to. Invite them into your family, like Kathy invited me, and know that if God gives you the chance of a lifetime and you take it, you will never be disappointed.

Brian Hudson
President, Showcase Media & Management

1 MOMMA

In typical Kathy fashion, I have just polished off a piece of birthday cake for breakfast. The cake was so generously delivered to my daughter Kelly's tour bus last night by a Facebook follower who knew about my cake addiction. One of the perks of being on a tour bus is the amazing food people randomly bring, and one of the joys of my life has been to sit on a bus with family and drink in the friendships of those that come bearing cakes and such. Last night was one of those nights. So today I had my eggs, flour, and butter for breakfast. It just happened to be in the form of cake with buttercream icing—you know, the white birthday cake that is sinful from the first bite to the last. A piece of cake and a can of Diet Coke is what I would consider my "breakfast of champions."

My view is that of the last golden, orange, and butterscotch-colored leaves falling from my lush backyard, which is more like a cliff with a balcony hanging high over the base of the trees. I am perched here in my favorite "cat" gown, which happens to be *the* gown that has seen it all, been there for the drama, the tears, and the good times too. I've had it for at least a dozen years and at least a million tears. So it seems only right that I wear it while I attempt to finish my story. I am staring at the face of the mountains and I feel God looming in the distance, sending me gentle breezes. It is a cool morning, and will be a 65-degree day by noon. It is perfection, but what else would I expect?

I sit in a rocker that looks a hundred years old, and instantly my mind becomes drenched in memories. I can close my eyes and see my momma. She was 5'2"—which is stretching it, in my opinion—and about 110 pounds, though she may tell you 105. She dressed amazingly chic in her younger years, wearing lots of pencil skirts and belts (to show off her 19-inch waist). She was a health nut before it was en vogue to be one. She didn't go to the gym (we didn't have gyms), but she walked every day, rode a stationary bicycle, and would lie on the floor while talking on the phone to her buddies and do leg lifts the entire time. She was one of a kind.

I close my eyes and I can hear her high-pitched voice. No one had tones like my momma. She could shatter glass and make dogs howl and cover their ears. Sometimes I did the same thing. This morning, I can hear her singing about the blood and the cross, and the power we had in the blood. She sang about the power and you believed her. You believed that her shrill voice and that old radio could point you straight to Jesus! For in those days Momma, Jesus, and that big radio were larger than life to this 5 year old. Music, Jesus, and Momma have molded me.

In the eye of my 5-year-old memory, I can see her scurrying around a little "hard rock" maple breakfast table in our kitchen, complete with red checked ruffled cushions, singing that song and a half dozen other Chuck Wagon Gang favorites, all the while working to ready some unknown concoction she was cooking. She was doing all this and ironing, too. She was always ironing. She would set her ironing board up in the dining room and iron for hours, putting that old radio on a gospel station that came out of Munfordville, Kentucky. We would try to guess what song would be the featured song of the day. She always picked a Chuck Wagon Gang song. That radio—you know, the huge ones that had knobs as big as Oreos—well, that radio would be instrumental in shaping my life. The early seeds planted through the music would prove to be the seeds that got pushed down to the depths of my soul, down into that fertile soil that is called life. *That* seed would bring forth fruit, good fruit, generational fruit. I learned to love a song. I made songs a priority, always.

Singing, hurrying, *and* ironing … that was my momma, and she always talked on the phone. She loved a phone. She had a BFF back in those days. Her name was Chlorine, pronounced Corine. She and Chlorine were great friends, but Momma was always rushing, and Chlorine was typically trying to get Momma to relax and chill out. They spent many days zooming to their destination in that little Volkswagen that Momma drove. Chlorine talked with her hands, but Momma listened with her heart. They truly had a life-long friendship. I am thankful that Momma taught me to make friends and keep them. These two are buried side by side in a Kentucky cemetery. My dad is on one side, Chlorine on the other. Yes, they planned it that way.

Momma met Chlorine at church. They were a lively pair in many ways. Chlorine was the more vocal of the two, unless you were talking about Jesus. When the Jesus talk started, Momma cranked it up! Momma believed in Jesus and would tell you if you talked to her more than five minutes that you need Him, too. She attended small, independent churches. She had a firm grip on healing and believed in it 100%, but she didn't embrace the Pentecostal doctrine. She believed in "Jesus name baptism," but she didn't believe in speaking in tongues.

What she believed was unusual, but hey, that's okay; it worked for her. She planted Jesus in us at an early age. I didn't smoke. I didn't want to. I didn't drink. I didn't want to. I didn't smoke pot. I didn't want to. I also had this built-in thing. Some would call it a "goody-goody" factor, but I call it reverence for Momma. I always felt that she was vulnerable and that my bad behavior would devastate her. Of course, I was less than perfect, but I typically confessed immediately and told on myself. Momma kept the guilt meter turned up pretty high at all times. I suppose the psychological factors of this are a bit negative, but it kept me out of jail, rehab, and the abortion clinic. I colored inside the lines.

I did make some horrible choices, but they were unopposed choices. There were no adults speaking into my life. No one sat me down and said, "Kathy you are loved. You are smart. You are pretty (I don't think I was pretty, but someone should have lied). You matter. You have a future. Stay in school. Stay disciplined. Let's choose a life path for you!" No one said that to me.

My dad died when I was 13. He had a massive heart attack that left me fatherless within a 60-second time span on a Sunday afternoon in 1969. Boom: he was gone. No more chances to ask him questions, no more chances to ask him how much he loved me, whether I mattered, what he wanted for my life. Gone. In the amount of time it takes to fix yourself a glass of water, he was gone. However, back to Momma and Jesus for now. I will get to Daddy later. He is his own story.

Momma took me to church on what seemed like eight nights a week. We went to a lot of storefront churches and white country churches with potbelly stoves and creaky plank floors that had that certain smell and a certain gleam from the decades of wear and tear. I used to sit there and wonder how the women looked in their dresses back in the "roaring twenties" and how the music sounded back then. No doubt it hadn't changed much, for these churches were the old-fashioned "Power in the Blood" churches, with the last verse sung 15 times on a *slow* night. By the time I was 9, I was pounding out those three-chord songs. Evidently, there was a shortage of piano players back then. I would sit and play on an old upright, out-of-tune piano, for *no one* had their piano tuned back then. If you factor in the weekly freezing temperatures when there was no one building a fire in the stove, well, just imagine how *out* of tune that baby was!

Anyway, I pounded on those awful instruments, sometimes with a guitar player, sometimes with a dozen guitar players. In those days, even visitors would come "be with you," carrying in a guitar case and a notebook full of songs and saying, "Well I didn't come to sing, but in case I was asked, I wanted to be prepared!!" This would be followed up with, "Don't listen to the way I *sang*, I ain't no *sanger*, but listen to the words!" I never understood why they would say this instead of letting the "real" singers sing, but I kept my sarcastic comments to myself.

In my 9-year-old mind, I was thinking, "If *you* say you're not a singer, what do you think *we* are going to say, and *why* are you taking up time when there are a dozen *good* singers in the crowd?" Yes, I was an early bloomer when it came to sarcastic comments in my mind. I was also learning to be a straight talker at an early age. Lord, help!

However, in the end, I learned about the "touch" of God that just seems to come down and wash over a service and mesmerize everyone. I learned that some nights are about conviction, confession of sin, and the Spirit drawing the lost. Then I learned that sometimes there's a special "sing it until you get the victory" song for those who have had all they can take and *must* get the victory. The eloquent may do it differently, but in Kentucky in the early sixties, we sang ourselves happy. It worked. We used it instead of medication and alcohol. Novel idea, huh?

My momma wasn't perfect, but she was close enough. She loved me with all that was within her. She was entirely too passive after my dad died. She checked out. She moved 100 miles away, and I was left behind to live like a sad little gypsy. I just wanted a home, warm food, and, most of all, to be normal. It wasn't to be. The years from 13 on would involve bad choices and many mistakes that were rooted in being a "lost little girl" and feeling like I didn't belong. I felt a bit alone, like I wasn't worth much, and never felt pretty enough. However, because my momma had planted Jesus, *He* would be enough. Because she had this part right, I would survive. Lesson learned.

Many things weren't perfect in my life, but the Jesus message would be my anthem. It was buried deep inside me. It was enough. Generational? Yes. The Jesus message has been the one thing I have done right. Among the bad decisions I have made as a parent, the Jesus message survived. Yes, it's generational.

STRONGER

2 THE CREEK

I know it was February, and I know it was cold. I think it was the first Sunday of the month, a few days before my 10th birthday. According to my memory, it was about 30 degrees. The red-faced preacher in his starched white shirt told the congregation that he wanted to have a baptism, and he asked, "Who wants to go?" I found my skinny little arm popping up. I thought, *Did I just do that? What will Momma say? I know she will like the idea, but can she take me? Where will it be?*

Back in those days, there were no baptisteries in churches, so the man of God gave us directions to a remote creek within driving distance that he frequented for this sort of thing. He would gather the saints and bring the new converts for water baptism. I wanted to do this! I was almost 10. I thought that I was mighty close to adulthood. I mean, after all, Momma now let me pluck her eyebrows and tease her hair. I was the church piano player, too, at least most of the time. Didn't that make me old enough?

I was anxious for the singers and the testimonies about wayward children to stop and for the service to end. I wanted to ask Momma if we could go. After all, wouldn't a trip to the creek be the best day ever? Would that little part about the water possibly being icy make Momma start the whole "You will catch a cold" thing and say no? Hurry, people! Be done already! I want to get in that car and talk to Momma. He dismissed, finally.

We got in that cold car. Momma drove a VW bug, as always. She had many of them; Daddy bought her a new one every other year, and she would put 100,000 miles on it those 24 months. I would ride shotgun for most of those 100,000 miles, because by this time in my life my siblings were grown and gone. They were not a big part of our daily routine. I was, and will always be, the baby.

Anyway, that was my momma; Momma was always zooming

around in her bug and getting to every destination before anyone else. I think she had lead in her foot and probably made the angels nervous. I would say being Momma's guardian angel would have been a bit nerve-wracking as it related to her driving. She once pulled out in front of a semi, got hit by a train in her trusty bug, and put her car in reverse at a stop sign because she had pulled up too far. She was always in a hurry. She gingerly backed up, but when she accelerated to pull out, she had forgotten she was still in reverse and we *creamed* the car behind us. Yes, she had various other "bad judgment" accidents, too. That may be another chapter, or another book. Remember, this was before seat belts! Jesus took the wheel *a lot*. Truly, I should have written that song after growing up in a car that my momma was driving.

Anyway, we got in that little black bug, which was as cold as Alaska, and I said, "Momma, I want to be baptized today."

She said, "Yes! I will take you."

She stopped talking. We drove. I looked over and saw tears dripping from her face. We said very little. Momma really didn't talk a lot. She actually didn't talk enough, but on this cold Sunday, she said almost nothing. She just cried and drove. We got food. I don't remember what; it was probably very little food, because Momma didn't believe in eating much. Eventually, food would end up being my rebellion, my sin, and my weakness, but until I was grown and out of her home, I was a skinny girl. We ate very little. I think we stopped at a country grocery for gas and got crackers and a sweet. Momma did like a daily sweet. That was her weakness, but she was a portion-control queen, and the sweets were in small amounts. So it worked for her. She stayed thin until her death.

Anyway, the drive to that creek, pronounced "crick" by many country folk, was long. It seemed to take forever. I remember Momma being worried that my dad would be concerned, but there were no cell phones back then to let him know where we were, and we were out in the boonies! I remember coming around a bend and wheeling onto a dirt road. We were following church people. By this time the sky was a bit gray, at least for a minute, and I was starting to wonder just how cold that water would be. What would I wear home? This was unplanned, so I had nothing to wear that was dry. We didn't have a towel, not that I had thought that far ahead until now. I saw a few people getting out with towels. Our house was too far away for us to swing by after church as these folks had done. We lived a good 45 minutes from the church. But hey, Momma wasn't saying a thing about it, so neither did I.

The middle-aged preacher opened his Bible on the creek bank and began to talk about why this was a special day for those of us who had chosen to brave the cold, cold water. He began to talk about decisions that would make us all different and choices that would set us apart. I, for one, believed him. I somehow knew, as I looked up at the Kentucky sky on February 6, 1966, that this day wasn't just *any* day. In my 9-year-old mind, I began to understand destiny. It was the beginning.

The choir consisted of elderly women who had hair hanging down their backs and wore no jewelry or makeup. They would pray at the drop of a hat and drop the hat. They knew Jesus. One lady was blind, but when she sang, she sang the glory down. She was 100%. She didn't have a bad night. When she opened her mouth and started rolling the lyrics out, the rest was history; the spirit fell. In my opinion, she prayed so much that He was constantly with her. She didn't have to look for the Spirit; her constant companion was the Holy Ghost. They began to plunk out a C chord on an old guitar and sang, "Shall we gather at the river, the beautiful, the beautiful river?" That brave pastor beckoned us to come, us shivering men, women, and children who were to step into the 30-degree water and follow Jesus.

Immediately, I couldn't feel my legs. My breath became shallow. I wanted to cry, but I didn't. I waited my turn. I had never been this cold. I continued to wait. It seemed like days, but was probably less than five minutes. No one wants to stay in water that cold for long. That poor preacher persevered. No matter what you believe or agree with, you must admit the seriousness of his calling. He believed in the Gospel of Jesus Christ!

I was finally next. They placed a "spotter" behind me, and then the preacher took my little hand and asked, "Do you plan to follow Jesus?"

Somehow I got out a "Yes."

Then, he said, "God has His great big hand on you, and I want you to understand that as we bury you in this cold water, your life is going to change! I baptize you Kathy Jo Coppage in Jesus' name!"

Down I went, and I came up shouting. My momma didn't shout; my grandma didn't shout—we weren't shouters. But on this day, I shouted. I've shouted twice in my life, and this was the first time. I came up with arms lifted to glory, praising, and drunk on the spirit. It happened; I never forgot it. This experience is a brick in my foundation of *faith*. This "block" reminds me that sometimes He touches us when we are very young.

This memory stayed vivid to me in times of struggle, and when the enemy tried to say that I was crazy, I took him to that cold creek. When the devil asked why I would drag my kids around on a tour bus and waste their lives, I took him to the creek. When the choices of others cut through my heart and dragged my soul into a pit, I would remember the cold water and the realness of God. When the world turned dark overnight, I would remember. This was my genesis, my birth, the beginning of a long journey where everything would change and a new life began. Many times life would shift and change would unsettle me, but I would always return to the icy waters and remind myself that I was the girl in the creek, that I was the one that felt His touch. This *was* my cold-water experience.

The lesson here is that once Jesus touches you, you are *never* the same. You may be in a prison or a crack house; you may be lying under a man who has paid you for sex; you may be reading these words with your computer browser opened to pornography that has enslaved your mind. However, if you have ever been touched by Jesus, you are living with the knowledge of knowing that He is all you need. You know that. You can run, but you can't hide. You know that you need Him, and He is the only one who can deliver you.

Where was your creek? When was your "cold-water experience"? You know the one I'm talking about. Close your eyes and remember it. Remember the outfit you were wearing, the color of the carpet, the smells in the air, and the feel of the altar. Wherever you were, stop and remember it. It's the beginning of *your* story. Let the Jesus moments, not your failures, define you.

Back to the wet girl at the creek: we got in the bug that had almost *no* heat. I had on wet clothes and no towel. I was *cold*—I'm talking shivering, blue-lips kind of cold—but I survived. On the drive home, Momma cried some more. She told Daddy. He seemed emotional, but he said little. I still love Kentucky creeks. Now you know why. The next day there was no sore throat, no cold—nothing. I had been forever changed.

I wish Mom and Dad were sitting on this porch with me today. I would like to read them this story and ask them how they felt that day. I would like to hear their take on the story of their aggressive 9-year-old who insisted on being baptized in 30-degree weather in a creek. I would give all of my worldly possessions to hear their version of the story.

3 THAT SUNDAY

My dad always smelled a bit like motor oil and gasoline. He owned a pipeline construction company and worked from sunup until sundown. He was what one would call highly ambitious. He embodied the term "self-made man," having worked his entire life taking risks that others wouldn't, working harder than others would, and prioritizing "the job" and "the bid" over everything.

He was not a hands-on dad. He was never home; he worked *all* the time. However, my short 13 years with him are surreal as I think about the folk-hero image he embodies in my memory. I knew who he was. He said little, but did much. He exuded loyalty. Most of his family—cousins, brothers, and nephews—worked for his company. Were they the best choice? Maybe not, but he was loyal to a fault and was provisional to all. If Jean Coppage was involved, the money was good and the details were smooth. That's how he rolled. As a child, there was never a day I worried about money or security. I knew he had it. *He* was my security. I called him Dad or Daddy, depending on the situation.

It was March 2, 1969, and I was 13. I had on a yellow dress with wide sleeves that looked like the arms of an angel costume, only the dress was yellow crepe and was three or four inches above the knee. It was March, and I was *so* ready for something new to wear. Momma agreed, so we bought the dress. I liked it, but in reality it was probably dreadful.

We went shopping on Wednesday or Thursday of that week, and I chose this frock for a church dress. It looked a bit like something I had seen on TV, and I thought I looked like Goldie Hawn in it. That was when I was about 90 pounds and would brave any kind of fashion that covered up all my "stuff." Momma didn't allow no "stuff" to show, and I had no problem with that. All I know is that I was wearing it on Sunday because we were going to Brother Sosh's church in Louisville. It's possible that I would be asked to play the piano, and Momma thought a new dress would be a good idea. So, we bought it. We shopped on "the square" in Elizabethtown back in those days. We didn't have a Macy's, or for that matter, a mall. We frequented the locally-owned clothing stores on the courthouse square. Sometimes Momma would drop me off after school. I could go in and look, get a counter check, forge Daddy's name with no questions asked, and buy what I wanted. Some of you don't know what a counter check is. This was before the identity-theft days, when a checkbook to each local bank was available at the retailer's checkout counter. You filled in your account number and signed it—no computers, no phone calls. This was how it was. I was allowed to do this. Daddy didn't care. He was the most generous man I had ever known. I was always terrified of disappointing him; I don't think I abused it. He would possibly have a different story.

I cared deeply what he thought of me. This may have come from the fact that I was the "oops" child, born the year he turned 38. I was *that* child. I was so many years behind my siblings that I have few memories of living in the same house with them. I was the child who would never be called pretty, but always called bright, intelligent, and funny. I was the child who was always quick to have an opinion and an answer—that is, until my dad was in the room. He seemed larger than life, but he was only about 5'8" and 140 pounds at his heaviest. He talked very little, but when he spoke, oh my, I listened.

To say I spent lots of time with him would not be true. My parents didn't have a smooth relationship, and my mom seemed to migrate to weekends in Ohio County, where she would go to church. Dad found himself on the lake and at the airport on Sundays. He owned airplanes and boats. He was a bit adventurous, but my mother was anything but. This was the 50s and 60s. Women raised their daughters, and I wound up as my momma's shadow most of the time. Occasionally, Mom would go to the lake, but only after we had driven an hour and a half to church. I, too, like boats. I am not a huge fan of flying, but I do it when it's worth it, which is often.

My dad didn't speak much, as I said, and I didn't see him much, but I will always remember the things he said. My dad would occasionally pick me up from school, and every time he picked me up he would say, "I feel sorry for those poor kids in your class. How could anyone compete with a girl as smart as you?" I am not sure if he was bad at conversation and that was his go-to line, or if a part of him knew that I would need the confidence of an army general to make it through the life that was ahead of me. Another thing he always said to me was, "Make up your mind quick, and change it slow! Trust your first answer." This rule has shaped my life.

By the time I was 8 or 9 years old, I started to realize how unfair life was in my little school on Morningside Drive. I was a candidate to be a liberal based on this story. It was clear that the disparity between the children being dropped off at school in those huge tank-like Lincolns and the kids from Stand Pipe Hill who walked in the rain and the snow weighed on me. At lunchtime, it was more than I could handle.

In those days we didn't have free lunches. At least the kids at Morningside Elementary didn't have them. While we ate our grilled cheese sandwiches and no-bake cookies, other children ate very little from crumpled brown paper bags that were used over and over. Sometimes they brought cheese but no bread, because cheese was given as a commodity item, and had a long shelf life. Folks, this was before food stamps and EBT cards. The poor were delivered cheese, peanut butter, beans, and rice, but no bread and no perishables. Times were very different.

If you know me well, you know that nothing upsets me more than knowing that people are hungry. If you know me *really* well, you know that I am going to rectify hunger in my little part of the world. That cafeteria with the shiny tile floors on Morningside Drive became my first mission field. By the time I was about 9 years old, I was gathering up all of my classmates who couldn't buy a lunch every day. In the 60s, we were allowed to walk home for lunch, be picked up by parents, or walk to a little market and get a burger. We weren't scared of anything; it was the 60s and times were oh-so-different. So, because of this, one day I had an idea. Would *he* care? Uh, probably not. Oh well, it was worth the risk.

I would march my classmates up the little hill to the market on Miles Street, where we get could get six ham sandwiches in a bulk pack. They were made daily just for the school crowd, and my little friends loved them. Score! My friends loved the shaved ham and cheese sandwiches, which they guzzled down with the chocolate milk in cartons and Milky Way candy bars that I handed out on the walk back to school. They were all boys, and they were all "brown." They were hungry, and they always seemed to want my opinion. They didn't like white girls, but they liked me.

After this, I also soon learned that the market would let me charge a five-dollar bill to Daddy's business account. I was 9. I think this would have made him nervous, had he known. However, he didn't know. When I charged the five dollars, we could go across the street and get cheeseburgers and milkshakes for everyone for that five-dollar bill. We decided this was superior to shaved ham. So my friends ate, and my dad paid, though he didn't *know* he was paying.

Then one day Daddy said, "Kathy, Mr. Spicher said I have been paying extremely high monthly charges to the School Market on Miles Street." Mr. Spicher was the comptroller for my dad's construction company, and I lumped him in the same category with the devil. When his name came up, I got in trouble. "Your momma says she hardly buys anything at the market!" Dad quickly started explaining just how much I was spending. I remember thinking, *Holy cow, now what should I do?* He gave me that gaze that was more powerful than screaming and threatening, which he never did. Dad never raised his voice; I mean *never*. "The look" was powerful enough to make the truth spew out of my mouth.

I said, "Daddy, the little boys from Stand Pipe Hill live in houses without windows. They say they have cardboard over their windows. They are cold at night. They stay at school as long as possible because we have water fountains and heat. They don't have lunches. They are skinny and hungry."

"The look" softened, and Daddy asked, "Are they white or black?"

My self confidence had evaporated. I was scared, but I had to tell him the truth. I confessed, "Dad, they are black. They are my friends, and they are hungry! If they can't eat, I am not going to eat. I have been going to the market and getting money on your charge account so we can go across the street and get cheeseburgers and milkshakes."

He asked, "You do this every day? During your lunch break?"

I reluctantly replied, "Yesssss, Sir." I don't recall saying that I was sorry, even though I was technically stealing from my dad. I knew I was going to get it! I was in trouble. He had never spanked me in my life. It was coming. I cringed.

He said, "Do you realize how much money this is?"

I replied, "No, Sir, not really."

He continued to tell me that the amount I was spending monthly was more than our house payment. At that time, a school lunch was a quarter; I was spending 20 times that every day. Jesus help me. I was going to get a beating.

Dad walked toward me, put his arms around me, and said, "Kathy Jo, you're a smart girl." That was it. No lecture, no beating, no punishment. We never spoke of it again. Once or twice I overheard him tell employees about it. He would chuckle and describe my "creative" charging tactics that funded my "feed the friends" program. He always smiled, and I realize now that he loved my heart and my tenacity. He loved the "get up and do something" attitude.

I told him, "I won't do it anymore."

He retreated and said, "No, it's alright. I will tell Mr. Spicher to pay it. As long as it's during the school year, that's okay."

The cheeseburgers with my friends continued for years. One of those little hungry boys became a professional baseball player. When I saw the news story back in 1973, I rejoiced that he was leaving poverty behind, as I remembered his little skinny legs, those thick milkshakes, the best cheeseburgers in Kentucky, and a 9-year-old white girl who created a viable cash-advance system to feed the hungry kids. I was learning about the greater good! My dad was truly the hero. He allowed an environment of creativity and entrepreneurism to rank above staunch rules. He also allowed generosity to trump stinginess, always!

Looking at my dad now through the lens of a 59-year-old daughter on this side of life, I am pretty positive he was in the top five smartest people I have ever known. I am aware that dead people are perfect, but I think I nailed this one. He was one sharp cookie. He was self-taught, self-made, and owned a successful pipeline business. He didn't attend a single day of high school to my knowledge, but he never wanted for anything. He worked hard, always had a plan, and finished what he started. That's a pretty simple formula—and guess what? It's a timeless formula. This man who should have worn a suit every day wore a uniform so he could get his hands dirty when there was a crisis in a ditch. I think there must be a spiritual application here somewhere.

Anyway, back to the 13 year old and the yellow dress. It was Thursday, I think, when we bought the dress; Dad worked late so I didn't get to show it to him, and I went to school on Friday. After school on Friday, I begged Momma to let me spend the night with a friend. I stayed over until Saturday and begged to go to another friend's house to stay. Momma said okay to that too. She rarely said no to anything, and yes, a pattern was forming. She picked me up on Sunday morning. I had on "the" dress. I was sheathed in *all* my yellow glory. One of the small tragedies of this dress memory is that I looked dreadful in yellow. Oh, word. *Dreadful!* My hair was a coppery brown, I had freckles, and I didn't wear makeup at that age. Well, I was only 13, but I didn't start wearing makeup regularly until I was 25 or so. Someone should have told me how dreadful I looked! This was not a good look. But hey, I didn't get the memo. I thought I was *awesome* in that dress.

We drove to Louisville from Elizabethtown to church. I played the piano.

After church, we went to Anneta's, my oldest sister's, to eat. She got married when she was 16 and I was 2. She lived in Louisville at the time. She was 27 and had two boys, Marty and Ronnie, who were 9 and 10. Marty and Ronnie were more like siblings to me than Anneta was. I liked going to her house. She had food and she loved me. She was almost like a second mom to me and would prove to be my stabilizing force in later years. Anyway, on this Sunday she had cooked, and I was happy. Momma wasn't a great cook. Anneta was no Paula Deen, but she was a Godsend to a hungry 13-year-old who lived with Elaine Coppage, the queen of "that will make you fat, so we aren't going to eat it!" So all in all, a new yellow Goldie Hawn dress and lunch at Anneta's, where we would probably have mashed potatoes and rolls with butter (which Mom would never allow) made it a pretty good day. We ate and I played with my little niece Donna. We argued with the boys over what we were going to watch on TV. Then suddenly, with the simple interruption of one phone call, my life changed forever.

My entire life changed when that rotary dial phone rang. In that moment, my innocence was gone, for the voice on the other line would deliver a life sentence to this little girl. The Kathy Jo Coppage with *parents*, plural, became Kathy Jo Coppage with *parent*, singular. My dad had suffered a fatal heart attack. He was dead. He was 50. I had been 13 for two weeks. How was I supposed to do this?

I looked at the yellow sleeves and decided I hated this dress. In that moment, I started dreading Father's Day and his birthday. His birthday was next week. When did I see him last? *Oh, God! I can't remember when I saw Daddy last.* What had he been wearing? Was he eating eggs and sausage at the table in his blue uniform? *Please God, help me remember*, I prayed. *Why did I leave? Why didn't I stay at home so I could remember that last time? Why was my memory locked?*

Mom was in shock. As always, we got in the car and drove. The drive was only an hour, but it felt like it took days. The silence was almost more than my young mind could endure. I needed hugs, reassurance, explanations. *What was a heart attack? Why did this happen? Someone, please talk to me!* When we pulled up to our ranch style brick home that my dad had proudly custom built for Momma—that home on Navaho Drive in Elizabethtown, Kentucky, my home since I was 5 years old—it no longer seemed like home. I was suddenly alone. I didn't know what to do. Even though I was unaware, this day would be my initiation into the club of "the Strong." For on March 2, 1969, Kathy Jo Coppage had to get tough or die.

Upon arrival at our house, we were greeted by Dad's employees and their families. They informed us that he had been on the phone with an employee discussing a bid when the phone went dead. They immediately called for an ambulance to be dispatched to his office. They met the ambulance there. He had been taken to Hardin Memorial Hospital and they pronounced him dead on arrival. I have no doubt he left this world while sitting at the desk in his office on Highway 62, on the phone, trying to plan his Monday, his week, his month, his life. This was always rooted in his immense desire to provide amazing things for his family.

He didn't smoke or drink and wasn't overweight, but the doctors said it was heart failure. 45 years later, with the development of cardiac medicine, we know more. We speculated after my sister and I had failed valves and open-heart surgeries. The surgeons speculate that our valve problems are congenital. Now we understand. Daddy had a bad valve. Would things have been different today, with medical advances that might have been able to detect and treat his condition? There was *no* surgery in those days, so we lost him to heart failure. What would my life have been had he lived? Different? Yes. Better? Yes. But in the end, God is God, and He is good. I accept His decisions. I am not a victim, nor am I disadvantaged. Some people have no parents. I am blessed.

We chose a funeral home, a casket, a minister, and singers, and I chose a dress. It would be "the" yellow dress. No one asked why the 13-year-old daughter had on a bright yellow dress at her dad's funeral. The 13-year-old daughter wasn't sure why she had it on; she just felt like she should wear it. It looked like spring, like a daffodil. Daffodils made sense, for Mom told me that the night before Daddy died, he had privately told her that when spring came, the flowers would be blooming on his grave. It appears he knew. I wish he had told me goodbye, and I wish I could picture that last glimpse at that Coppage face, with its strong nose and big deep-set blue eyes. How I want to remember, but it never happens. I often ask God to make it happen, but it hasn't. But this 13-year-old daughter wore the daffodil-colored dress, hoped I looked pretty, and prayed that somehow Daddy knew how very much I loved him. Life would never be the same—not even close.

Here's my hope: Dad wasn't a big churchgoer, but he was a believer. It's complicated, and I won't spend time on this subject matter. All I will say is this: contrary to what many people will tell you, God is God. He is our judge, and His blood saves us; not works, not men, not our own righteousness. I will see my dad again. I hope there's a blue uniform company in Heaven, and I hope Daddy is wearing one when I get there.

Once again, how I know Daddy would love this view of the mountains I have while I write. He would probably want to go ziplining if he were here with me today. He loved to be above the trees and, for that matter, above the clouds!

Dad, if you can hear me, thanks for the gift of the adventurous spirit. Lord knows, with Elaine for a mom, we needed the gene pool to be livened up a bit!

4 43 STITCHES

I close my eyes and force myself to remember.

September 5, 1973.

The weather was mild. It was truly an Indian summer night in Hartford, KY. I was 17 and a newlywed. After all, it was Kentucky. Why was I married? That's a really good question—but the point is, I was. I had been married for three weeks. My husband was an older man. He was 19. I worked part-time for my sister at a high-end clothing store, and I had been a bit of a lost soul for many years.

Four years earlier, after my dad died, Mom had moved us back to various places in Ohio County and the stability factor evaporated. These four years are murky at best, and there was enough dysfunction to make the Kardashians look normal; not in a Hollywood-immorality kind of way, but in a "*Think* about what you're doing" kind of way! My dad's death did a number on my mom, which in turn did a big number on me. He was our stability. He was our income. He was always her voice of reason, and he was gone. Soon after he died, people moved in on her. She was *so* vulnerable. The buzzards were swarming, and they were toting Bibles. I won't give all of the details, but a gold-digger type moved in on Mom a couple of weeks after we buried my sweet dad. I was angry; I hated him. I created an enormous problem for them. I was a 13-year-old dependent child who didn't want *that* man in my dad's house. Mom had to provide me with a place to live, and I wasn't going to live with this man. When I saw him in my dad's chair, I became ill. When I came home from school to find that he had changed the name on our mailbox, I lost it. My dad had been buried less than a month and he was changing the name on our mailbox?! The buzzard was aggressive with his prey. My poor momma would eventually figure him out, but it took a few years, a lot of tears, and a small fortune to get rid of him. He extorted her, and I knew he was doing it. So did the rest of the family, but no one seemed to have the influence to make her see who this jerk really was, at least not for a while. She became somewhat naïve and childlike, while I became hard, quick on my feet, and a bit jaded. Life regressed. I will omit the details, but know that it was bad.

Consequently, I found myself in a mobile home, otherwise known as a trailer, in my Aunt Net's back yard. I was close to 14 and on my own, if my memory serves me correctly. Mom had plenty of money, but she had lost her ability to reason. She bought a house in Owensboro, then a different house in Elizabethtown, then the trailer for me to stay in. She bought this mobile home for me to stay in and put it in Centertown. All of this happened within a few months. She was lost. I was in and out of Aunt Net's care for about a year. Mom was going through something, and it was a deep something. We all have those times. She was human. The bad news was that she had a very dependent child who had to get tough or die. My world was gone. I had lived in the same house since I was 5; now it was gone. My dad now resided in the cemetery; my mom was living here, there, and everywhere while she was being used like a personal bank for a certain gentleman who claimed to be a minister, a "man of God" (pronounced "Gawd" by this arrogant, narcissistic man). He was more like a swindler than a gentleman. I knew he was spending our money, and so did my sisters and brother, but no one seemed to have the influence to make it stop.

So there I was, I was in a relative's yard, in a trailer, virtually alone. In a short year, the world had shifted. There was no gravity; there was no structure. My normal was oh-so-abnormal. I had no parents, no transportation, and no purpose. Life was out of control. But hey, I was a kid. I couldn't even drive a car. What was I *supposed* to do? As I think back, this was my first real experience with hypocrisy for profit. This man who hijacked my momma was the hypocrite from Hell who turned the "preacher voice" on and off as needed. He was a phony. My little heart felt guilty about the disdain I harbored for this man, but I knew too much. He was using us. He had a "script" and lived behind a facade. This would be like basic training for the little girl who would be used by many and loved by few.

If not for my Aunt Net's biscuits and fried chicken, there wouldn't have been much to look forward to in those days. She made sure I was safe. She had a house full of kids still at home, but she always loved and fed me. My Uncle Truman was a good singer and possibly the most humble man I have ever known. He promoted "good" singing and taught his kids, Bruce and Portia, to sing amazing harmonies with him. I know their life wasn't always easy in those days, but even so, you could always depend on hearing a good song and eating a good biscuit in that house.

Once again, a good gospel song was the highlight of my life. The next few years would be spent honing my minimal amount of talent by playing for an array of local gospel groups comprised of various friends and cousins in many combinations. When I had nothing, I had music. When no one was there to love me, I still had my Rambos albums. Many times the convincing lyrics would keep me grounded. I knew that there was too much to gain, too much to lose. Music was the medicine for my sick soul, my broken heart, and my orphan existence. Even when I was all alone, I had my songs. The pattern continued. Pain would be frequent, but great lyrics and soul-stirring melodies would be my friends forever.

Somewhere along the way, when I was a freshman (no, I am not kidding), it was decided that it was okay for me to quit school. This can't be blamed totally on me, but it can't be blamed totally on my mom either. She was passive, and I was probably clinically depressed, though that phrase was an unknown term in 1970 to folks in Centertown, Kentucky. Depressed people were called "sulky" or "hateful." We didn't have the medical profession encouraging us to help the mentally ill like we do now. I am not saying I was crazy. I wasn't. I was in need of a good counselor and some mentoring. My world was inverted and spinning. The shame of being a dropout nearly destroyed me in later years, but the truth will set you free, however it may shame you first. Anyway, I was a 14-year-old high school dropout with a relatively high IQ and nothing to do. In the meantime, my sisters Anneta and Linda decided to move the 100 miles to the area. This would be a game changer for me. Anneta was my oldest sister, and by this time she was approaching 30. She would prove to be the greatest influence on my life. She opened a retail business and gave me a job when I was 15.

Other kids my age were in school, but I worked, played piano, and listened to the Rambos, the Goodmans, and the Downings. I grew into a bit of a song critic. I didn't voice my opinions in that day, but I sure had them. This "song sense" would serve me well many years later. When I listened to these vinyl recordings, I felt God. I would listen to them all alone, in that little trailer, and I would feel the Holy Ghost. I cried; I always cried. The Holy Ghost makes me cry, always. That's okay. This 14-year-old girl who felt abandoned and ugly had learned that those tears somehow made me feel connected to a God who had placed this "tear factory" in my eyes. Those tears were so commonplace it was almost freakish, but somehow they attached me to the Holy Ghost. I knew the tears made me feel Him, and I was happy to own my tears; I still am. If the day ever comes that I don't cry, you should worry.

I regretted leaving school daily, but I was told repeatedly that I would have to start my freshman year over and be a year behind, which would be much too embarrassing. After all, the only thing I was known for was my intelligence. Well, so my daddy had told me since first grade. He had convinced me at least. So to be a year behind was not happening. Given that, my pride couldn't handle being a year behind. So I hatched a plan. In those days you could take your GED at 16, but you couldn't get your diploma until your class graduated. So I took the test as soon as I was eligible. It was easy. I passed, and truly, under my breath, had a lot of "na-na na-na boo-boo" moments when I saw other kids studying for finals and sweating homework. I knew that my diploma was waiting and that I could attend college if I chose to. I knew I could attend *anytime*, even when I was older. Once again, my untraditional approach worked, but it certainly wasn't the preferred route.

Now, let me tell you here and now, I don't recommend this path. It's dangerous. Crack houses are full of dropouts. Prisons are full of dropouts. However, let me make this point very loudly. Sometimes the four walls of a classroom are overrated. Sometimes life struggles, or gifts and opportunities, dictate a different path. Intelligence and education are not one and the same. Intelligent people aren't always educated, and educated people aren't always intelligent. Let me clear that up for some of you. Half of *all* college graduates this past year were unemployed. Graduating college doesn't necessarily guarantee a job. Many graduates are in minimum-wage positions with looming debt due to the cost of the education. I am not anti-education, but I am pro-common sense.

Anyway, back to my story: I was a 17-year-old high school dropout who had been married for three weeks. Remember, I had a job. I loved working, *always*. I was in my white Levis, driving my bright yellow 1973 Z28 Camaro (thanks, Mom!), and on my way to the laundromat to wash clothes. I felt pretty awesome. I was rocking those size-five white Levis. I still didn't feel like I was a pretty girl, but all in all, I have always had a self-confidence that leaves beauty in the dust. I am bright enough to know that people are drawn to confidence, and that has served me well. I was never the pretty girl in the room, but I was always the busiest girl in the room: no victim here.

While my clothes were washing, I decided to get a good ole Dairy Queen milkshake at the best Dairy Queen that has ever been: the one in Hartford, Kentucky. My friend Sheila was in the hospital, and I felt like driving a couple of blocks to check on her and bring her a milkshake. So with the normal swiftness of a 17-year-old who happens to be the "hurry-up" daughter of Elaine Coppage, I quickly got the shake and zoomed over to the hospital to see Sheila. I parked in the first spot by the front door. It was about seven o'clock. I went in, visited a bit, and then decided to go put my clothes in the dryer at the laundromat. Sheila had told me that she was a bit hungry, so I planned to grab her a cheeseburger from the Dairy Queen while I was out.

So, once again, in typical "hurry-up" fashion, I quickly walked to my car. By this time, it was dusk, not dark. I was in a hurry. I was also in Hartford—population 2,000. I didn't know anything about fear. I wasn't scared of anything or anyone. Little did I know that within 15 minutes that philosophy would be changed forever.

I jumped into my unlocked car, turned the key before I closed the door (a habit that I still possess), and a large hand grabbed my door window, preventing the door from closing. I looked up to see a very tall man with blondish-red hair. He looked to be in his late twenties, and he was dressed in khakis and a polo shirt. Honestly, he looked *so* normal, but what he said was anything but!

He pushed me as if to push me into the passenger's side of the car. As many of you already know, the console in a Camaro prevented a quick slide through to the passenger's side. He pushed, but I stayed firmly planted in the driver's seat. Within a few seconds, he said, "Move over. I am going to drive. If you scream, I'll kill you."

What happened next has played over in my mind like a slow-motion film no less than a million times. I *screamed*. It was one of those screams that you hear in a horror movie: a blood-curdling scream. Then, I pushed the accelerator of that 350 engine all the way to the floor and kept it there. No, I was not that street smart. It was pure instinct, or maybe it was the hand of God. I felt the man brush my body, rub my face, and then scratch my neck, but to my relief, he ran across the parking lot and then disappeared into someone's back yard.

Immediately I ran into the lobby of the hospital. I didn't close the door of my car. I didn't even turn my car off. I left it running! I was in shock. I remember this warm sensation and thinking, *Why do I feel warm, and why are my white Levis red?* I bolted into the lobby, through the door to the unit, and approached the nurses' station.

In those days, this little hospital didn't have a doctor on call in the emergency room. The closest thing there was to a physician was the charge nurse at the station located about five feet inside the door from the lobby. I excitedly lunged through that door so I could tell the staff that there was a man who had tried to kidnap me. I was beginning to see black. Everything was spinning, but I made it to that nurse's station. Nothing could have prepared me for the next thing the nurse said. "Oh God, she's going to die! Get her to the ER! Call a doctor!"

They threw me on a gurney and ran with me to the emergency room. All the while, someone was holding compression on my neck. I still didn't understand why. I was slipping into unconsciousness, but a nurse said, "Stay with us, stay with us!"

As we settled into the ER, a local doctor rushed to my side. As it turned out, Dr. Price had been a block away standing in a parking lot when he heard the screams coming from the hospital. So of course he dropped everything and went to care for the emergency at hand. By that time, I had been told that my throat had been cut and that I must be still and calm. I described the object in the hand of the man who cut me. Someone said, "She's just described a scalpel." This explained the smooth cut. He cut me with a scalpel. That's why the pain was minimized. Oh wow. Who would be carrying around a scalpel? This was so weird. A well-dressed man with a scalpel in his pocket. Why would that well-dressed man have been carrying around a scalpel?

Now mind you, all of this had happened in the span of about six or eight minutes. My blood-soaked clothes now made sense. The warm sensation was blood and urine. I had gone into shock. When I did, I peed on myself. I was losing massive amounts of blood. My white jeans were now bright red. They let me feel my neck; I'm not sure why. It was an experience from which I will never recover. I felt the gaping flesh pulled apart, and the warm, moist tissue that was fully exposed, probably a couple of inches wide and about seven inches long. The doctor quickly assured me that the jugular vein was completely exposed but not severed. He told me I would have died in the parking lot if it had been severed. Could this really be happening? Was it a dream? Someone wanted me dead. Why? Who?

My Aunt Net, Mom's younger sister, worked at the hospital. About that time, she walked in. I immediately told her I thought I was dying. She assured me that they were telling me the truth and that I was going to live. I believed her. It would be a stretch to say I calmed down, but I became still and cooperative at her insistence. Dr. Price put 43 stitches in my throat with the precision of a plastic surgeon. He knew it mattered. A "butchered" job would make me look like a horror movie character. He took his time. I felt many of them because the local anesthesia didn't work, but I squeezed my Aunt Net's hand, cried, and let him sew me up. There was no true comprehension of what had just happened, not yet.

After about 25 minutes passed, my momma walked in. Now remember, there were no cell phones at the time. She had been at prayer meeting when this happened. That little church didn't have a telephone. No one had called, and there hadn't been enough time to get her anyway. The only family member who was there at this point was Aunt Net. My little bitty momma walked in. She had been in church when she stood up to interrupt the service, and said, "Can we gather at the altar and pray? Kathy is in trouble." They prayed. Then she left and drove the 20 minutes to the hospital. As it turned out, she had requested prayer at the exact same time this man had approached me. This is completely documented by the people at church and the hospital staff. I think it's safe to assume that she had a direct line to the throne room.

When she walked in, half of the church was behind her. They didn't know why they were there. She drove straight to the emergency room. She said she had a feeling that I had been involved in a car accident. This had been revealed to her in the spirit realm. She nailed it, almost.

When she came in, half the church came with her. She rushed to my side and said, "The Lord told me you were in trouble, but Momma prayed, and you are going to be all right. You're *His* child and you have much to do!" I have no words to describe how many loads of faith were delivered to me that night. I received probably 50% of the faith I still pull out of my gut when the devil is trying to crush me that night. That's some stout stuff. That's the "I know, that I know, that I know" kind of stuff. God is God. Can He disrupt a service and speak specifics to us concerning our family? He sure can. He did.

Within an hour, there was an array of law enforcement officers surrounding me, hurling questions at me left and right. Most of the questions were stupid and felt irrelevant. This monster had cut my throat and left me in a hospital parking lot to die. The police officers kept asking me if a black man did it. Then, they would throw out names of family members and friends. I kept saying, "No, no, he was about 6'2", a white man with reddish-blond hair. He had on tan pants and a polo shirt, like an insurance man or a realtor would wear." They didn't get it! They waited until it started raining to check my car for prints. Remember, the man had grabbed my driver's side window. My door was still open. There would have been a great opportunity to get a set of fingerprints for a positive match. However, when it started raining, they lost their window of opportunity. Fingerprints would not solve this attempted murder.

My frustration was rising by the minute, and I didn't feel safe. Where had the man gone? Would he come back? They promised 24-hour security outside my hospital room,   but I doubted them. It appeared the mistakes were high, and no one was listening to me—no one. They wanted to make the attacker someone they chose, someone on their list of ex-cons; or at least that's how it felt to a 17-year-old who had never had so much as a speeding ticket. I knew nothing about the workings of small-town law enforcement. I was beginning to feel very much like a victim. There seemed to be this attitude among those in charge that conveyed this back to me: "When you get ready to *talk*, call us."

I *had* talked. They didn't listen. However, it happened on about the fifth day of my hospital stay. Someone brought me the local newspaper. In the paper was a picture of *him*. (No, not what you're thinking.) The picture was a business-community announcement welcoming this man to our community. He had apparently just gotten to town. How nice that we now had this amazing gentleman here in Ohio County, or so the newspaper said. But there's one little problem. This monster tried to kill me the first week he was here! The little newspaper "welcome" sent me into a manic state that was followed by depression when I realized that the law enforcement authorities didn't want this to be their man. The man who sliced me was a highly sought-after professional, and the community was welcoming him with open arms.

I started screaming and crying, "Get the detective! Get him here *NOW!*"

However, I was only to be told, "Now Kathy, honey, I know you are under pressure, but this couldn't be him!"

By this time I felt like I had *no* value at all. They didn't care. The truth was inconvenient. My living hell made *zero* difference to these people! I sank into a deep, dark place. My mind couldn't take any more. I was so scared. I needed someone with me 24/7 by this time. My dreams were fragments of horror. My sleep was in five- or ten-minute intervals. Nightmares were the norm. I had ten or so every night. When I was deep in this darkness, the devil came to me and said, "You lose!" I wrestled Satan daily. I fought for my sanity. I fought to feel valuable. My near-fatal attack wasn't as important as the stories the locals chose to believe. The truth was inconvenient and would create circumstantial problems if acknowledged, so no one acknowledged it. They ignored me, and their little "house of cards" stood for a season. I was bitter and angry.

This nightmare went on for 15 years. He was questioned at the time I saw the newspaper, but he had an alibi. He *was* at the hospital at that time. That was proven. He *did* have on the described clothing. That was proven. He *was* on foot and left walking through the parking lot. That was proven. But a nurse, who seemed flattered to be his "friend"—in fact, a nurse who was taking care of *me* at the time—said she was giving him a shot in the medicine room at the exact time I ran in with my throat cut. This was per her handwritten chart. It was not a computerized clock, but a handwritten "chosen" time. She lied. The end.

I could write much about the struggles of the next 15 years, the hell my kids suffered, and the fear in which we lived. I could talk about my 14-year-old nephew Marty, who stayed with me every night so that my husband could work his night shift at the mines. I could talk about all of the times I called the police because the man was parked outside my place of employment, just *staring* at me. I could talk about coming out of dressing rooms at department stores, only to see him lurking and watching. I grabbed my kids and ran for the car, locked the kids in, and then had a complete meltdown. *NO ONE DID ANYTHING!* This lasted for an eternity. It would have made sense to move, but to leave my family and friends would have left me without the much-needed support. What was I to do? I needed therapy. I was in Beaver Dam, Kentucky. We didn't have therapy in the 70s. We barely had dentists and doctors. I had no clue how badly I needed it. If I hadn't been a believer in the Word of God, I would have been a statistic. Many times, the temptation was there to make it all go away. The fear, the torment of no one believing me, the hellish nights of struggling to sleep, and the overprotection I had inflicted on my children was dysfunctional and miserable. Again, what was I to do?

I prayed. I worked. I protected my children. I learned to talk it out. Remember, I had quiet parents. I am not from a family of talkers. Through this attack, I learned to do self-therapy. I talked to anyone who would listen. I often reasoned out the answers for myself. It's the only way to survive something this horrific. Unresolved issues will not stay inside; they *will* come out. Isn't it better for it to be when *you* choose to deal with it? On your own schedule? Many people wait until the unresolved issues of a past problem ruin a new relationship and a new life. Do *not* be that person. Deal with your "stuff" daily! Talk through it, be honest, and move on. *We must!*

Rumor had it that the perpetrator raped a young lady in the community a few years after he tried to kill me. There were various rumors; all of them were chilling. We will never know how much horror he was responsible for. He was good at evading conviction, but the community began to talk. His reputation was finally being marred. The folks who couldn't believe that he would try to kill someone began to listen to the rumors. However, no charges were ever filed. Imagine that. Today, he walks the streets as a free man. I have managed the fear with God's help.

I have come to realize that until God calls me home, no man can take me. I trust God, but it doesn't hurt to have my big, brave husband, a Smith and Wesson, and a great security system with cameras.

Was there justice? No, it didn't happen. I was a bitter girl for many years. Honestly, I still am, but only a pinch. I used to have gallons and gallons of bitterness; now it is 1/8 of a teaspoon. However, if I have learned anything in my life, it's this:

To be blessed and live a big life of miracles and memories, you have to get up and face the world. Becoming a bitter, angry, reclusive girl would have been such a wasted life for me. So I refused to sign up for fear and reclusiveness. I wrestled with the devil for many years to maintain control of my "sound mind," which my Bible says I can have. Was it easy? No. Did I have my bad days? Let me re-phrase that: *do* I have my bad days? Of course, we all do, but fear isn't my GPS. It doesn't make my decisions. Retribution has never been an option. Did I *want* to retaliate? Yes. My husband is seething as I type this, but the law of the land will be our compass, and God will be my attorney, judge, and protector. I know that sounds super-spiritual, but these are the facts. I often say, as I am sure you do, "I wouldn't want to be _____on Judgment Day." This blank has been filled in with many names in my 59 years. About now, all of the folks who have wronged me are thanking God that Kathy Crabb Hannah is not making the decisions. Let me give you a tip: don't come up behind me in a parking lot, parking garage, or any other situation where I may think my safety is compromised. I will hurt you. This post-traumatic stress didn't go away. When I don't feel safe, you'd better run.

Now, if you think I am crazy, maybe you know why. If you think I am as tough as an army general, maybe you know why. If you think I over-communicate, maybe you know why. If you think I am too hard on people when I say, "Get over it! If you're not dead, get up and shake it off!" maybe you understand me a bit more. We are resilient people if we choose to be. God is able to help us if we will get up and help ourselves. Quit obsessing about yourself and you will get to a better place quickly.

Somehow, like many things in my life, this didn't kill me. It made me stronger!

5 FEAR, CASTOR OIL, AND BEAUTY

It was about September 12, 1973, and I was being released from the hospital after being attacked. I decided to go to my sister Anneta's house. Anneta cooked, she loved me, and she would make sure I was safe. Steve, my brother-in-law, owned a gun, and I was pretty sure they would do everything in their power to get me through this.

My entire family was in distress from the attack on my life. My brother Danny was making threats here and there. (If you know Danny, you are smiling about now.) All my cousins, aunts, uncles, and certainly my mom and siblings were in protective mode. We were frustrated and uncertain about what should come next. All I knew to do was to go to my safe place, which was Anneta's house.

I spent the next year of my life like a gypsy. I stayed with Anneta for the most part, but sometimes I would go to my friend Linda Beth's house. She was a newlywed, and they opened up their sweet little home and life to my husband and me. We would go there and stay for days at a time. One day, both couples decided to go buy new Mustangs. We were young, stupid, and lived in the moment, but we didn't do drugs, drink, smoke, or anything that would make our mommas ashamed.

We were settling in, and I refused to go home to our little place. I couldn't be alone. Also, Anneta was cooking and I was eating. I noticed my clothes were tight. It was weird. I was nauseous in the morning and ravenous by five p.m.. We would eat roast beef, gravy, mashed potatoes, corn bread, and watch *The Brady Bunch*. Anneta's house looked like the *Brady Bunch* house, with orange shag carpet, 70s furniture, built-in appliances, an in-ground kidney-shaped pool, and a recreation room with "barn lumber" walls. Anneta has always believed in making her home inviting, beautiful, and comfortable. She is and has always been an amazing decorator, designer, and builder. I loved the feeling of belonging, the feeling of having a home, though truly I didn't feel well. Everyone was saying that the eating thing was my nerves, and the nausea was also probably my nerves. Okay. I guessed they would know. So I kept eating and being sick in the mornings.

Finally, my mom said, "I am going to take you to Dr. Norsworthy." Dr. Norsworthy was an aging doctor whom my momma really liked. He gave me a pee test and sent it to the lab. It seems like they didn't call me until the next day, when I was getting dressed to go visit my friend Bridget and play Rook that night. Then, I got the call that went something like this:

"Hello! This is the Ohio County lab, and we got your results. You're pregnant!"

"I can't be," I said. "I am on the pill."

"Well, Dr. Norsworthy says the levels are high, so you definitely are."

"Was I pregnant when I got my throat cut?"

"I don't know. You need to see an obstetrician and get a due date to know that."

I swooned. I was dizzy; I was *scared*. I didn't plan to have kids until I was older, like 25, or 30, or never. I knew how you got them out. That was going to hurt. I was 17. Was I even *allowed* to have a baby? Did they let people have babies who didn't know anything about them?

I told my mom, sister, husband, in-laws, and extended family. I went to Bridget's mom's house and played Rook for six or seven hours in a stupor. I couldn't believe it. Could this be? What if I was a little bit pregnant when I was attacked, in shock, and subsequently medicated with *lots* of medications while in the hospital? That was barely a month ago. Could it be? Would my baby be healthy? Would this baby be healthy? Oh God. *Help* me. My mind was spinning. My nightmares wouldn't stop. This poor little baby, was it okay?

As soon as I could think clearly, I called Dr. Harrison, an Owensboro obstetrician who was the doctor of choice at the time. I remember retreating and letting fear hold me until the appointment. I couldn't speak my fears to anyone. Somehow, I thought if I didn't speak it, it would possibly be okay. However, leave it to Momma. About a week after the test, but before my appointment, she said to me, "You know this baby may be marked, and if it is, you have to love it anyway!"

Oh, my word. That was Momma. She was a bit pessimistic at times, and a bit blunt in certain situations. She meant well, but her words rolled over and over in my mind for the next eight months.

I went to the doctor. The due date was May 29. Based on the size of my abdomen, I was about six days pregnant on the night of the attack. This estimate was an unscientific projection that was little more than a guess. My body was nurturing a six-day-old fetus when that awful attack happened. "Jesus, help me!" was all I could think about that day.

I spent time with family and friends 24/7. Anneta had a business to run, so I spent a lot of time with my in-laws and my momma. My mother-in-law was an amazing cook. I learned from watching her. She is the single reason everyone loves my cooking. Did I just brag? Sorry.

Anyway, we passed the time as best we could, but the cloud loomed. There were no tests in those days to ease my mind concerning the normalcy of this child, and even if there had been, I didn't want to know. I was trusting God, but I was a 17-year-old, soon-to-be 18-year-old girl. I needed to maneuver myself into a position to support myself, go to school, and have a career. If I had a child with disabilities, it would mean a one-income family and a poverty-level household. However, I would ultimately accept God's will.

My honest answer is that I was terrified. I was convinced that this baby was "marked"! I was certain that Momma was right. Her fears were my fears. At 17, we think our mommas know everything. What did I do? I ate. I became a chubby little pregnant girl. The weight of 120 came and went, 130 came and went, and 140 came and went. At delivery, I weighed 142, and I thought I was a *cow*! I would give a farm in Texas to see 142 again. It's amazing how much your idea of an acceptable weight changes as you get older!

May 29 came. No baby. I was anxious. I was also huge. It was hot and I was miserable. I tried walking, swimming, cleaning, and walking some more. Nothing worked. I had to have a babysitter every day due to my fear of "the man." The state police detectives were still working on the case; they interviewed people occasionally and then supplied me with feedback. All of it was to no avail, and it kept the waters of my mind troubled. I knew who had done it. The mystery was solved, but they didn't get it. They didn't care. The pandering and occasional call was an insult to me. They didn't believe me when all of the evidence was there. I was bitter and afraid. I was constantly reminded that *he* was out there, a mere two miles away, and I was pregnant with a child. I worried about it 24/7. I suppose I hated him. That's not a spiritual thing to say, but it's honest. God understands.

On June 4, I went to stay at Anneta's all day, because her sons Ronnie and Marty, who were 15 and 13 at the time, were out of school and would be at home with me. They were old enough to make me feel as if I wasn't alone. I was so large "with child," and I was *so* ready to do this. We had a normal summer day. We swam, and I dove off the diving board and jumped on the trampoline for hours. No one had ever told me that these things could endanger an unborn child. Apparently, I was a total idiot, but I didn't know. No one had ever told me not to roller skate, dive, or jump, so I did everything other teenagers were doing. Later that night, Mom called and said, "I bought you two bottles of castor oil. I want you to come out to the house and take this drink I am going to make you at bedtime."

My reply was simply, "Okay."

Lord have mercy on anyone who drinks two bottles of castor oil at one time. She made me an orange juice and added both bottles of the oil. I drank it. Immediately, I wanted to throw up, but I went to bed instead.

It was 4 a.m. Wow! I woke up with a vengeance. Where was the nearest bathroom?! I went to Mom's bath off her bedroom, where I had been snoozing. The *pain*! *Oh, dear Lord, help me*! That pain, part laxative overdose pain and part labor, all mixed into one huge wave that put me physically on the floor. Momma, help! I thought I was dying. Help!

Momma came into the bathroom and said, "Spread your legs and let me see!" At this point I knew I was going to have to spread them wide real soon, so I let her have a look. Oh yeah, we needed to go to the hospital.

Momma had delivered five babies at home. For a few of us, the doctor didn't make it for the delivery. That was how it was in the 40s and 50s in Kentucky. You had babies at home. So Momma was an old pro. She always said, "Your Aunt Mary Emma can deliver a baby as good as any doctor!"

Since I wasn't all that cool with any of that nonsense, I was going to the big hospital in Owensboro, the neighboring county. We grabbed the bags and left. I was admitted and put in a room by around 6 in the morning. They broke my water for the convenience of the doctor's schedule and gave me Pitocin to speed up my labor. They also gave me Demerol and codeine, both of which I was allergic to. I was so drugged that I don't remember a lot. Legend has it that I was throwing up and the castor oil was working at the same time, all the while I was in delivery. Sorry, Krystal; I suppose this first glance at life was a bit disturbing for you.

I don't remember much, but I do remember when the nurses handed me a beautiful, blue-eyed, black-haired baby girl. This was 1974, and we didn't even know the gender until she arrived. She was perfect. I counted her toes and her fingers. She had hair on her back like a monkey, but the doctor said that was common with babies who had lots of hair. The questions of an 18-year-old mother are a bit silly; I get it. She could have had a ponytail, she had so much hair. She was over 8 pounds and only 19 inches long. She was stunning!

God had protected this child. God had shown Himself to be faithful once again. If she had been born with a severe disability, God would *still* be faithful, but I praise Him daily, especially on her birthday, for this miracle. This child is now a 40-year-old woman who is a mighty woman of God. She is extremely healthy and active. She is a sold-out Christian, and there is never a day I worry about her commitment to Christ. She took the long route to get there; many of us did. However, she made it. She is a force to be reckoned with. She, too, is strong. When she wakes up in the morning, I believe demons tremble.

It's a miracle she survived the shenanigans of an 18-year-old mother who was always on the go with baby on board. I went everywhere. I took her. I rarely left her. When she was 2, she could talk to you about any and everything. She read early. She was a mini adult. The reason? We didn't have a television for a long time. No, we weren't that spiritual; we just didn't have an antenna. It wasn't my fault, but I was *so* okay with the "no TV" thing. I didn't try to figure out a way to get the antenna. It was better for her. She learned. It has served her well. She is a natural problem solver. I will gladly take the credit for that.

So in the end, my nightmare was still a nightmare, but I had this live baby doll to take my mind off of things. Is that recommended? I don't know, but it worked for me. I stayed sane. I didn't take meds. I took care of my baby. I dressed her in frills. I cooked for her. I taught her the Pledge of Allegiance. I played with her. The poor-me victim mentality had no fertilizer in my baby-focused environment. Suddenly, nothing was about me. Time passed. I survived. So did Krystal.

Babies   are   resilient!   Sometimes   adults   are   too.

6 THE BLIZZARD OF 1978

It's cold in these mountains this morning. I wanted to sit on the porch and look at the view of the Smokies, but I must settle to be inside by the fire. The temperatures dipped to a frigid 20 degrees last night, and this morning isn't much better, or at least it doesn't feel much better to me. It's not warm enough for the outdoor office setup that I had earlier in the week. I was at a crossroads on what to write about, so I let the cold weather be my guide. Let's pick Kelly. Cold weather takes me back to the "first" Kelly story.

It was January 1978. We had experienced an exceptionally snowy month with colder-than-average temperatures. I was seven months pregnant. I was large—no, huge—no, *mammoth* with child. This time I had topped a whopping 145 pounds! What I would give to see that now.

So I was a round pregnant girl. I wasn't working for the duration of this pregnancy, and I found myself stuck inside entirely too often for my "busy-bee" nature.

Krystal was 3, soon to be 4, and I spent most days playing with her and waddling. I did lots of waddling. I am a sweller, and even though the temperatures were cold, I still had so much swelling. So you get the picture. I was fat, stuck at home because of icy dangerous conditions, playing Barbie dolls and watching *Mr. Rogers*. Full-blown Mommy times had arrived.

On January 26 it started snowing, and snowing, and blowing, and blowing. It was like nothing I had ever seen before. Now mind you, schools had already been closed for a month due to snow, but this wasn't like that. That was just snow, you know, five or six inches at a time; it was enough snow each time to wreck the schedule and create highway havoc, but the plows could still plow. Four-wheel drive trucks could get through—and remember, this was Kentucky in the late 70s. Every manly man had a four-wheel drive, oh yeah.

The coal industry was our number one provider of jobs, and the good jobs were there. So most of the guys who had the nice trucks that were jacked up with big tires and big antennae worked at the coal mines. These guys all had a CB radio in their four-wheel drives. They wore Carhartt coveralls daily, boasted about having the nicest thermos and "dinner bucket," and played eight-tracks of Hank Jr. every day just because they could. This was Ohio County, where most men had blue-collar jobs. In these kinds of rural communities, where everyone owns a four-wheel drive, men are "manly" and not afraid of work, and they're always game for any kind of inclement weather. These men were all about the storm chasing and enjoyed offering their taxi services to the community. The elements were no big deal for these guys; after all, they had the macho trucks, the "hoss-cat" four-wheel drives. Neighbors took care of neighbors. That's how it was in Beaver Dam and Hartford, back in the day.

Anyway, January 27 blew in, and we were freezing. The depth of the snow was starting to be enough to make the kids giddy. They were thinking about snow tunnels, not snowmen. By the time that snowfall stopped, all of our roads were impassable. The National Guard was called out. We had two feet of snow, a full-on blizzard, and drifts over the heads of the tallest men. Those four-wheel drive vehicles were no match for this storm!

The doctors couldn't get to the hospitals. We lived next door to a couple of doctors, and one was a general surgeon. There was an emergency appendectomy, and the family had walked and brought this man on a sled to the hospital. Our neighbor, the Asian doctor, needed to get there. The neighborhood men said, "We can get you there!" However, the snow had drifts 10 feet high on Iron Mountain Road, and that was the only way in and out of our neighborhood. There was no success in getting a vehicle through that. So the good doc dug tunnels through all of the drifts. There were many of them. This was several miles, and he walked. People were trapped in cars and homes and froze to death in parts of Kentucky. This was declared an emergency. People lived without electricity for weeks. The death toll from this storm topped 70 in a three-state area. It was freakish.

What if I went into labor? Oh my, what if? I was nervous and wouldn't leave the house for weeks, not even to walk to the neighbors', for fear of falling. Thankfully, we had a huge supply of food, and I don't remember a long bout without electricity like others had. So we were safe but stir crazy! Can we say cabin fever? I had been stuck in that house for two solid months!

Kelly was due the last week of February. By 1978, Dr. Harrison was giving a due-date window that spanned seven days. I think my due-date week was February 20-27. February came and went. As of March 1, we still didn't have a baby. The snow was still on the ground. The kids had been home from school for two months. (I didn't have kids in school, but neighbors and friends did.) Many people had lost weeks of work. Yes, I was still stuck in that house. Everyone was! Moms everywhere were declaring that they were planning a group check-in at the mental institution in Hopkinsville. It was the most nerve-wracking time ever. Here I am, 36 years later, and I find it important enough to write about. Remember, my inspiration for this book is my kids and grandkids, and the things I want them to know. So Kelly, I was sick of being fat and snowbound, and you were late. There, I said it!

March came in like a lion, with more snow falling onto the blizzard covering that still hadn't melted. Would we ever have warm temperatures again? Would I ever see a pool, a field of flowers? I was sick of gray skies and the salty film that collected on my hardwoods from the icy boots. I was tired of the prints that left a salty residue on those plank mahogany floors I just *had* to have in that house. We had built a new home in 1977, and I was in my glory. Krystal's room boasted a yellow chandelier and navy and white polka dot wallpaper, with an accent wall of a companion paper that was still polka-dotted, but with a yellow tulip overlay. We had bright yellow carpeting, a bright yellow chandelier that I would give anything to have now, and a room full of navy and white polka dots. White furniture and a plain white ruffled bedspread and curtains finished off this look. Oh my, that look was timeless. Krystal, to this day, is always drawn to a navy-and-white polka-dot *anything* with yellow accessories.

The suggestion of style begins very early. By the time your child is 6 years old, they have developed their taste, or lack of it. Now, that's not to suggest that a 6 year old will choose what a 50 year old would choose, but let me explain. If I asked my granddaughter, Gracie, what I should wear and give her two or three choices, she knows what to choose. And be assured she will correct me if the accessories, shoes, or purse are not right. She was born with "that" style sense. It's in her genes. You can't teach style to 25-year-olds. 25-year-olds can mimic the style of others. They can memorize "looks," and they may know what they like when they see it, but they can't create a look from scratch; they can't create a fresh, new style that stuns. Krystal, though, can create. She is amazing at style, anything that depends on an eye that analyzes color, texture, fabric, and arrangement of items. Whether it is clothing, furniture, or art on a wall, she gets it. Actually, all of my girls get it; the grandkids do too. It's a gift of creativity. Music freely flows among the family, but so does opinionated fashion flair. And I, for one, love it!

Back to Kelly. She wasn't born when we built the house. We suspected she would be a boy. Wrong. So I did that "dorky" nursery that wasn't a total sell-out to either gender. The nursery was yellow and green, with teddy bears and yellow and white striped fabric for the bedding and windows. She would hate it. It wasn't a good choice for the real Kelly, so it's a good thing we changed it before she was old enough to truly understand what I had done to her.

Anyway, I was *ready* to have the baby. After all, Krystal was ready for that little brother, who would most likely be named Andrew or Nicholas. It warmed up for a day or two, and the snow began to melt; not totally, but the roads were good. We could get out of that stupid house! I heard that the new Towne Square Mall was open in Owensboro, and I wanted to check it out. We did. I walked, shopped, walked some more, ate at the Briarpatch, and decided I *had* to have this baby, like, *soon*!

Mom suggested the castor oil caper again. I just couldn't do it. I gagged and nearly threw up at the mention of it. She kept insisting, telling me not to smell it, to hold my nose and chug it down. I put her off for a day or two. I was now looking at March 15. I was at least two weeks late, or possibly three, depending on the doc's calculation. Something had to give. I finally told Momma okay on the castor oil.

It was spitting snow again, but Momma brought the "diarrhea cocktail" to me and made me chug it. I threw it up immediately. I just couldn't do it. I was frustrated; we all were. The next day I said, "I am packing a bag and going to the hospital in the morning. I am telling them I am in pain and I want them to break my water."

Now in those days, they didn't schedule deliveries like they do now. Most of my grandchildren's births have been scheduled on a particular day so that the family members who travel could be at home. Well, not in those days. Common stories circulated of girls who had gone to the emergency room and were sent home if there was no dilation. I feared this happening, but I was beginning to know that this baby was getting too big. I didn't want my baby to be ready for kindergarten and still be in my belly!

So we went. I played the "soap-opera" version of labor pains. They bought it, broke my water, and started Pitocin. In hindsight, with my overdue condition, they probably would have admitted me without the drama, but my 22-year-old personality was a bit more intimidated by the "godlike" obstetrician. So, I played the drama queen for all it was worth. Now, I would never do so.

Labor was hard, with lots of "ouch" moments. This baby was cruel to its momma. Everyone was saying, "Well, boys are harder to have. Right?" I wouldn't know.

A nurse said, "Do you realize it's St. Patrick's Day?"

I said, "No!"

"Well, it is. You need to make sure this baby is named for the Irish."

Well, I instantly decided that this little boy would be Patrick! Yes, Patrick Andrew, or Patrick Jean for my dad. My dad's name was Jean, the French spelling. However, it was pronounced Gene, unlike the French name. He wasn't French, but evidently his momma had seen the French spelling, or someone was being cruel. Anyway, they named him Jean, and his middle name was Elvis. Now this was many years before THE Elvis. My dad was the *original* Elvis. When I use his middle name in the identification process, you know, security questions, the person who's taking my security info usually chuckles and says, "Really? Elvis?" So my daddy's name was *Jean Elvis Coppage*. Unique, huh? My mom was always a bit bitter, because her parents didn't give her a middle name. I would say, "Mom, they had 10 kids! They ran out of ideas!" She would snap back, "Well, they made sure everyone else had a middle name, didn't they?" This was a bit of a sore spot, but to me it was funny, and I brought it up far too often just to get her stirred up. She was *so* funny, and we all enjoyed this petty side of her. It was her sore spot, her "jealous pot" moment. We all have them, and we *all* enjoyed hers. It was hilarious! An 80-year-old woman was still complaining about not having a middle name!

My sister was allowed to name me, or so Mom always told me. She chose "Jo" for my middle name. Yes, Kathy Jo. Not Katherine, a classier choice, or Kathleen, a timeless choice, but Kathy. That is so 50s, and Jo is *so* wrong! Anneta, that wasn't nice. I know you were only 14, but really?

So by 2:30 in the afternoon on St. Patrick's Day, the Pitocin had done its job. No epidurals in those days. We had to bear it and could get a "saddle block" at the very end. I signed up for the saddle block and was screaming for it. This baby was a meanie—pain and more pain. Saddle block time was here. That big needle was in my lower back, and then total numbness that stopped the pushing was the reason for the forceps. They used forceps. That looked so scary, and truly it was.

So now I was numb, I was feeling pretty good, and this little baby was almost here. The forceps pulled and pulled. I could see the head: another head full of black hair, just like Krystal. The doctor commented that the shoulders were crowded and the face was chubby. Then he said, "Miss Kathy, this is the prettiest baby I have ever delivered!"

He pulled the baby out and held *her* up for me to see. I tried to see if I had a boy. I was pretty sure the equipment wasn't there for a boy, and I asked the nurse. They didn't hand babies over as readily in those days as they do now. I was squinting to see. I had bad eyes and no glasses or contacts in. The baby looked like a little Mexican. She had lots of thick black hair and rolls upon rolls. The doctor said, "Those extra weeks in there have put some weight on her!"

I asked, "It's a girl? For sure?"

He grinned, "Yes, it's a beautiful baby girl."

Well, what do you know? I had two girls! That's okay with me. I know about girls. I know about frills, polka dots, china, ruffled socks, and patent leather shoes. I was happy. There may have been some disappointment, but it wasn't from me.

They cleaned her up. I held her, brushed her hair, and went to sleep. I was tired. The next morning, I wasn't sure what I would name her. I talked about Heather. Yes, I liked Heather Layne, for my Mom Elaine and my sister Anneta Lane. Anneta came with Mom, and she had an idea. She had a name for her. I told her to go for it. She got with Kelly's dad, and they went and filled out the birth certificate. They came back to the room and told me they had decided to name her Kelly Layne. I remember thinking, *Kelly? I am not sure I like that name. However, (things that matter, things that don't), on the other hand, Krystal's monogrammed items can now be hand-me-downs!*

So, I was good! Her name grew on me quickly. They brought her in so that I could see how yellow she had become. She was jaundiced, and I remember thinking, *She looks just like a Kelly!*

Well, this little St. Patrick's Day baby will be 37 on her next birthday, and she has lived a blessed life. I tend to steer away from the Irish description of lucky, just because we of faith prefer "blessed" over "lucky," but call it what you may. Through many storms and dangers she has already come. Grace has brought her, kept her, and will lead her on. I think she knew by the time she was 4 or 5 that she was "called." Mom always claims that Kelly told her when she was about 4 years that she was going to sing for Jesus. I am sure a lot of kids have said similar things, but Kelly was different. She hungered for His touch, and that seemed to keep her on the straight and narrow. She wanted to please Him always. Her story is pretty much drama-free, unlike mine and Krystal's.

Everyone has a struggle and Kelly has hers. Don't we all. She is passive to a fault at times, and I don't think she inherited that from me. In the end, she got her dream. She married Mike Bowling when she was 20, and she has lived a life of ministry and family. They have three girls; it hasn't been easy living a life on the road and raising three kids on a bus. It ain't for sissies. The laundry is a mountain every Monday. The schedule is crazy, between school schedules, activities, music/group rehearsal, road responsibilities, interviews, special events, TV tapings, church, and *all* of the commitments that the Bowling family *must* keep. It makes for a stressful, busy life, but she does it. She organizes, packs, unpacks, and matches shoes, hair bows, and clothes; she totes backpacks, band instruments, cheerleading bags, and anything else that one could imagine in and out, on and off the bus every week. She and her family live in a state of constant motion. That's hard for a person to do, even if it's only for yourself, but add three kids to that. Wow! Respect Kelly Bowling, people. She deserves it.

She and Mike married when she was 20, and we approved, even though he was in his early 30s. He looked like a mere child, and he had no baggage. No children. No ex-wife. So morally, the age difference isn't a spiritual or moral issue. It's just a bit odd when you don't know music from the same decade. You know, little differences like that. The age difference has brought challenges, no doubt, but the fact that there are no exes or children from previous marriages made this road easier.

The age thing is not all that difficult when the circumstances are right.

However, when their story is written, it appears it will end like this: Mike and Kelly Bowling married in April 1998. He was the lead singer for the Perrys. (Remember songs like "When He Spoke" and "Not Even a Stone"? Well, that was Mike.) They traveled separately for a year. She was with us, and he was with the Perrys. We elected to do a tour with the Perrys so life would be easier on Mike and Kelly. Beckie Simmons got on it, and we made it happen. We were in a major "growth" mode in those days. Our flats were nearly doubling every year or so. We did the tour, and it was good. We called it "Family Ties," and we saw good things happen. Then Kelly got pregnant. Mike declared that he wouldn't be away from his child. The end. Bye-bye Perrys. Hope was 6 days old when we loaded her on that big red bus. A bus and the road is all she has ever known, be it good or be it bad. Farmers raise farmers, preachers raise preachers, doctors raise doctors, and singers raise singers. But singers must travel, and sometimes that's a sacrifice. Kelly's children are the only children that travel full time. The other grandchildren stay at home with their moms or both parents. Kelly's kids? They go. They don't have a normal life. Is that a good thing? I am not totally sure I know the answer to that. But of this I'm sure: they are rich in experiences, music, people skills, and God. The ability to convey emotion through a song is as much a part of their skill set as reading. They live, breathe, and sleep music. What else would we expect?

The year Hope was born, we invited Mike to come on board to be a "built-in" opening act. He agreed. We did a solo record of him and put him on the Crabb Family bus. Actually, we bought a second bus, raised our flats, paid Mike a salary like everyone else (from Krystal, the oldest, down to Terah, the youngest), and made him share in his product sales with the other kids. After all, we were communists in that everyone shared and dispersed profit. It worked. He moved to the piano a few years later and was still an opening act plus the Crabb Family piano player. I went home. I had no choice. Life happened. The Crabb Family was reduced to the five kids plus a band. The kids were in a great place spiritually. They had this. They were fasting, praying all night, and finding out how *big* God was.

Mike and Kelly weathered and thrived under the Crabb Family ministry. Years later, in 2006, when she got pregnant with the "oops" child Gracie, Kelly wanted to leave and go with Mike to form a family group. The big divorce bomb had exploded at my house. My days were filled with tears and hurt, and I felt that soon, very soon, I wanted a life change. The kids were struggling with direction, musically and personally. I knew that Jason needed to follow his musical dreams. Aaron wanted to be with Amanda, and Adam and Terah could make it. I told Kelly to go and start building her own heritage! She did.

They took little Kate-Kate and Hope, who had been on a Crabb Family bus since she was a week old. By this time, Hope was about 6 or 7 and Kate was 3. They loaded those little girls off the Crabb bus and right back onto the Bowling bus. Kelly became Mike's business partner. The Bowling Family had officially started. Gracie was born later that year. The rest is history: Hope is 15, Katelanne is 11, and Gracie is 8.

Mike is one of the most talented singers to ever sing a song, and he's as loyal as he is talented. Kelly made a good choice the day she said "I do," but don't anyone tell him I said that. Additionally, the kids seem to be blessed with a great gene pool when it comes to music. That's always a perk. Their future is bright. Mike and Kelly carry an anointing that comes with sacrifice. They have suffered, but God has kept them, and His grace is amazing, truly. However, that's another chapter, where you will see what made them stronger.

I think I need a cup of hot chocolate and a back porch chair for a minute. I will brave the cold to see that view. I have much more to tell you, and my time in this cabin is running out.

7 DAY ONE

It was the summer of 1991. I worked for a General Motors dealership in Owensboro. We were a bit of a lively bunch, and many of us were close friends. I was the business manager, and VeLoyce Keown was the office manager. By this time, I was divorced from Krystal and Kelly's father, and I desperately needed friends and mentors. I always need friends. I have many, and I love each of them.

VeLoyce and I frequently found the courage to go to a local eatery that was rumored to have roaches. It was a hole-in-the-wall kind of place. It was there that she had a "light bulb" moment! I worked with a great group of girls: "Little" Kathy was the younger of us two Kathys, so she got to be Little Kathy. Little Kathy, Debbie, Paulette, VeLoyce, and yours truly rounded out the crew. We were friends, and we would always look to find a reason to have an outing or an event. Well, since we had a few musicians who worked there, someone suggested a musical *Hee-Haw*-style family picnic in the park behind the dealership. We all agreed, and I was in my element. That day at the roach restaurant, VeLoyce figured it all out.

She invited employees to participate, and the singers and musicians were tickled pink. The weekly practices began. This show was a fork in the destiny of many lives. Stay tuned. We sounded like a VFW country wannabe band, with a heavy emphasis on Travis Tritt hits and Merle Haggard oldies. When you mixed a bit of "don't hand me no lines and keep your hands to yourself" with "when I get behind closed doors," truly you had a bit of redneck heaven, because heck, I could play that country piano intro. So we had to do that tune! Anyway, Hank Jr., the Head Hunters, and all the rowdy hillbilly sounds were happening.

The dealership band was a motley crew: Roger, Perry, Doug, Bubby, Little Kathy, and me, with VeLoyce at the helm directing traffic and making us adhere to her schedule. That was VeLoyce. She was the poster child for "take charge." I got along well with her, because if she would take the lead, I could have a rest. Seriously, we were friends.

The day was finally here. The families were coming. There would be alcohol, which I didn't like. My girls were coming, and I didn't want them to think I was okay with the alcohol. VeLoyce said, "You can't control other people bringing beer. Get over it." She was a church girl, but she wasn't so heavenly-minded that she was irrelevant. She would say, "They're not going to put a gun to your head and make you drink!" She didn't drink either, but she was a bit older and had mellowed. I wasn't involved in church much, but because my brother was an alcoholic I hated alcohol. I hated wild parties, and I didn't participate, divorce or no divorce. However, I chilled and enjoyed the fun of the night. We played our hillbilly music. I will never forget this day, not if I live to be 120.

I was in my office when a little girl walked in. Her name was Terah. I worked with her dad, and we had become close friends. Her dad wanted me to meet her and her brothers, so meet them I did. We were immediate friends. She was a bright-eyed 8 year old, and I had lots of experience with little girls. We chatted for a minute. She was mesmerized by the computer and the office supplies in general. She loved paper, markers, staplers, scissors, and anything that made her feel like she was an "office" worker. She told me that day, "I want to work here when I get older."

Terah had some serious issues with her hair, and I wanted to get her a hair bow and fix it. Wait, I had a better idea. I said, "Terah, come with me. We are going on a shopping trip!" This was on Saturday. I worked every Saturday, and rarely took lunch on Saturday, but on this day I was taking a long lunch, just because I wanted to! I called Little Kathy in the showroom and said, "Come with me to the mall." She came right over. I asked Terah's dad if I could take her, and we left.

When Terah tells this story, she says she had never seen anyone drive that fast on the off ramp. Well, she had only just begun. Little did we know that I would later become her bonus mom. She would end up living with me a few years later and teaching me about unconditional love.

Anyway, on that day, we got out of the car and busted up in that mall as if we were on a scavenger hunt. She left with a new outfit, head to toe, and a hair bow; she truly looked like a doll. We were quick friends. She made me comfortable from that first day. I think she had some knowledge of the future as it related to me, but she was just 8 years old. How could an 8 year old grasp the choices of 30-something adults? She knew that her world had been turned upside down. In later years, she would share the hurt and pain. She would describe the tears and fears—but in that moment, she was smiling. On that Saturday, she was happy. She had solid ground under those two little feet.

I am fully aware that my "spoil meter" was turned *way* up in those early days. I am also aware that kids are drawn to spoiling, but they are also drawn to safe places, places with boundaries and provision. Kids want to feel secure. Even though we had navigated troubled waters, my girls always knew they would have what they needed and then some. I got many things wrong, but providing a stable, safe home with rules was not one of them. I believed in rules, homework, and a home where children did not take on the adult responsibility of finances.

Terah had seen her share of heartache. She had been in a parsonage for her early years, but that life had evaporated. (Many of you have heard different family members tell these details.) Her world had been blown up and she was vulnerable. There are days when I look at all six of these kids and my heart breaks for them; their pain relates to divorce and brokenness, which was someone else's choice, not theirs. They were all damaged goods, and to some degree, they still are. Adults are selfish, me included. Children are the victims, always. The damage was done. She had moved out of that parsonage a few years before and, like my girls, had made the best of the choices of parents. It's not my job to assign blame to anyone. This book is not about wrong, right, or anyone's thoughts but mine. However, of this I am sure: kids get the shaft when their parents don't protect their marriage and stay married. All six of these kids suffered. Period. I am not judge and jury. If I were, there would be plenty of blame to go around. But this isn't that. This is my observation of flawed people that God managed to continue loving. At times I think about those days and I ask God how He could take that mess and use it. However, somehow, He did.

I married Terah's dad in September, her birth month. She wasn't present for the wedding, and I couldn't bear to miss her birthday. I am a birthday kind of mom. Those who know me already know that. I once flew to Vegas because the Crabb Family was singing there and it was Kelly's 25th. I wanted to surprise her, so I did. It seems like we have a birthday party every week! But hey, that's okay. You can't enjoy a party or a cake after you're dead. Let's celebrate each other while we can!

So I insisted that we wait until after Terah's birthday to leave for a honeymoon. We waited two days. On her 9th birthday we went to her school and brought her a "Wedding Barbie," which she loved. I didn't regret waiting, and it was the first of many birthdays I would celebrate for Terah, the baby girl, the little girl with a head full of hair and an unsure smile. Terah, the teenage girl I protected from the vultures when I knew she was scared and nervous. Terah gets nervous under pressure. I have always protected her, and I dare anyone to demand she do something that makes her uncomfortable. I was on immediate "Momma Bear" alert and meant business. I still do. Don't mess with her. I was never a replacement for her mom, but I know she loves me, and she knows I love her. Period. We have walked through fire, floods, wind, and any other disaster you can imagine, and our love has proven to be golden. It was spawned from the hands of guidance, dependency, and the knowledge that I would never leave her no matter what. You could ask her today, at 32 years old, if our bond could be broken. Her answer would be no. Don't believe me? Ask her.

The kids all thrived with the blended family dynamic. Life was exciting on the music front, and Terah met and married her sweetheart, Jon Penhollow, in 2001. Jon came from a musical family, and is the youngest brother of Charlotte Ritchie. Charlotte was a longtime friend who happens to be an amazing talent. Her husband Greg was always one of my favorite people in the world. Jon was smitten with Terah, and Terah was smitten with Jon. Our personal lives were challenging during this season, but we managed a beautiful July wedding at the Belmont Mansion in Nashville. Terah's decision to have an out-of-town wedding was welcome news for me. Under the circumstances, it seemed to be the right thing.

They settled into our old Delmar Drive house and life was good. But the summer of 2003 brought changes. We were all moving to Nashville. The plan was made and the excitement was mounting. However, for Terah and Jon, it wasn't to be.

In September 2003, I woke up to a nightmare. Terah was leaving! For a year she was gone from the Crabb Family ministry. She decided to pack up and leave. She was hurt, and her struggle with the choices of another made her run. She cleaved to her husband, tearfully told her siblings goodbye, and left. The scars were deep, and only God knows how much that little girl suffered from the autumn of 2003 to the autumn of 2004. She was heartbroken and couldn't quite understand, but she knew what she knew.

It wasn't until after Terah left that we learned she was pregnant. I cried every night. It was a ritual. The previous year Krystal had left. Krystal came home and Terah left. Yes, there was a pattern. I went into work mode again. If I hadn't immersed myself in work, I wouldn't have survived, for I truly felt like my heart was ripped out. I was carrying things that only my family knew about. We were beginning to have cracks in the armor.

Christmas came and went; no Terah. Her absence was pure pain. Spring came and summer was almost here. I saw a picture of her, and she was *so* pregnant. It broke my heart. I was missing this, and I wanted to see her. I wanted to have a long lunch, laugh, pat her belly—you know, I just wanted normal. What should I do? The resolution wasn't a simple one. God, please help. I need You again. Mend this problem like only You can do.

On May 25 Amanda (Aaron's wife) and Terah both went into labor, both a few weeks early, in two different states. Terah was in Georgia, and Amanda with us in Tennessee. It was the first child for both couples. I was there for Amanda and Aaron when Eli was born, but not for Terah. This is one of the biggest regrets of my life. We couldn't have physically gotten there, and Terah knows that. However, I should have gotten into my car and driven to her months before to let her know how much she was loved, no matter what it cost or whom it displeased. Period. I regret it.

Sweet little Logan was born. We saw photos, but hadn't seen him. The summer passed. I cried every single night. Would we ever have the family together again? How could I continue to pretend that all was well?

September came. I was praying Terah would come to the National Quartet Convention. The kids were all praying and fasting for a resolution. Jon was working for Jeff and Sheri Easter and they were living in Lincolnton, GA. I heard that Terah might come to Louisville to the NQC. I hoped. . How would she look? Did she want to see us? We wanted to know our baby boy! Was she missing us? I didn't know. All I knew was that my pillow was tear-soaked every night. All I knew was that there would never be completeness until she came home. All I knew was that I would give up every worldly possession I had to have the dysfunctional junk be gone and for there to be harmony again. Terah held her own, and she had become strong. That was the part I didn't know.

I was a bit anxious. I kept walking by Jeff and Sheri's merchandise table in Freedom Hall, but no Terah. Their money was tight. Jon was the only income now. Terah had a baby, and I wasn't sure she would drive to Louisville from Georgia. However, as with everything that God orchestrates, He took care of all the details. He told Melissa Mann, a long time friend, to mail Terah money. She did. It came in the mail just in time to be the gas money for this journey back to Kentucky, where it all began. It would bring her to a place that would start a soul-cleansing journey of forgiveness. She drove and arrived on Friday. She was finally there.

Things were tense. Then it happened. Big Jon was provoked. The conflict that had been brewing for a year finally ensued—in an aisle at NQC, no less. The moment we had all dreaded became a tense conflict that produced a head to this awful year of hell. The "mess" would soon be in the history books. It was tense—like *Jerry Springer* tense. We watched. News traveled those aisles quickly. The entire family was anxious. We had prayed for an end, but would this come to an end for the better? It was looking doubtful. Jon had stood his ground, and the old grudges were solidly in place. But then, some way, somehow, the situation began to relax. God was at work. Common sense and calm replaced heated comments and anger. We were praying, watching, and waiting, all in that aisle at NQC. Then someone had a brilliant idea: take the entire family to a private room. There were some private rooms off the stage area. I am not sure who arranged it, but I am thankful for them, whoever "they" were. The room was about 12 by 12, but all of us piled into that room to talk, and pray, and experience a miracle of sorts.

That room became an altar, a place where apologies were offered and accepted. A cloud of glory covered the room. Heaven opened up. I was totally drunk on the Spirit. I think most everyone was. Terah made peace with the issue. She forgave, and then she walked toward me. I went to grab her and hug her, but that wasn't what she needed.

I will never forget that night. She touched my face. She kept feeling my facial features. She rubbed my cheeks and touched my lips for what seemed like a gloriously long time. Then she said, "Is this real? Am I really here? Is this really you?" She traced the lines of my face, and she cried. I cried. We all cried. Truly, it was indescribable. In my 59 years, I have never witnessed joy like that. We were all swimming in joy. We were swimming in the waters of thankfulness. There was so much unity in that room anything was possible. It was one mind and one accord that night. I was holding our precious baby, whom I had never seen. Big ole Jon-boy was reduced to a puddle of tears. God knows we were grateful.

I am sitting here, 10 years later, and I can see her in that t-shirt. I can see that baby, his little face and his fingers. The anger had evaporated. Those of us who witnessed it from the sidelines felt like Heaven and Earth had kissed and we were in the middle of it. That day was the best day ever!

To summarize a long story, by October of 2004, Terah and Jon were back in TN, living across and down the street from Terah's siblings. God had been faithful. My babies were all home. She went back on the road by mid-winter. The chickens were back in the nest. No more Christmases apart, ever.

Today, I love having all of the kids close to me. I love them. Jon and Terah currently live about three miles from my front door; Logan is a Tennessee Titans superstar in training. He is poised to be a football star, in my opinion. He is a sweet little boy who is taller than his granny. Jon and Terah have weathered the storms of life and bad schedules and managed to get it right. The hand of God is solidly on both of them, and I, for one, am awaiting the next chapter of their lives to see where God takes them.

Now, I need a fresh Kleenex and a bottle of water. I've cried my eyes out while writing this! God is good. He is gloriously good!

8 THE CLOSET

My reminiscing is on overload today. I remember something, write it down, remember some more, write it down, and soon enough, voilà, I have a chapter. They are sweet memories. I may have selective memory syndrome. I choose to remember the good and dump the ugly. Well, that's okay. It's actually pretty healthy. These mountains seem to mellow me a bit, make me want to take the "high road" today. Truly there's no congestion there.

It was a Sunday in late April of 1994. I was at church in Philpot, Kentucky, in the third pew from the front left side if you're looking at the pulpit. We were the pastors. This building was *old*. The sanctuary structure was built in the 1800s, with Sunday school rooms added onto the back in the 40s. These were our current living quarters. Another Sunday school wing had been built on in the 60s.

Behind the church lived several goats. They were fenced in, but found us strange things to look at and always tipped their heads when looking at us. Once I fed them a bucket of wallpaper paste. They loved it. (Don't call PETA. They lived.)

The newest wing was brick. It had a kitchen, a water fountain, bathrooms, and was considered modern when compared to the sanctuary structure. The floor sloped, and not totally because it should have. I remember the foundation being massive blocks or stones. I am sure a truck with a hoist didn't come out to the build site and bring uniform concrete blocks in the 1800s. I was always a bit nervous about the structural integrity of the old sanctuary. It had a certain smell. That mauvish, pinkish carpet had that certain look, but we made it work.

This would be the place of beginnings, the alpha in the book of chronological information about the organized musical efforts of my family. Songs would be written here, tears would be shed, dreams would be dreamed, and confusion would be encountered. On certain days I was uncertain how I got here, but somehow I was in a matriarchal position to a small congregation and a house full of kids. It was here that music was practiced, harmony parts found, and starry-eyed kids dreamed of a stage. The good news is that they loved Jesus more than the stage. That has kept them. A person who is called craves the delivery of the message, and they were called. They were learning to deliver and refill, deliver and refill. They played and sang for hours while people prayed in the altars. They played without stress and learned to wing it because no one was listening anyway—or so they thought. The truth is, everyone was listening, and their reputation spread quickly.

We had put together a program of sorts and wandered outside this church to do a few special services for some friends in the Western Kentucky area. There were certainly some rough edges, but the important things were there. The talent was solid, the anointing was heavy, and the work ethic matched the talent.

So in the span of a couple of years, I went from the divorced mother of two who lived in a nice subdivision with a "normal" brick home to living in a wing of Sunday school rooms built in the 1940s in Philpot, KY. I sold my home and bought a church. I had married a man who has self-professed the issues with which he struggled. I will let you read his version if you are uninformed. I could tell you, but I won't. My family was mortified, my friends thought I had lost my mind, and my employer would just scratch his head and stare at me, all the while chewing on that stupid cigar. At times I questioned my decision too. This wasn't a real smart choice to any onlooker. I now had my two girls to support and four new kids who had the exact same needs as mine, and I was the main breadwinner in our home.

I had vowed never to be a "typical" stepmother; you know, the kind who says "Don't take that; that's *my* daughter's shirt. Let your mother spend that child support money on you if you want a shirt like that." You have seen it many times, yours and mine, and they *think* they are going to blend, but in reality? Not a chance. When I agreed to the marriage I made it perfectly clear to my children that we would all live on the same economic level. It's possible that I was a bit delirious that day, and I know that on this side of history, looking back, my girls had to be a bit perplexed. I mean, seriously. They barely knew these kids, and their mom was telling them that her paycheck has to be divided in such a manner as to buy for six kids, not two. They knew the economics of the decision. But if they got mad, they didn't tell me. In all honesty, to be angry would have been normal. I didn't break the news gently. I never do. I was a bit abrasive. I still am. They did pretty well with the news. My girls tell me I have the personality of a man; you know, no weakness or softness. This book will enlighten you as to the whys of that.

Well anyway, the gist of this point is this: Krystal and Kelly were on the brink of a recession! Kelly was 13, Krystal was 17, and they were spoiled. The mall was a weekly outing. I worked hard so that they could have whatever they wanted. I now realize that this formula isn't always a good thing. Kids don't need everything they want; I am *just* learning this, and it may be a tad bit late. Who knew? However, the message from me to all of the kids was always this: if one child got to go out to eat, everyone got to go out to eat. You get my drift. Everyone went to sleep and woke up in a communist world. We shared everything—clothes, shoes, cars, burgers, beds—and now they were also sharing parents. All six of them got something they didn't sign up for: a new family and a foreign environment, created by an adult who was not their blood parent, an adult with their own ideas on what the future would be, and the kids didn't get a vote. That's what blended families are like, typically.

Let me expound a bit on this. If you are a stepmom or a stepdad, don't wait for the child to love you first when you start parenting. If you parent them, if you protect them; if you love them, they *will* love you back. *Always.* You are the adult. They are the kid. Adults need to behave like adults. Your stepchildren are not your competition; they are your responsibility. You took on that responsibility when you married their parent.

Too often blended families fail because the parent in charge isn't willing to allow love to happen. The strife over money, clothes, braces, child support, visitation, and a hundred other adult issues are used to badger the child, to encourage anger at the other parent. If you are part of a situation like this, stop. The divorce is over. Spend your time loving and getting to know these kids. Spend your money spoiling them. I guarantee you that if you always buy for yours and his in the same proportion, if you love and honor them all in the same proportion, they will be there when you take that final breath. Love isn't dependent on blood. Prioritize his kids exactly like you prioritize your own: no shortcuts. Kids know that money isn't everything, but they also know it's the number one thing divorced parents fight about, and the kids are caught in the crossfire. Don't do the minimum for this child. Rather, do all you *can* do. Generosity is the key. I am not suggesting that you "buy" them. I am suggesting that you undergird their fragile and undetermined place in life by making the child feel secure emotionally, financially, and spiritually. It works.

I was a "tell-it-like-it-is" communicator, and I was a workaholic. I didn't watch movies or play video games. I had never had the time, and I believed these things were a *waste* of precious time. Was I right? Not entirely, but partially. I am driven and motivated; I didn't want to pass a life of poverty on to these children, who adapted quickly to my ways. I am confident that it wasn't easy, but that's how they were conditioned: to adapt. That's how they rolled. Don't speak up and don't have an opinion. My girls?

They *always* had an opinion. I like opinionated kids; I always have. However, my girls would soon become less vocal, at least for the most part. That seemed to be what worked best in this new dynamic. I regret allowing some of this to transpire, but hindsight is 20/20, and those who criticize my effort can assess the result and know that I did my best with the juggling act that was the new normal.

Time passed. We survived a ton of struggle, emotions, feelings, and unresolved hurt. Those six kids learned to love. It wasn't the demanding love that was most likely expected in the beginning. It became the "time-spent" kind of love—the bonding and nurturing that only comes when you share secrets, hurt, and socks.

However, the constant was music and church. We went to church, *all* of us. We looked forward to it. Krystal was in college during this season, and then married. She was caught up in a subset of problems, no doubt, but, she too had learned to love, and those new siblings loved her. They loved their pretty big sister, who was cool and a bit too sassy. Krystal wasn't always at church, but she came when she was at home, and I think she drew strength from it. Even though she didn't have it together, who did? We were a case study in dysfunction, if the truth be told, but our lives are a testimony that dysfunction ain't nothing for God. A mess brings a message, a test a testimony!

Things were far from perfect, but the five younger kids were beginning to love music more than sports, more than clothes, more than anything. They bonded with Kelly; this was a bond that would last for a lifetime, a bond that would transcend the storms of life. I told them that I would always be there for them, and I meant it. We are still a family. We choose life over death. We choose love over hate. We choose light over dark. If you don't realize that I am committed to all six of those kids, their spouses, and their babies, mess with them, and you will find out. You will also be sorry. I have a mean streak when it comes to them. I would run to Terah as quick as I would to Kelly. I have tried with everything in me to be faithful and supportive, and guess what: they have reciprocated. They, too, are what they say they are. They love.

Back to Philpot, 1994. They listened to Michael English 24/7. Occasionally one would sneak a country artist in and get in big trouble. We were a "no secular music" zone. We decided that gospel music would be the only music allowed. I could tell you why, but I won't. It's not my story. There is *much* I could say right here, but I will move right along.

These were the years that I matured into a woman who would understand what "the greater good" meant. I would become the person who bore the load quietly so that ministry could be furthered. I became the behind-the-scenes workhorse to propel others to the front. I would also suffer greatly. I know and God knows, and that's enough, but in the end, I feel blessed just to have been used. Was I a great singer? No. Was I a great piano player? No. I wasn't even average by Nashville standards, but I was enough for a start.

I insisted that the kids learn harmony parts. I insisted that they learn to sing together. It's tough to have a group when you don't know how to sing together. After all, I had been in local groups, several of them, starting with the Songbirds when I was 8 and continuing with the cousin group known as the Young Believers in my teens. I was an expert. (Yes, I am being *very* sarcastic.) However, I always knew I had an ear for a great song and for talent. I guess I thought I was a bit like Kentucky's own Simon Cowell. My playing was best described as "better than nothing." Truthfully, good musicians, in those days in that little pocket of Kentucky, were rare. So I guess that, compared to others, I was probably pretty okay. The difference in me and most aspiring singers and musicians was this: I have ears, and I use them. I know capabilities; no narcissism here. I know that nothing is about me.

The Crabb Family had several winning components. I admit it readily. The components were the work ethic of a workaholic, great singing, great songs, and above all, the anointing on the innocence of those kids. That is what made the Crabb Family. It gave the name "Crabb" a brand. No matter what anyone tries to take away from me, I share in that story. I know where the money came from to buy the first bus; it was my 401K. For fear of sounding like a braggart, I will shut my piehole.

Once again, back to Philpot and the story. On this night I had on a cotton floral one-piece flowing jumpsuit. The legs were big, and it almost looked like a dress. It was my go-to Sunday night outfit, and I had gone to it. I played for the song service. Back then, I called it the song service. I hadn't gotten the memo that it was "praise and worship" yet. I'm not sure anyone in rural Kentucky had. It was a "business-as-usual" Sunday night. All of the kids were there, and Jason sang "Daystar." They did "Saved by Grace." (Okay, call me a freak for remembering this. I couldn't remember the code to the cabin door today. Such is life.) The kids sang the glory down, and we settled into the sermon. I was distracted. I was trying to get with it, but I was having so much trouble. I kept getting this strange sense that God was speaking in my ear. It was so different. I am not an overzealous "God told me" person, so if I tell you God told me, *God told me.* I am a bit practical on spiritual matters. I believe the Bible is our guide. I also believe that prophecies line up with the word of God. I once had a preacher tell me that God told him, while he was married with children, that He was going to send him another wife who could help him in ministry. You know what I said? "God doesn't speak contradictory messages. That wasn't God. That was you and the devil."

So back to the third pew, right side, Sunday night service. God spoke with clarity during the service: "If you will work as hard for the message of the cross, the gospel, as you do for General Motors, millions will know Him."

It was profound. It forever changed my life path, and those of many.

However, I was thinking, *what? Me? Are you talking to me, God? No. I am the wage earner, the sole support, and God, You know, I tithe. You know how much I support this work ... God, well, don't you know that I can't subject those kids to poverty? What would I do in ministry? I know you are probably talking about the singing thing, but God, that's a one-in-a-million shot. I am not stupid. Remember, I don't quit jobs or change paths unless the money is better, much better. But God...*

God was finished. He wasn't planning to get into an argument with me. He spoke. He had my attention.

The service was wrapping up and I was glad. I was a mess. I needed a quiet place.

We dismissed, the people went home, and the kids went to bed. After the house was quiet and I knew everyone was asleep, I got up. I went to the closet under the stairway. It smelled like a mixture of mothballs and stinky feet, but I didn't care. It was private. No one would find me. I got on my face and prayed this prayer:

"God, I heard You, but it's a community decision. If I tell the other party, he won't agree. If I quit my job and I am wrong, I could come up short on providing for their needs. I need to know that this is *You*. I can't make a bad decision. The world thinks I'm crazy for buying this church and selling my house! So here goes, God. I have a fleece. It's a doozy. God, You know the lady in our church who's dying; I want you to heal her. I want her to raise those four children. I know what the doctors have said—I know that she is on life support—but I have to be sure. This is a big thing, so I need You to do a big thing. God, I am sorry if I sound like a used-car salesman, and I am sorry if I am doing this wrong, but You know better than anyone that I have no experience with this sort of thing, and You know my heart. You *know* my heart. If you heal her, I am willing to eat bread and drink water for the rest of my life if it means that millions will be saved, changed, and delivered. Lord, if You can provide the minimum, I will return all that I have: my time, my mind, and my trust."

I went to bed and went to sleep.

The next day, I decided I must tell someone. I did. Again, this part of the story is well documented on video and testimonies. I got a cold reception to this idea. I was a bit shocked. However, I made it clear at a Shoney's restaurant in Owensboro, Kentucky, during my lunch break, in the midst of a heated conversation, that if God came though, I would do the same. Subject closed. We left. We didn't speak of it again.

The idea of leaving my job wasn't easy. I liked working; I liked making money. I liked the perks of trips, health insurance, dental insurance (Terah was in braces), a free car, free gas, and a great base pay plus commission. I had a great job, but I worked long hours and had many other responsibilities outside my job. There was never a day I wanted to quit. In many ways, my job defined me. I was independent. That's what great income does: it makes people independent. They choose their life, typically. It doesn't choose them. We were busy at work. At this time, it was May and we were very busy. Life was normal—well, as normal as our life ever was. Remember, we lived in a church.

Then we got "the call." Our old-fashioned answering machine had a message. The message simply said, "Please come to Lexington to the hospital!"

It was the sick lady's husband—the lady I had included in my fleece. (We have disclosed their names before, but I shy away from doing that now. For some reason, I feel the need to omit the real names. We will call her Ann and him Bill.) They were new converts. She had four children, two of whom were under the age of 4. The other two were from a previous marriage, and I remember them being about 10 and 12. Ann was very sick; she was an experienced nurse and knew what she was facing. She had a disease called myasthenia gravis. She had a severe case and her heart was weakened. She had lost all use of her limbs. She had been on a ventilator at the University of Kentucky Medical Center for some time. Lexington was at least a three-hour drive. The family was suffering and Bill was missing lots of work. The kids had to be cared for. Ann hadn't been able to lift her baby for weeks. Her muscles were gone. Now it appeared, from what we had been told, that the heart muscle was weakening—hence the ventilator. I hung on every word I could get from the family. I was perplexed about the "whys" of this situation. I struggled to find a happy place most days because of her suffering and the suffering of her kids. She was my fleece. This woman, in her early thirties, whom I had known for a few short months, was my fleece to God, the deal breaker in the negotiation between a sovereign God and a girl in a floral jumpsuit.

I was reminded of a lamb in the thicket, the staff that Moses used, and the oracles that followed a command straight from God. Could it be? No. I am no prophet. I mean, I don't shout; I don't talk; I rarely testify. Had I really heard God speak? I mean, it's me—lowly little me. I said nothing, but I thought of every possible scenario. However, on this day, I kept my thoughts to myself. We drove to Lexington. There was a spoken consensus that she may be dead. The family had informed us earlier in the week that their attorney had drawn the will and the power of attorney, and a notary had gone to the hospital to get an X on the dotted line. The family thought death was imminent.

The burden I carried for this family was easy for those around me to grasp. It was a heart-wrenching story. She had those babies still in diapers.

They would cry for their momma, but she wasn't there, and it appeared she was never going to be there. So gloom was easy to accept after knowing the facts. I tried to prepare myself mentally for the bad news. That would break my heart and also speak to my doubts about what God had said. It would prove that I was in the flesh with my fleece. Maybe I was. I was not a confident dealmaker with God, that's for sure. It wasn't like playing cards and bluffing your way through. This was a vulnerable place; our future was on the line. I had shown my faith, or my ignorance, whatever the case may be. I was feeling like the least spiritual person in the car, that's for sure. I actually regretted telling anyone. However, it was too late. We rode, and rode, and finally, there was the city limit sign. Lexington was in sight.

When we arrived at the hospital, we immediately saw Bill walking toward the waiting area. He spotted us and his face lit up like a country Christmas tree! His cheeks were red, and he looked excited. It was telling. I almost exploded inside—but patience, Kathy, patience. He said, "You all won't believe what happened yesterday. Something happened. She rose up, took the ventilator out, rang the bell, and told the nurses to come help her get up! The nurses freaked out and called a doctor immediately. They were trying to make her stay in bed, but that wasn't happening."

Now remember, this woman hadn't fed herself or brushed her hair in months, and now she was getting up and taking the tubes and IV out.

We said, "Take us to her!" We walked in, and she looked as healthy as I did. She was sitting up, raring to go home.

She told us, "It was like I felt something come into the room. It overtook me. I was well, miraculously, in that moment. Done."

She was a nurse, and she began to use medical terms and descriptions of the removal of tubes, monitors, and such. I was almost in shock. Why are we surprised when God does what we ask Him to do? Why? It was surreal. I still remember how much I struggled to finish the visit.

She told us she would be coming home in a few days, as soon as the doctors ran a plethora of tests. To say they were shocked would be an understatement. However, it appeared that they accepted the facts. They gave her a letter that stated that a divine intervention had occurred and saved her life.

We drove home. I spoke little more than this sentence: "I know what I am doing tomorrow. I am giving my two weeks' notice. If God did that to convince me, I'm in."

I had no idea what was ahead, but I didn't need to know.

Ann was discharged by the end of the week. On Saturday, she helped us paint the fellowship hall. On Sunday, she was in church with her husband and four babies.

I worked for two more weeks, hired my replacement, got a book of leads from Laura Colston, who was a gospel singer and songwriter for her family group the Kindlers, and hit the phones to cold-call pastors. I emptied my 401K and bought an old 4104 Buffalo bus from David and Gary Roberts, who were mere children at the time. Seriously, they were young. We had a house full of kids and nowhere to live. We had to move because we had decided to bestow our investment in the church to another ministry. We wanted that flock to have a shepherd, and we knew we wouldn't be around. So we had nowhere to go, no money, and no jobs. Sounds like we were crazy people, right? However, when God does something that big, there are no fears. I was fearless and focused. I was in that closet that night. I knew that I knew.

And that, my friends, was how the Crabb Family, the music entity, began. My faith was on steroids. We spent the next 15 years working day and night. My personal goal was the obvious: to see God change lives. However, I had a second goal too: I wanted to brand the name Crabb. I wanted to prove that it could be done. When asked why I continue to use the name in a hyphenated manner after I married Steve, here's my reply: I spent 15 years marketing the name—why wouldn't I keep it?

9 THE PASTOR

I met Aaron the same day I met Terah, Adam, and Jason. The year was 1991, and he was 11. We were doing the dealership music show, which was more like karaoke in the park, and he was there along with my girls and his siblings. I know they have vivid memories of that night. I have heard them describe it and laugh about their first encounter with Krystal, Kelly, and I. He grinned a lot. Actually, he and Adam laughed a lot. They laughed about everything. If one of them got in trouble for laughing, the other one started. It was a twin thing. I suppose that's where Ean gets it. He smiles and laughs like his Daddy!

I don't remember anything said that day, and honestly, the fact that there were three boys and that Adam and Aaron were twins was a bit overwhelming for me. To remember what each of them said would be impossible, because I was getting them confused. I didn't have boys, and admittedly, I didn't know anything about them. Our common ground was Kentucky basketball, Mexican food, and music. He loved Chi-Chi's restaurant, and it seemed that we made that the birthday celebration spot for the twins starting the first year I was in their lives. He wanted to play acoustic and bass, and he practiced for hundreds of hours to learn. I played piano for several years, and he was the bass player. He was a joy to watch. He loved it. He loved every note to every song. He listened to the Nashville players and learned their licks. He had discipline. He still does.

We ate out a lot, and Aaron and Adam weren't used to that. One night in particular, we went to the Beaver Dam Pizza Hut. We had our pan pizza and pitchers of Coke. The boys were thin, and I always encouraged them to eat. (Anyone who hangs with me will eat, no doubt!) Anyway, we were all there, and we ate and laughed and destroyed those pizzas. It was time for the check. I picked it up and grabbed my purse as we all got up to leave. The check was collected at a cash register by the exit door. I had nonchalantly plopped a $10 bill on the table for the server. The kids looked at it and thought I had mistakenly left it. Aaron gave me one of those "Aaron" looks, a quizzical look that said, "Really?" Someone else went to pay the check, and Aaron ran over and told me I had left money on the table. I explained to him that it was for the server, a young lady who had done an excellent job. He responded, "Are you kidding me? You're just going to give it to her for no reason?"

I said, "Yes, we are."

He ran over to the server, tapped her on the shoulder, and said, "You won't believe this! They are giving you $10! They left it on the table!" All together everyone say, "Awwwwwww." That was his first experience with tipping! That's our Aaron: innocent and honest.

Boys aren't mushy like girls. They also don't do drama like girls. When these boys came into my life, they were only 11, but let me tell you, Aaron Crabb didn't give me 10 minutes worth of trouble in his life. He was the picture of obedience. The other kids always said that he got the most spankings as a little boy, but I didn't see that. With me, he was maintenance-free. We used to get ready to go to bed on the bus, and I would say, "Aaron, what did you eat?" Many nights we would go into the restaurant for a meal and he would stay on the bus and practice. It would be midnight or later, and when questioned about his meals, he would say, "Oh man, I forgot to eat today!"

Kelly would say, "Really? I sure wish I would forget!" Terah and I would shout a big "Amen!"

That was Aaron. He was disciplined and selfless.

Aaron is a passive soul until it comes to things that matter. Then he has a backbone. He is now my pastor. That's a role reversal of sorts, but in the natural progression of life, we concede leadership to the next generation. Those who do it with grace are the ones who are blessed. Aaron is now my spiritual leader. I know him. I know his heart. There is nothing that could be more natural or fulfilling than this. For you see, I was there when the 12-year-old Aaron stepped into the pulpit in Philpot and preached his first sermon. He was wearing an outfit that I had shopped in consignment stores to find. It was tough to find dress coats to fit skinny 12-year-old boys. The department stores typically didn't have anything unless it was Easter, and Owensboro was about the extent of my shopping reach back in those days. So I would go on my lunch break and look for the twins' church wardrobe. They looked so cute in their little ties and dress slacks. They occasionally wore a Jesus or Noah's Ark tie—you know, the cheesy ones—but somehow they could pull it off. We didn't know they were cheesy then. We frequently bought ties and t-shirts at concerts, and trust me, those kids represented the message well. They wore those "statement" items everywhere! I remember the one that had the hand with the nail being driven into it. I think I have a picture of each of them in that shirt at different times.

Aaron preached a sermon that made his entire family proud. I think I always knew that he was the one. I knew that he was the one who would build a church and be the shepherd. During the five years he was in Texas, I waited. About once a year, I would text Amanda and say, "Will you be needing a house in Tennessee soon? If so, give me a heads up." She would say, "Not yet, but one day!" There were days I missed them so much, knowing they were 18 hours away, that I would block it out of my mind. Aaron now says he did the same thing. However, we understand that there are seasons. The experience he gained will be invaluable in the work of Restoring Hope Church. The time spent in San Antonio was boot camp for new pastors starting a new work. The opportunity to work and learn from John Hagee was the favor of God. Aaron is one of those people who walks in favor because he's the real deal.

I remember the day that Aaron met Amanda. We were at Amanda's home church and Lyn, her mom, came to the product table. She told Mike, "Introduce Amanda to one of these boys!"

Well, for those of you who know Mike, this is like telling a pig to go get slop. He was immediately trying to make the hook up. However, being the parent, I was the last one to hear the result of these romantic road stories. Aaron wasn't a big talker, and he was drama-free, so there wasn't much on my radar.

To my recollection, Aaron was about 19 or so when he and Amanda met. She was probably 18. Well, after the introduction, it seemed they hit it off. I heard rumblings from the other kids that he *really* liked her and that their romance was catching fire.

I was pleased, because the last girl Aaron dated wasn't on my list of girls for whom I cared. I wanted him to dump her. I truly watched the girls who chased boys with an evil eye. I was always giving those "I'm watching you" looks. So I remember thinking, *I am happy Aaron is no longer interested in that other girl.*

Some time passed, and it appeared this was getting serious fast. There was concern. They were young. Aaron was asked to slow it down. He was obedient, so he did. There is much I could say here, but I will not. They weathered the storm. That 16 months they spent apart was sad for me. Aaron was grieving, but he was disciplined. They were honorable, more honorable than most can imagine. (Ephesians 6:1: Children, obey your parents in the Lord, for this is right.)

However, there was a limit. It appeared they loved each other. They now say that the Lord gave them appreciation for each other in their months apart. I didn't live with Amanda, so I can't speak to the daily comings and goings in her life during their time apart, but I lived with Aaron seven days a week. I know what he did. He prayed. He respected. He exercised patience, and long suffering, and temperance, and forgiveness. I think he would have served seven years to get her. He was a bit like Jacob, right? One day Aaron woke up and said, in so many words, "I am a man. I am an adult man. I want to be with her. She wants to be with me. God is in this. I am going to see her!" Aaron, you were so right! And the rest was history.

Truthfully, I always say Amanda is my "mini-me" (only prettier). We are amazingly close and very much alike. She is a "get it done or get out of the way" person. So am I. If you're going to be in ministry, this drive and aggressiveness can be your best friend.

Together, Aaron and Amanda are dynamite. They look like a Hollywood couple with their good looks, but make no mistake: they're not playing church. These two are sold out to ministry, not branding. They are kingdom builders, not building builders. They get it. They know it's a soul count, not an awards count. Don't get me wrong: awards are great. Notoriety is good and can be used to draw people, which in turn means souls. I understand that. I could write that book. They were willing to walk away from weekly exposure to tens of thousands and pack up the U-Haul, and head back to Tennessee. They didn't have a flock (except the immediate family), no guarantees, no one making the way for them. They would just do it because God spoke—that's a ministry after souls. They are walking a complete faith walk. They trust Him 100%. That's when He can be big. Truly, it's *so* exciting to watch.

Aaron and Amanda are now the pastors of Restoring Hope Church, which is located in Hendersonville, TN. They have three beautiful, gifted children: Elijah, Eva, and their little "surprise" Ean! Eli is 10, Eva is 7, and Ean is 4.

Not to be repetitious, but I will say exactly what I said about Terah: I have been a "go-to" person since Aaron was 11. There has never been a day I wouldn't have walked to Texas to help them. I am part of the stability factor that has allowed Aaron to pursue his destiny. He is part of the beautiful life I have been blessed to have, part of this front-row seat that God gave me. He is part of my investment. I have loved Aaron and invested in him, and it's been easy. Everything with Aaron Crabb is easy. He is the easiest person on the planet to love.

That day many years ago, God told me that if I obeyed Him, millions would hear the gospel. That promise is still alive through these ministries. I get to sit, cry, and watch with pride every soul whom Aaron and Amanda have a part in winning. I see the promises of God repeated and repeated, generation after generation. I watch God give Aaron and Amanda dreams and visions, prophecies and wisdom, sermons and songs, discernment and strength, and yes, I still have a front-row seat. That's how I like it. Blood is thicker than water, but love is thicker than blood. Love is stronger. And once again, I have all of my babies within a few miles, and I like that.

It's like this: I may not see them every day, but I know where they are, and they are close enough to borrow a cup of sugar. That sure beats thinking they're 18 hours away in Texas.

10 TRUTH SHALL MAKE YOU FREE

Krystal may be the child who is least known. She doesn't sing, doesn't seek attention, and enjoys a normal, private life these days. However, she is my oldest, and I have the most years spent, the most struggle, and an amazing story of triumph about her. I will take the opportunity, with her permission, to tell you the story of Krystal Lynn. I hope you are ready for this!

As you know, she was born in 1974—on June 5, to be exact. She was a bright little girl, with big blue eyes and a huge vocabulary from an early age. We were young parents, and I am sure our mistakes were immense, but she thrived.

After 15 years of marriage to her dad, I decided to get divorced. It was a rough time for all. I was about 32 or so; Krystal was 14 and Kelly was 10. I worked long, grueling hours for several years. So there I was, a divorced, single mother of two, working tireless hours as a business manager for a dealership. I am confident that I wouldn't have won any "Mom of the Year" awards. I know I failed miserably. I failed by being absent. However, the mortgage had to be paid, and clothes, food, and cars had to be bought. You all get it. We all live it. My job was 6 days a week, at least 10 hours a day, plus a 45-minute commute. Life was tough. I missed band concerts, cheerleading, and any and all school activities. I was an overcommitted mom. This is on my list of *big* regrets.

I was the breadwinner. Money was good, and I had been blessed to some degree to have been trained in sales and finance. I spent four years working at a bank in my 20s and went to college to study business and accounting for two and a half years. However, as with most plans, a curve came. When I was in college, my husband lost his job, so I had to find one. I quickly found out that my years at a bank, and the communication skills I learned there, made me a candidate for a sales job at any dealership. I worked a couple of years as a bookkeeper, but I soon realized I was missing the money boat. The income was in sales, not bookkeeping. I transitioned to finance, which also has a commission-based salary. My income went to six figures. This was the 80s, in Kentucky, and I was a woman. Truly, it was nothing but favor from God.

The economy in that part of Kentucky had been decimated during Jimmy Carter's reign of terror, and anyone who derived their income from coal was in trouble. The trickle down was insane. The county had been forced into a state of poverty 10 years earlier, when the massive layoffs happened, and the recovery was truly never there. My choices were this: work for $10 an hour and live at poverty level, or make a big salary and sacrifice the time. I chose the latter. Would I do it again? I am not sure. Probably, but I would be more demanding of time off. I wish I had realized that I was the "cash cow" (no jokes please), and I should not have allowed myself to be bullied by employers. It's called a rearview mirror for a reason. It's pretty easy to see from here.

As my independence grew, so did my longing to be happy and my dissatisfaction with my home life. We agreed on the terms of the divorce and signed. My girls would go with me and I would support them. I was willing to do that as long as they were with me. I couldn't do without them under any circumstances.

I don't hate their dad; I never did. I was young, and so was he. We had different ideas about raising kids, church, and life in general by the time we hit our 30s. We didn't have a Biblical reason to divorce to my knowledge, but we did it anyway. Don't judge. I am being honest. There was so much unhappiness in that home. My girls were suffering. We all were. This marriage was prime for intervention from spiritual leaders and counseling. I mentioned it, but no dice. It was over; the divorce was final. I made mistakes, serious mistakes, and so did he. I made choices that were always rooted in insecurity, but in my heart of hearts I had always wanted one thing: a Godly home, and that was all. I had voiced that for many years. Now that I was divorced, I still longed for it. However, it proved difficult to see myself ever having a husband who was interested in God, church, or destiny. People looked at me like I had two heads when I started talking that "church talk." It was a different world, this divorced world.

Fast forward several years, which I will not expound on in this chapter, and I find myself living in Philpot, KY, in the back of a church that was built in the 1800s. I moved my girls from a nice home to this. Why? All because I had married a man who said he was called and wanted to preach. If the opportunity was going to present itself to preach, it would be up to us to provide a sanctuary, due to circumstances. This has been openly discussed and documented many times. I will choose to disclose only things that are already common knowledge.

Anyway, we lived in a parsonage that many would consider a dump. It was crystal clear that I wanted this to work so much! So what did I do? I talked it up to my girls, because they would be living there—you know, like all-the-time living there. No plan B for us.

Kelly's first reaction was, "I am *not* living here, Mom. This is awful!"

My reply was, "Little girl, you will live wherever I say we are going to live. You are not the decision maker!"

So we painted, put in a bathroom and a kitchen, wallpapered, and shined that place up. It was roomy, and the kids could spread out. They learned to sing together there. This was the genesis for the Crabb Family the singing entity. This was the place Aaron preached his first sermon. This was ground where fertile prayers were prayed, and liking became loving to a bunch of kids who were a blended family and told they would be siblings. They didn't have a choice in the matter. The "holy grail" of the harmony lessons and songwriting attempts for these kids happened here. In the end, they decided they liked it, Kelly included. They also decided they liked singing together. They enjoyed the hours upon hours spent honing their parts and learning instruments. So we were living in an old building behind a church. The kids had been through many changes, and they were kids.

Everyone handles things differently, especially when they get things that they didn't sign up for. Let me make a point right here. Divorce is nasty. I have seen kids, grandchildren, and spouses abandoned and devastated. Not all marriages will last. However, the way you treat people after you don't need them is a true snapshot of who you are. This is my number one anger moment! I have seen total abandonment of kids from people who want to be highly esteemed and regarded as spiritual! It's amazing how they can walk away from children and grandchildren! It's amazing how the value of a human being is determined by the current "story" of the user. When the storyline changes, dump the kids. New wife? New life. People aren't trash. You can't dispose of people. How do you turn the love on and off? How do you do that to children? This is a question I will take to my grave. Oh, the pain of selfish adults and the web it does weave!

Anyway, Krystal was beginning to be my "stress" child. We had struggled with her choices regarding boyfriends and her choices in general. She didn't tell me the truth. She would disappear for days. I bought her five cars and took them all away for not obeying rules—all in the span of four years. I am sure that she would have *her* side of this story, so I guess when she writes a book, we will get it. Anyway, you get the picture: she was rebellious. She was not dealing well with the hand she had been dealt. She often said, "Oh Mom, you don't know the *real* bad stuff!" There's a *big* part of me that appreciates that honesty.

Once we took a family vacation to Disney World, compliments of General Motors, and all six of the kids went with us. Those sales contests made for great vacations! This was the first time my bonus kids had gone.

My girls had been multiple times, but Adam, Aaron, Jason, and Terah had never met my dear friend Mickey. I was exhilarated to introduce them!

We had a vacation that would rival the Griswolds, truly. We stayed at a Disney resort and lived and breathed Disney for the better part of a week. This blended family was finally feeling like a real family. It felt like Krystal, who was now 19, was turning a corner. We were spending more time with Jason, and I was starting to feel a bond forming between all of these kids— and me too, for that matter.

Too soon the vacation was over, and I went back to work. The kids went back to school, and life returned to normal. At this point in our lives, I was the only wage earner in the family, and all six kids were in school. We had three teenagers with cars, car insurance, braces, glasses, and lots of tennis shoes to buy. My stress level was high, but let me tell you a little secret: when life happens, you don't get a memo to prepare you. It just happens.

Krystal let me know that she needed to talk to us and preferred to do it at the church. I said, "Okay, no problem."

I walked in, and she had brought a friend, which confused me. I am fuzzy on the details of the conversation, but it went something like this.

"Mom, you know how I told you I am not seeing _____ anymore? Well, that was a lie. I am seeing him, and I am pregnant!"

I don't remember what I said. Once again, maybe Krystal will tell us in her book. However, how do normal people handle mistakes? I cried, then I cried some more, but we came to a resolution within an hour. I believe in sticking with people I love. I don't throw people away. We circled the wagons, told the truth, tried to talk her out of marrying the guy to no avail, and continued to love her. She married him. It wasn't a good thing, but it happened.

However, on July 15, 1994, my world was rocked. Welcome, Eden Nicole, to planet Earth. The world changed that day. It suddenly had a new center. I thought I loved my kids. I thought I had "Momma Bear" instincts for their safety. This exceeded that. This little redhead would eventually be by my side. She was my sidekick and was constantly saying, "Granny, get off the phone. You talk to Beckie (Simmons) too much, and you need to talk to me!"

The marriage ended about 20 months later, and Krystal came home. She was in bad shape. I won't elaborate, but it wasn't good. She hadn't been allowed to have so much as an opinion in two years. We had rarely seen her. At this point, I had spent very little time with Edie, and I wanted her more than anything in this world. Time passed. The Crabb Family was front and center. I had devoted all of my time to creating, branding, and promoting the music of these kids.

We had moved back to Beaver Dam, to a house that my brother sold us on owner terms—because truly, it's a pretty tough thing to get a mortgage when you recently quit your job to manage the career of your unknown children. This was my life. The banks said no, as I had known they would.

I prayed this prayer: "God, You are able to provide us with a house. I don't see how it would be Your will for all seven of us to live in an apartment, but if that's what I have to do, You alone know that I will. You know what You told me. You alone know the entirety of the marching orders you gave me, so I am trusting You for a place to move these kids—a place that's a home, not an apartment, God. You own the cattle on a thousand hills. This is small stuff for you!"

I drove my old blue GMC van down Highway 231 and prayed that prayer. I was going to look for an apartment at that very moment. I actually had a cell phone then. As I drove, I noticed that I had a message to call my brother, so I called him. He said, "Kathy Jo, you know that house we've got in Beaver Dam? Why don't you move into it? I can carry the note. Get those kids, and get your stuff moved. I am not having you move into an apartment. You have owned a house most of your life. You're not moving into an apartment now."

Sold! I went and looked at the house. It was pretty nice. It was certainly nicer than the old Sunday school rooms we were living in. We settled in nicely. It was small, but we were gone so much that it worked out pretty well.

Krystal got a job with one of my former employers. At first I thought this was a good thing. She needed to support herself. She was living with us, so all six kids plus Edie were there. We had nine people in 1720 square feet. We didn't even know we were crowded. We loved it. She was living at home and driving to Owensboro to work. However, something didn't feel right.

One morning, the phone rang super early. I recognized the number and the voice. I knew this person. He was an atheist, and probably 25 years older than Krystal. I said, "If you have intentions toward my 22-year-old daughter, you better be prepared for war! I will take you on." He lived a life of influence and was not accustomed to rules. The deep pockets of his family had offered influence in this Kentucky town!

I asked Krystal about the situation, and she denied any wrongdoing. I didn't believe her and told her so. We clashed. We clashed a lot during that time. We truly had the classic mother/daughter relationship that depended on her growing up, and growing nearly old, before I think she had any appreciation that I was smarter than she thought. Anyway, back to the 22-year-old Krystal.

In the meantime, the Crabb Family needed a platform. We decided that if we could showcase the group on our turf, with our rules, and with our people, then Nashville would pay attention. We needed a booking agent.

We thought we needed a record company. We were green, so this "build it and they will come" philosophy became our daily routine. I scheduled a meeting with Steve Chandler and the entertainment committee at the Executive Inn in Owensboro. This was a Vegas-sized showroom that seated a thousand people when it was packed out. I had been there many times to see country acts. I'd seen Ricky Skaggs there at least four times, and had dragged my children there to see him as well. They resisted, but now thank me for the experience. It was a room that was built out over the river, and you could listen while you watched the barges go up and down. It looked much more glamorous at night with its lighting, water, and music. People loved it.

So I went there to pitch gospel music with the Crabb Family opening. I had known Steve since I was a kid. He was a local engineer and lived in Owensboro at the time. He was extremely influential in music circles and had influence over the decisions for this venue. He was also the road sound man for the Happy Goodman family when he was a kid. Now you get it. Everyone thought Steve was a big country music guy at the time, but he and I had a bond: Gospel music. So I pitched the idea to him.

It wasn't as easy as I thought. No one had even remotely heard the name "Crabb." Steve, who ran the place, didn't even know me by the name Kathy Crabb, so no dice on the date with the Crabb Family opening. I explained to Steve that I had remarried and that my husband was a singer-songwriter and all of these kids were singers. I explained that I had quit my job and was planning to spend the rest of my life promoting the gospel. I think he was a bit shocked, but after he absorbed it, I am sure he knew that I wasn't crazy.

Even though all of this sounded a bit crazy, he later called me. He said, "Let's talk. I think I can get them to rent the room to you one night a month. Let's see how it goes. You make money, you keep it. You lose money, you pay us anyway. It's a gamble, but hey, I think I can get Howard and Vestal to come!"

Wow! I am a player, and this is called playing. We said yes immediately. Here's the long and short of it: it worked. We booked almost every group that was touring. Some sold tickets; some didn't. We paid everyone like we said we would. We filled the room and always made it appear successful. I knew that empty rooms do not invoke excitement. So if we had slow sales for an artist that had assured us they would be a major draw, we gave tickets to youth groups, begged all of our family to be there, and guilted our friends and family into coming. They came. But ultimately, the word on the street was this: they are having great crowds in Owensboro. I had a natural instinct to "fake it until you make it" and this was that! The kids put up posters every week. Every storefront in three counties had a poster. The funny thing was this: the kids were the singers, the musicians, the grunt workers, the bus cleaners, and the stamp lickers. They learned to work! Those early days taught them the true price of success. It is my gift to them. A few criticized me for ALWAYS working, and ALWAYS making them work, but it's possibly the most valuable lesson they have ever been taught. We worked, and worked, and worked some more. Nashville was coming as our guests. I mean, who would turn down a hotel, four-star restaurant, and concert tickets, all for free? We invited everyone. They came. In the secular world, it's called "wining and dining!" It was like putting a career on speed dial or steroids, or like having a fast-forward button. We invited everyone, including radio people, all of who came. We worked ourselves to the bone. Radio started happening. Life was heating up. Make no mistake about this, though: we were working like plow mules! For you that don't understand my lingo, that means we worked *HARD*!

So we were at the Executive Inn for a Friday and Saturday weekend extravaganza. I am struggling to remember the Friday night artist, but I think it was Vestal and Howard. They gave us a large oil painting and autographed it to us that night. Sweetest thing I have ever seen. Dottie Rambo was coming the next night. Friday was a huge success, and we had rooms to stay in at the hotel for the weekend. We had enjoyed our late night dinner with friends in the restaurant, and now we were headed to bed. All of the kids were with us except Krystal. She had given me some sort of story that I questioned, but I was to the point that my hands were tied. I had no proof; it was all speculation. Edie wasn't with us, but she was safe at a relative's house. So I checked off my "where is everyone?" list and went to sleep.

At 3:15 a.m., the phone rang. I thought I was dreaming, but finally, I awoke. The voice on the other end said, "Ma'am, this is Officer Smith with the Bristol police department in Bristol, Virginia. Do you have a daughter who's petite, blonde, and would be in Bristol?"

I couldn't do this. I quickly handed the phone to Doug (Gerald). I couldn't get news from a police department about Krystal. I couldn't do this. I started crying, having a meltdown. I thought she was dead. After hearing a few sentences of dialogue I decided that she wasn't dead, just injured. I grabbed the phone back. Jesus, Jesus, Jesus! I was hyperventilating. Jesus, help!

The officer said, "She's alive, but we need to talk. Okay?"

I agreed to compose myself and was trying to believe what he was saying—the part about "she's alive."

He said, "Your daughter is in the emergency room here in Bristol. Apparently someone gave her some bad drugs that were heavily laced with a hallucinogen. She was hallucinating and ran out into the traffic. She crossed eight lanes of traffic, running erratically. She wasn't fully clothed. Several people called the police. They were very worried that she would be hit by a car before we could get her. They kept calling and saying she had no sense of where she was and was just running and running!"

By this time, I was crying again. I told the officer I should hang up and leave. I had to go to Bristol, now!

He said, "Wait and hear me out. We arrived at the area where she was running through traffic, quickly grabbed her, realized she was hallucinating, and got her into an ambulance. She was breathing shallow and starting to be fearful. I asked her what her name was. All I could get out of her was, 'My momma is at a hotel in Owensboro and my family is in ministry.' She then asked me to lay hands on her. I prayed for her, but it appeared that I wasn't rebuking the devil with enough authority. I could tell she expected a Pentecostal prayer, but I'm a Baptist. I prayed like I know *how* to pray. She was obviously very afraid that she was dying. She even asked me if she was going to die. Evidently I wasn't convincing enough with my prayers, because she started praying for herself. She was rebuking the devil and telling him that he couldn't have her soul. She kept saying, 'I plead the blood of Jesus, I plead the blood of Jesus!' Ma'am, she touched God. She immediately got better. I will never forget this night. I have never seen anything quite like this."

I was in a puddle of tears by now.

He continued, "Miss Kathy, I don't know you. I have never heard of you, but this I know: I was on that run for a reason. I am a believer. I am a Baptist, and maybe not Pentecostal enough to lay hands on people without being told to, but I know this much. I called directory assistance for a hotel in Owensboro. They gave me this hotel first. I asked the switchboard operator if there was anyone staying there who's in ministry. She said, 'Sir, there are 800 rooms here, but wait, I may know who you're looking for.' She rang your room. You answered. You are her mom. With two clues and two minutes on the phone, I found you. This is about your daughter. I need to tell you more: it appears that she has lost her way, but when she was looking Satan in the eye, she started rebuking him. She went straight for the blood! Whatever she's going through, never forget what I am telling you tonight. She understands the power of the blood!"

This conversation would be my go-to for the next few years. It was God who put this man there to convey this information to me. God assured me that night that she was promised to me, that she would someday get it right. He also allowed me to see that deep down in her soul, Krystal had the hidden key to life figured out. She knew how to pray for herself. When the room was dark and everyone was gone, she had learned to draw the "bloodline"! She understood the power that we possess in the tongue, the rebuke, that authoritarian stance that positions us, the blood bought, in a superior role over our enemies. Simply put, she understood the blood. The struggle continued, but the blood would cover it.

With this, he gave me a number to call to get an update on her condition. I got up and got dressed and readied myself to leave.

I called, and the hospital information person told me, "Some man came and got her. He had been in jail for giving her the drugs, but he made bond and picked her up!"

I highly suspected the man was the wealthy businessman . It had to be him. I knew his wife and dad. My next call was to the wife, followed by a call to his elderly father. Sin is sin, and truth is truth. I wasn't sure how long it would take Krystal to get over it, but I knew that I was required to tell the truth, even when it was about one of my own. The wife divorced him.

Krystal moved out of my house and took Eden with her. It broke my heart, but I couldn't stop her. The relationship with this man lasted for a short season. Sadly, it appears that he never found peace. Many years later, this man chose a dramatic ending for himself. On his 60th birthday, he prepared detailed directions for his employees regarding what they should do upon his death. He then called 911 and told them to come and check out the garage area of the dealership, that they would be needed there soon. Then, he went to the wash bay and shot himself. He shot himself in the dealership he had grown up in, inherited from his dad, who had inherited it from *his* dad. It was the dealership where I worked, the property where I met Adam, Aaron, Terah, and Jason, and the location of years of labor for me and my friends. It became tarnished by the self-inflicted gunshot wound of this troubled man on his 60th birthday, the man who enticed my young daughter, the man who thought Christians were crazy. He ended his legacy in a manner that made an entire city gasp. He seemed tormented, and that truly made me sad.

About six months after the bad drug incident, Krystal started missing the family, and we invited her to the Singing News Ski Retreat. She had been nearly estranged from me, and I missed her terribly. I also missed Edie. I saw Edie occasionally, but I missed the days when she lived with me. I had found a new kind of sad, a sad that isn't understood until there's a grandchild involved. We were thrilled to be going on this ski trip, and I was more thrilled now that Krystal was going. Maurice Templeton, who owned *Singing News Magazine*, hosted all of the young singers in a beautiful ski lodge and paid for all of us to stay, eat, and ski. The lodge was beautiful, the scenery was breathtaking, and we were in Heaven. The lodge provided a place for fellowship around a fireplace at night. Those were glorious times, simply glorious. Krystal went with us, and something clicked. Without fanfare, she went home and broke the relationship off with the older man. She moved back home. We were all together again for a season. I was incredibly happy. The times we shared in that little house on Delmar Drive in Beaver Dam are catalogued in my mind. The photos are in color, and include a little redhead, giggling twin boys celebrating their 16th birthday, a house full of teenagers on any given night, and a big old Silver Eagle sitting in the drive out front. Always. Charlie Burke had signed the note for us to buy the current Silver Eagle . Charlie Burke was a well-connected businessman who I had never met from North Carolina. We needed a new bus and a friend told me to call Charlie for advice. After a 30-minute conversation he told me to buy the one we had our eye on. It would cost twice what we had paid for our house. I was nervous. He said he would arrange the loan and sign with me. I was like, "Seriously?" We did, and he did. We paid it off early, and Charlie remained a close friend until he went home to be with the Lord a few years ago. The bus we traded in was another miracle story. It was our second bus. Our first bus was a primitive existence. And we desperately needed adequate heat and some air. We also needed beds and a water source. It was rough. This wasn't a "want" situation; it was a "need" situation. God knew. We spotted a bus in a "Thrifty Nickel" want ad while in Nashville. I called to inquire about it and learned that bus had belonged to Ricky Skaggs. We made an appointment to see it. Compared to what we currently had, this million-mile Eagle was a dream. It had bunks, a bathroom, a television, heat, and air conditioning. We thought it was "up town!" We wanted it. There was just one small problem. We didn't have any money. Two of my relatives stepped forward and offered to loan us $40,000 to buy it. There was another problem. Ricky was asking $60,000 for it. We were an unknown group at the time and Ricky Skaggs was a star. I was intimidated, but I wanted to talk to him somehow. I wrote Ricky a letter and faxed it. I poured my heart out. That "you have not because you ask not" would not stand in my way. I was asking.

We were in Leitchfield, Kentucky, working a Wednesday night service at the Church Of God, when I called Ricky's office in Nashville to see if they had received the fax. The sweet lady assured me they had, and she informed me that she had given the letter to a courier to take to Ricky. He was at the Ryman sound checking for a show! I had goose bumps! My letter was at the Ryman. She conveyed that it wasn't likely he could take that price. He had much more invested in the bus and it had appraised for more. I was still a bit hopeful, but the confidence that was so easy to find when I was writing the letter was disappearing. I almost felt stupid. Almost.

This was the bus he had during his early years—you know, the "Highway 40 Blues" years. I wanted it bad. We all did. However, the $40,000 would be every red cent we had. After the service was over, I used the pastor's phone to call my answering machine back at home! Well glory! I had a message from Ricky. He said, "Come get the bus. I prayed about it and God said to do it!" These Kentucky hillbillies went and picked up a Silver Eagle from a superstar. What a memory. Ricky is now a friend, and I have thanked him many times. This story always invokes a smile between friends that realize that God had a plan.

We didn't know what we had. We didn't complain; we worked. We appreciated God, each other, and the simple things like cheeseburgers, buses with heat, and guitars that would hold a tune; yes, the simple things.

Within a few months, Krystal began to travel with us occasionally. She really hated it, but I wanted to be in church with her, so I insisted. She met Ben Isaacs. They dated, married, had another little girl named Cameron, and moved right next door to me. Things seemed good. I often refer to the five years that Krystal was married to Ben as my years of innocence. All of my kids were my neighbors. We ate together; we played together; we worked together. The entire family worked for the ministry, with the exception of Ben, who continued to work with his mom and sisters. The Isaacs were extended family to us. We worked with them a lot during those days, and everyone grew close. Time passed; life was good. Krystal and Ben were celebrating five years of marriage. All was well, or so I thought.

On October 1, 2002, I came home to an unusual anger. Doors were slamming and attitudes were flying. Something was terribly wrong. My stomach hurt so badly! I knew that something unseemly had gone down. The information that I received that day would forever change my life. I decided that denial might be my only option. What was I to do? I was trapped. I had so many responsibilities, and I had to keep the boat floating, didn't I? One wrong move could sway the public opinion, and that would lead to suffering. Krystal thought I should let the chips fall where they may. She thought the offender should be "outed" and rejected. I was scared. We needed a plan. There wasn't an easy fix. The events that Krystal discovered would disappoint her in such a personal way, and truly there is no way to convey this in a few sentences. These facts are not for public consumption anyway; just know that it was devastating for all of us. Consequently, Krystal was very upset with me because of my passivity. In my opinion, she felt abandoned. I will not elaborate. I can't elaborate. However, the result was this: she shut everyone out, including Ben. Ben wasn't the issue, but he would lose his marriage anyway. Ben was blindsided. Watching this broke my heart. Ben was stunned and confused; we all were. She actually filed for divorce. Their five-year marriage would end, and I don't think they had ever had a real argument. Krystal left her job; I actually fired her. I felt like she had allowed the rebellion to occupy her thinking, and she was now making her own bad choices. She decided that hypocrites were far too prevalent and she didn't need this mess. She was finished. She threw out the baby with the bath water. She walked away from Ben, me, and her siblings. We weren't the ones who had hurt her, but we would be the ones who suffered. In that moment, Krystal was finished with all things ministry.

It was such a horrible time for me. She felt that I compromised. She felt that I had turned my head and pretended not to notice the obvious. She was right, but I had to have a plan.

This is all very personal, but I will summarize. After the separation, we saw Krystal maybe twice in the next year. I saw her children maybe a half dozen times during the next year. *I was broken.* That timeframe was one of the most painful things I have ever walked through. I remember seeing an 8-year-old Edie riding her bike in a parking lot. I sat in my car and cried while I watched those red ponytails bounce, longing to take her for an ice cream, but it wasn't allowed. Krystal had divorced her entire family when she divorced Ben. Ben allowed me to see Cameron when it worked out. Krystal was burying her pain. She wouldn't talk about it, and she was once again allowing the rebellion to own her. She had lost respect for others. She considered me too passive with a particular situation. She wanted me to be the big and bad person who didn't allow the world to mistreat me. I disappointed her. If I had it to do over, I would do things so differently. I would go deep, eradicate the problem, and refuse to grant grace to the ungrateful. I would wise up in situations that were profoundly personal. Had I faced the real enemy, this year of separation from Krystal might have been avoided. But once again, hindsight is 20/20, and trying to deal with the secrets of others will always leave you in a fog. I was in a fog, that's for sure. In this situation, I can't be totally candid. I would truly love to be, but for the sake of the innocent, I won't be.

We all went to Hawaii on a family vacation in 2003, a few months after Krystal had pulled away from us. Everyone went except for Krystal. She declined the invitation. She was resistant to the idea of spending time with us. We had a conversation in Hawaii, and I told the kids and all of their spouses that I needed to move. I had spent over 100 nights of 2002 in a hotel in Nashville. The business of the family was exceedingly demanding, and I was growing tired of hotels. I was also tired of the I-65 drive. Cell service was awful on the way to and from, and I needed to find answers to help maximize my time. There had been a couple of things that had prompted me to want to move in addition to this, but once again, that will go unspoken.

I had a new home, and I hated to leave it. Jason, Adam, and Kelly had built new homes. Aaron had just bought a house, as had Terah. However, on this beautiful day in May 2003, sitting by the pool overlooking the beach in Hawaii, we all agreed to move. Kristi was ecstatic because Nashville was near an airport. She was from Florida and went home to visit a good bit, so she was happy. Amanda didn't care either way, but I think Nashville made her pretty happy too. Mike was immediately in with, "Yes! Get me out of Beaver Dam!"

Jon was the same; it wasn't his home. Jon was from Maryland, and Beaver Dam was like a foreign country to him. I don't remember Shellye's reaction, but it wasn't a big deal to her either. Kelly and Mike had just built a house, and Kelly cried! Adam and Aaron didn't care; they would live wherever their wives wanted to live. So it looked like we were all moving! Everyone except for Krystal. It was bittersweet. My Cameron was growing, and Edie was too. Edie was so confused.

We moved and left Krystal, Edie, and Cameron. That made me sad, but Krystal had no interest in moving to Tennessee. I was heartbroken. We were all heartbroken. I cried myself to sleep most nights. When my workday was finished, my social commitments settled, my gown was on, and my teeth were brushed, then and only then would I give myself permission to think and cry. I missed those babies, and I was so worried about my daughter! I felt as if I was living in the tribulation. The 12 months of separation would equate to thousands of tears and mountains of fear. Would life ever be normal? Would the scar heal, would my daughter return, would the ground ever stop shifting? Did this family have a chance to survive and be intact?

There were other patches that weren't smooth either. Heartbreak had set in for this gal. I plastered on a smile, did the interviews and meetings, and promoted songs, people, and the gospel. Crabbfest was thriving. The group had made their first recording with just the five siblings. It was a hit. I was gaining grandbabies left and right, and life looked good to an onlooker. However, my heart cried, and I spent a lot of time begging God for answers.

It was early September, I think, maybe the first week of the month. I had an earache and went to an ear, nose, and throat specialist in Hermitage, right outside of Nashville. He wanted to do a CT scan. The doctor returned to the exam room to tell me that he had had it read and that it looked abnormal. They sent me for an MRI. It showed a large mass in my sphenoid sinus.

They called to discuss the MRI and said, "This doesn't look good. Let's get you to the surgeon as soon as possible. This mass is twisted around and involves your pituitary gland, so we are going to need a neurosurgeon to see you."

I was once again speechless. Should I tell my family? Should I wait and see? I remember sitting at the Applebee's in Hermitage trying to decide.

I called my friend Brian Copeland and he came and talked me through it. He was a fixer. So was I, but when it was me that needed fixing, I wanted some reinforcement. I opted to tell the kids. The short version of this long story is this: I had a pituitary tumor in my sphenoid sinus cavity. The doctors were extremely "gloom and doom" about it. It showed as benign in the biopsy, but it was near the optic nerve, and they recommended a big surgery.

Somewhere in the middle of all of this drama, Krystal came to see me. She came to spend the day and ended up staying forever. She didn't return to Kentucky at all, for anything. It was actually bizarre, but in a good way. We found a house for her and the girls. We bought furniture, clothes, and a car, and she transitioned school and their lives in less than a week. She agreed to take her old job back in the Crabb Family office, and she was back in our world. In the end, her love for those who hadn't hurt her proved to be stronger than her disdain for the one who had. We were complete again, at least for a minute.

My tumor is still there. The story is long and may be something I save for another day, another book. However, my health hasn't been compromised. I haven't experienced vision problems or any kind of peripheral issues. I still get annual MRIs and I am painfully aware that the tumor is large and intrusive. However, I still haven't had the surgery, and it's been over 11 years. My neurologist says that these kinds of pituitary problems can debilitate people. Thus far, I have been fine. I have peace that this is one problem the Lord has handled for me.

So back to Krystal. Ben moved to Hendersonville and bought a home about a mile from Krystal, and they co-parented Cameron. Krystal remarried in 2006. She married a Christian guy who was willing to move to Tennessee and leave his beloved North Carolina. I haven't been able to convert him to Kentucky basketball yet, but I am believing God!

Brian Lawing and Krystal got married in the spring of 2006, and he stepped into some big shoes. He married a wife and took on the struggle of a built-in family. He had never been married, and he's an only child, but we are a tribe. How would an only child do in *this* environment? Well, he has survived and thrived! They have attended church for the entire length of their marriage. He signed up to be a God-fearing, church-going husband, and that's what he's delivered. They added another little girl to the roster in 2007. Sophie Caroline was my 13th grandchild. She truly completed this marriage, and this family. Krystal works at Cornerstone Church in Nashville, and is mom to Eden, 20, Cameron, 15, and Sophie, 7. They are truly a beautiful family, and a walking, talking testimony about the grace of God.

If I had to list five people I know who live what they preach, Krystal would be on it. She's solid. She refuses to wear guilt and shame as an accessory. She is unashamed. She gave her blessing for this story to be told. When people are honest with the world, that's a pretty good indication that they're honest with God. Let this be an encouragement to those of you who have adult children who are wayward: there is hope. Sometimes they're struggling with hurts, anger, rebellion, and disappointment. They don't know where to put the pain. They medicate it, bury it, scream about it, try and tattoo it away, and in my case eat it away, when in reality we just need to submit. Strong-willed people struggle with submission, but here's the good news: once a "hard head" gets it right, they are unwavering in what they believe. That's Krystal.

Ben also remarried, and they have been an example of how people should act if they get divorced. I hate divorce, but in the end, it happens. How we act when it happens defines who we really are. Ben's family and our family never exchanged a cross word, and we have all remained close friends. I have never heard Krystal say a bad thing about Ben, nor Ben a bad thing about Krystal. They didn't avoid each other, and they communicated. After all, isn't that how adults should behave? So there you have it. After thousands of questions and lots of back-story gossip, here's the truth. Ben is still like family. We don't throw people away.

Life is full of twists, turns, and curves. In the end, it will be okay. If it's not okay, it's not the end. Most of us are still painting our picture, writing the script of our life. We fail and we get up. We fail again and we get up again. The thread that weaves the fabric of life is love. Love is stronger!

11 TATTOOS AND SMILEY FACES

On July 15, 1994, I became a 38-year-old grandmother. Wow! When I look back at how incredibly young I was, I write myself a "pass" for so many mistakes. Good gracious: at 38, when most people are parenting toddlers, I was trying to parent a house full of teenagers and starting on the grandbabies. The circumstances weren't perfect, but *she* was perfect.

Eden Nicole made her grand entrance at the Owensboro-Daviess County Hospital. We waited outside the door while she was being delivered. I could hear her cry, and I couldn't wait to see her. Would she have black hair like Krystal had when she was born? Would she have chubby cheeks and be a little round fatty? I was confident she would. We waited. Finally, we got to enter the room. She had blood in her hair. I touched her. I held her, and I was mesmerized. She wasn't a fatty, and her hair? Who knew? It appeared to still be dirty and bloody. I asked the nurse to clean her little head; it *must* still be bloody. She quickly told me to look at her eyebrows in the light. She was a carrot top! That's not blood—that's her natural hair color. We had a redhead! I was shocked, but I loved it. I remember thinking, *This little girl will hate her hair at first, but then she will love it when she is older and realizes how special and unusual it is.* I was right.

My redhead was incorrectly named Eden. She truly should have been named Demonica. She was mischievous! Actually, she was mean in a good way. I suppose a softer description would be spunky. She was spunky. When she was 2, Krystal moved back home and we became best buddies. We were inseparable. She was my shadow and often went on the bus with us. Her little red shoes sitting on the bus one afternoon in London, KY, would be the inspiration for our 1998 song "Two Little Feet." No, I didn't write it, but I have the video where the writer tells the story about her shoes, and I was there when it was written.

She didn't have a picture-perfect situation, and I always felt like I needed to be the extra something in her life, that person who assured her that she mattered. No disrespect to Krystal, but Eden's life had known much change, and I felt she needed me.

She is now a 20 year old who decided to turn down a college scholarship to take a job at the mall. I was upset. She got a tattoo; I was upset. She wouldn't listen regarding relationships and choices; I was upset. However, guess who calls to offer help when I need it? Eden. Guess who has her size 9 1/2 boots under my table on Thanksgiving? Eden. We love. We don't always agree, but we love. Abandonment is not how I roll. I have to suck it up sometimes. I don't necessarily like it, but I do it. Why? Because we love.

Edie is *my* grandchild. She has my big feet, blue eyes, and fierce ambition. At 20 years old, she single-handedly earns as much as the average household income in the United States, without a college degree. Is that the recommended path? Of course not, but Eden is a textbook study in hard work trumping a useless degree. All degrees aren't useless, but many are.

My brother had a saying that I love. My brother was an alcoholic. He owned it; he didn't blame it on other people. However, when he assessed humanity, which he often did, he would say: "Kathy Jo, people must have a redeeming quality. I know I don't do everything right, but by doggies, I go to work. I support myself and several others. If I am drunk on Sunday, I will still be at work on Monday. Work isn't optional, —it's mandatory." He would proceed to tell me about someone who didn't abide by this philosophy. Yes, you guessed it; Danny and I were cut from the same cloth.

Eden is also cut from some of that cloth. Her drug of choice doesn't seem to be cigarettes, alcohol, meth, pot, or food. Her drug of choice appears to be hard work. Work will never fail her. God won't either.

Eden is the oldest, and I could reflect on her and write an entire book, but that would stir the jealousy pot, now wouldn't it? So I won't write an entire book, but I must share two things.

The first of my Edie stories is the one of the mean little girl who hung out with me in Beaver Dam. She played and I worked. My work was Crabb Family work, which often involved me being on the phone. Actually, it almost always involved me being on the phone. She would say, "Granny! Hang up the phone and talk to me!"

I would put my finger over my lips, give her that look, and say: "You could be at daycare, but Granny wants to keep you. You know the rules. You must let me work, because Granny has a real job, and with real jobs, people don't get to take their little girls to work. You are just special and get to be at work with me, but you must let me work!" Actually, I have told all of my grandkids that at one time or another.

On this particular day I was making radio calls. I did this once a month, and it took me three or four days. It was exhausting, but it had to be done. Eden was there and had been very little trouble. We had just built a new house, and she had lots of room to play. They lived next door, and she was there most every day that we weren't on the road. On this day, I was babysitting her.

I was talking with a Mississippi station, and the on-air personality answered the phone. We were scheduled to do a concert there in the near future, so about 30 seconds into the conversation, he said, "Everybody, welcome Kathy Crabb on the phone. She just called to say howdy, and I want to put her on the air to talk about the upcoming concert."

So I was live on the air. This wasn't unusual, but there was usually a heads-up and a warning. Not this time, but no big deal. We talked about the concert. He was blowing it out! Truly, this guy thought, and still thinks, he is a Crabb Family trivia expert. He chattered, and I chimed in when given the opportunity.

In those days, we all used landlines. Cell phones were expensive and reserved for the road and important conversations. Cell phone bills were always more than my mortgage in those days. At home we had a landline phone in every room. You remember the cordless extensions? Many disasters happened because of extensions and the ability that one had to just drop in on an existing conversation. This was one of those times.

Edie picked up the extension from the powder room. A little 5-year-old voice interrupted the on-air interview and innocently said, "Granny, I *pooped*, and there's no toilet paper in here!! *Please* bring me some!"

Like any real professional would do, I hung up that phone and never called that station again! It was a charting station, but I didn't care. I can remember the name of the guy and the town in which it was located. This is a "forever" memory. Thanks, Edie! Someday you will get your payback!

Eden, the oldest, is the one who seemed to need me the most and listened the least. I have struggled to let go and let her make her own mistakes. I want to protect her, wave a flag and a flashing red light that says "Danger ahead!" I have watched as she was bruised and disappointed by adults who didn't consider her innocent heart. I watched and prayed; I watched and cried. Her cross was my cross. Her insecurities were my insecurities. Her triumphs were my triumphs. Life is full of winners and losers. Eden is a winner. She is also chosen. On days when I wonder where the road will lead her, I take the devil back to a spot, and I remind him who Eden belongs to. She belongs to God.

The second story involves a night in Echols, KY, when a little redheaded girl who couldn't have been more than 10 years old got a touch from God. I can see that image in my mind's eye: that troubled child whom I had poured everything into was experiencing God. That child, who had known more disappointment than happiness, was meeting the Father who would stay. This Father would never abandon her or throw her away like she was a dirty paper plate; He would dry her tears and be faithful. In an old-fashioned revival, on a weeknight, God touched her. As Pastor Betty laid hands on her, I saw it. I clung to it. I know what she got that night, and I know that *she* knows.

All in all, I love her heart. Her heart has been broken, but it still bleeds for the needy. For years I lived in a cesspool of anger as I watched the pain she suffered. She was thrown away in the same garbage can I was thrown in. She was emotionally injured, and she still is. However, in the end, the one who understands every tear and every choice will keep her. He has an abundance of love to cover her, grace to pour on her, and forgiveness for the long journey she is walking. That was enough for my life choices, and it will be enough for Eden's. The grace will even cover the tattoos, I suppose. My momma always said, "There won't be no tattoos in Heaven!" I think it would be appropriate to insert a smiley face right here, but no smiley faces are allowed in this book. I think Momma got this one wrong, but don't look for me to line up for my own tattoo. It won't happen. I am too old and saggy to pull it off. As I often tell Edie, "When you're 60, that Eiffel Tower will look like an apartment complex on your stomach!"

12 LONG AND WINDING ROAD

I made a decision that this book would *not* be a Crabb Family book. I wanted it to be more personal than the expected story about the music and the travels. I committed to write the backstory of my life struggles. That one-dimensional view of me as the bossy, tough-as-nails manager doesn't define me, and besides, people have heard it before. Well, some people have anyway. Those who have followed gospel music probably know that part of my life. I am confident that I got a bad rap on occasion. I took the blame for others back in the day, but that's okay, and I would do it again. If you were a Crabb Family fan, you may think you know me. If you ever did business with us, played our music, recorded at our studio, or cut our songs, then you probably know my role in this ministry. I was what is commonly known as the "fall guy"—or, in this case, girl. I made a conscious decision to be the bad guy when necessary and allowed the family to be innocent. I may be tough at times, but I am fair. I am aggressive, but I would give my last dollar to those who need my help. I won't apologize for either of these qualities. I have many bad qualities, so please allow me to bask in a couple of good ones for a moment. Strength and generosity are my strongest characteristics, and again, that's okay. If I were selfish, I would be rich. I know many people who are exactly like me, and that's no accident. I choose my friends carefully. My time is valuable, and I typically spend my time with likeminded, generous people. I truly dislike selfishness. Selfishness is at the top of the "bad" list, right beside jealousy. The litmus test to be my friend is that simple: don't be selfish or jealous and you're in! Oh, and bring me cake. I like cake.

I have tried to weave bits and pieces about the music days into the chapters, and I've been as candid as I can be. I committed to a "high-road" book, and I plan to follow through. I committed that to myself, not a family member. Truly, we are still in America, and we do have a First Amendment right. However, just because you can tell a certain story doesn't mean you should. It often becomes difficult to tell this story because of circumstances, but I have given it my best shot.

Please know that every word, every thought is mine. There is no ghostwriter, no cowriter, and no input from anyone with the exception of confirming factual information. I also got permission from Krystal to disclose her story. She welcomed it. She has found truth. I am proud. The truth shall make us free.

The Crabb Family started with only four members. All of the kids sang and played if it was local. However, when God directed me to quit my job and go, we had to be wise. We asked the kids to come only if they felt it was their time. We worked in the Kentucky area so much that all of the kids went to 80% of the dates that first year we were a full-time group. About a year later, Aaron came with us full-time. He hated to leave Adam, but he came. Terah was right behind him. Adam went on the road during the summer with us, and joined on local dates and some extended travel, but he was the last one to join full-time, paycheck included.

The boys were great athletes, and they could have excelled in college, in my opinion, but God put the desire in their hearts for the music. There truly wasn't time for both, and in the end, an ex-college athlete is probably not nearly as fulfilled as these boys are today. Right choice, guys! They're just now hitting their stride. Each child came in their own time. That's the way it needs to be. Not everyone is called to travel. Not everyone is built for the road. Let the Lord call people, on His watch, in His time.

I think it's so disturbing when moms, dads, grandmas, and grandpas "call" their children and grandchildren to the ministry. Let God do it. He will. I try to find balance between encouragement and pressure. To pressure a child to be in ministry when God truly gifted them to be a human rights attorney isn't God. They can be Jesus to little girls who are sex slaves. They can be Jesus to people who are being abused. To encourage a bright child who can't sing to be in a quartet because *you* always wanted to be in a quartet is wrong, and it's stupid. That bright child may find a cure for AIDS, or maybe he will become a Christian banker who helps churches fund and build buildings in Haiti. Ministry is not just in pulpits. Ministry is anywhere Christians meet opportunity, anywhere there's fertile ground.

I guess what I am trying to say is this: traveling is a tough life, and so is pastoring. It better be your calling, and it better be God. If it's you, you will fail. If you are in love with the stage, you're in trouble. If you need attention and need the approval of a crowd, become a country singer, because those needs aren't Godly. They aren't the stuff of which true ministers are made.

I slept for a year on the floor of a bus that didn't have bunks. It was an old Buffalo that didn't have an interior built in it. It had no generator and no rooms, just a long bowling alley-like space with no heat, no air, and no bathroom. We slept on a plywood floor; we couldn't afford foam mattresses for everyone, so no one had them. It was rough. People thought I had lost my mind when they saw the traveling conditions. I had a ruptured disc in my back that didn't get better because the floor was so uncomfortable, and the inflammation stayed for well over a year. The pain was intense, but the call was there, so I forged ahead. I have seen my family work when they were too exhausted to stand, eat, or talk. I have seen them work 300 nights a year in the early days and have bedtime be in an old bus without bunks, no comfort at all. It's not a glamorous life. It's not for sissies, believe me. However, their commitment to the call always rose above the "cares of life" struggle. It must. Be careful what you pray for, and be careful what you love. If you love it enough, you will pursue it and chase it. If you pursue evangelism, be it singing, preaching, or anything that takes you away from home, be prepared to be gone and miss life as it happens at home.

I will never forget a story about Jason and Shellye. They met before there was any success. We were so broke, we couldn't buy a meal at Shoney's. Jason met Shellye at an outdoor concert in Rosine, KY. The Kentucky Educational Channel was filming a special on Rosine. Rosine is the birthplace of Bill Monroe, the father of bluegrass music, and is only seven or eight miles from Beaver Dam. The Crabb Family was a little-known group at the time, but we managed to be invited to appear on this special.

My cousin, who was a young 40ish widow, had a new boyfriend. We were thrilled because she had spent a long season grieving. She told me the new boyfriend had three daughters who lived with him: twins who were 16 and an older sister who was about 18. She, my cousin Shelta, wanted Jason to meet the twins. Jason was shy and unsure of himself with girls. I know you don't believe me, but you can ask him. He was very shy.

Shellye, one of the twins, came to hear our group. She had recently told me that she had never heard of the Crabb Family at that time, and she had doubted that Jason could really sing as well as Shelta had told her! When Shellye and her dad got to the concert, we were already finished. Shellye didn't hear Jason, but somewhere in this process, they met. They were babies, awkward babies, but there were sparks. He started going to see her every day we weren't on the road. Shellye, her twin sister Kellye, and my Kelly became close friends quickly. Actually Shellye and her twin sister Kellye became close to all of my girls and hung out a lot at that old house on Delmar Drive with the hunter-green walls and the kitchen table that seated 14.

Prom was coming. Shellye was going, of course, but for Jason, that wasn't possible. We were booked in the Conway, S.C. area, and Jason's new single, "Still Holding On," was hot there. They had sold hundreds of tickets. This was one of the many early rules we adopted. Looking back, it was possibly wrong, but truly I don't know how we could have done anything much differently. Anyway, as with most families with brothers, Jason decided to corner the market on Shellye. He asked Adam, who was still not on stage full-time, to be her date. Adam accommodated his big brother. So that explains the hysterical prom pictures from the mid-90s of Shellye and Adam. Jason was living out his dream; for one night only, Adam shared it as the faux Jason, Shellye's prom date!

We missed many functions, but I always drew the line at missing the birth of the babies. We all wanted to be there. So, for the most part, with an exception here and there, they were scheduled inducements. Unlike births, dying isn't quite as planned or joyous. Funerals aren't as easy. When Momma died, the kids were about to host a family cruise. The ship was scheduled to leave the port on Monday. Momma died at 3 a.m. on Sunday. It was tough. The funeral director wanted to hold the funeral until Saturday to accommodate all of the kids. This would allow the kids to do what they must do and then be home to sing, preach, and love Momma for the last time in this life. I had a relative who was uncooperative and said absolutely not. I suppose there's one in every family. The kids were contractually bound; someone had to go. Kelly, Mike, and Aaron came home. Terah, Jason, and Adam went and hosted the folks on the cruise. They were devastated, but once again, the "do what you must do" qualities of an inconvenient life schedule were the gauge. I told them that Mom would understand, and she would want them to go host the folks in Kelly's place so that Kelly and Mike could come home. Mom helped me care for Kelly when she was a small child; Kelly had to come home for closure. I am not discounting that Jason, Adam, and Terah loved and cared for her. Believe me, they cared. They are the picture of unconditional love. They love the non-blood relatives with every ounce of their soul; we all do. However, more than anything, I could feel that they were devastated they weren't here for me, the living and the one who was hurting. They said so. I knew it already. However, such is life. Miles and distance don't diminish love. I felt their love that day. So did Momma.

Being a singer means that you must deal with the schedule, the commitment of the road, and the decision to live that life. The vocal fatigue, the mental fatigue, and the physical exhaustion of the dictated schedule, which is decided on months before, must be met. The schedule, which in reality produces that "what was I thinking" moment, is not easily changed.

I am often reminded of Jason's personal prayer. When he decided to become a soloist, he prayed for vocal strength. A soloist doesn't get a pass when he or she struggles. A whole group can lean on the healthiest voice, the voice that isn't weakened by a cold or laryngitis—but a soloist? Not so much. Jason prayed, "Lord, keep me healthy, and I will keep You high and lifted up, at the center of my message, and You will be my song." It has worked. God has been faithful, and so has Jason. Truly, this is amazing, but it's the truth. To my knowledge, he has never canceled a date because of vocal duress. How cool is that? How good is God?

In the early days of the group, there was a Beckie Simmons story that she commonly told. Beckie is the owner of Beckie Simmons Agency, which books many artists in Southern Gospel music. The story goes something like this, when Beckie tells it:

"Kathy calls me and says, 'Can we meet?' I say, 'Yes.' We meet at my office in Nashville. She tells me about the Executive Inn shows they had on the books. I was impressed. I pitch talent to promoters, and she needed groups to play at the Executive Inn. Then she says, 'Well, I may book other groups from you, but I am looking for a booking agent for my family. I am going to book all of my talent from the person who signs our group.' I didn't have a clue if they could sing. I had no reason to think I wanted a new group with a name like Crabb. Kathy asks me if I would just be willing to answer the phone, take the calendar, and fill in the blanks. Basically, I was to take orders for them. She said the demand was there, that the phone was ringing. That was 20 years ago. I said yes, and the rest is history!"

This is another funny story:

I took that same proposal to Jeff Harper, of Harper Agency first. He said no. We are now friends and this is now a funny story to both him and me. I am pretty sure if he had it to do over, he would have paid a bit more attention. But hey, why would he have listened then?

Another funny story:

I took "Please Forgive Me" to Ed Leonard of Daywind Music Group and did everything in my power to get him to do this record for me. Because Dottie Leonard Miller, his mother and owner of the company, felt disloyal to a friend who owned another label we were leaving, she said no. Dottie is loyal like that. I think that was 1996 or 1997. Eddie Crook, president of Eddie Crook Company, said yes. It became our first of 21 number-one songs.

The rest of this story is this: six or seven years later, we would partner with Daywind Music Group, Word, and WEA (Warner-Elektra-Atlantic Distribution) and do great things. Under the direction of Crystal Burchette (Daywind Publicist), Brian Copeland (Daywind Director of Publishing), Rhonda Thompson (Daywind Radio Promotions), Norman Holland (Daywind A&R Director), Susan Puckett (Daywind Director of Marketing), and of course, Ed Leonard, the Crabb Family would flourish. We had a machine. It was good, rocking good. I had these dear people at my beck and call on the music side of things, Beckie on the booking side, and Brian Hudson on the "special" projects that felt better represented by a nonfamily member. We were a well-oiled machine. The Crabb Family was our name, and exponential growth was our game. Times were rolling.

We were there because circumstances forced the change. The five siblings would be the new face of the Crabb Family. The parentless records were to be the turning point for the family, the point where it would be possible to grow the under-40 demographic, and these kids could go to Morocco and sing to 100,000 Muslims or the Grand Old Opry in Music City. They could pull off both of these feats equally well. They were diverse. Because they were youthful and pretty, they were the new face of the genre in a world where our music, Southern Gospel, was often ignored. Their product and concert tickets were selling, the Doves were landing, and the Grammy nods were falling.

Brian Hudson, President of Showcase Media and Management, was a friend and teacher. He taught me more than he will ever realize. Brian took me to school on bigger and better things. He had been a manager since he was about 5, I think, and had a sixth sense about all things Christian and all things music. He was also privy to many things I had walked though—let me rephrase that—*waded* through to get the kids to the other side of this mountain. He was a friend and family confidant. I would dare say he has wiped my tears, counseled, and shot it to me straight. Sometimes you can be in a fog of pain that mimics a forest. We were in that thing so far, we couldn't see. We needed friends with eyes to see for us, and enough guts to tell us the truth. Brian spoke truth to me, to all of us. The kids and I depended on him daily and entrusted him with the truths of our pain.

Brian also taught me that professionalism is needed to get beyond the realms of your current boundaries. I listened, and I encouraged the kids to listen. We like shouting services; we always have. Although the kids soon became professionals who understood a set list and a plan, if God wanted to interrupt, He was welcome. They became the kind of professionals who could deal with a live TV show where the announcer drops a glass of water and the set is ruined. They don't reduce to laughter. They save it by having thousands of hours logged on a stage in front of people. By the time they hit their 20s, they were seasoned professionals. That "starting early" thing definitely has some benefits.

I remember a family meeting in 2001. We made a decision, as sad as it was, to turn the record company that we started with the Crabb Family, Mike Bowling. and the Hoskins Family over to Les Butler. Les was another friend and confidant. He knew us. He knew the battles we faced. He knew what the quick rise had created. He knew the innocence of the kids. He knew the determined focus that I had. He knew everything. He knew the time necessary for me to operate the company must now be reallocated to the situation at hand. He wanted to continue the label, so we said okay. This event broke my heart, and I cried for days. The Crabb Family would end up at Daywind, as would the Hoskins Family and Mike. The label I dreamed of building into a catalog of masters for my grandkids was not to be. The kids and I agreed that this was what we must do, and so we did.

Sometimes I get a case of the "what-ifs" and a wave of bitterness sweeps over me. As always, God knows the details. When the reckless choices of an irresponsible person destroyed our dreams, it crushed me. As I reflect and assess, I admit that I occasionally struggle with resolving the anger and moving on. The label, the masters, and the publishing would have created a revenue stream for the entire family eventually. And yes, I feel like that was stolen from me!

My friends the Hoskins Family would go on to make great records. Mike would end up being the first Southern Gospel soloist to have back-to-back number-one songs, and the Crabb Family ... well, they did okay, too. But OUR label, our catalog of recordings, our shot at a "cutting-edge" Southern Gospel record company, was thrown to the winds.

Our next big undertaking was Crabbfest. It was a "one of a kind" spiritual experience, We had been hosting the five-day event for 9 or 10 years, and it had grown. I could write an entire "how-to" book after producing this event for many years. We had a staff that worked on Crabbfest year-round: Allison Stinson, Patty Murphy, Scottie Desper, Bobby and Sally Pinkston, and of course, Anneta and Krystal. It was a 52-weeks-a-year commitment, and it took a village. We did our own ticketing, production, food, everything, and we had 5,000 people per night. So this was a big deal, but it was part of our brand. It's sad to think that the Crabbfest brand is no more. Allison was a great event coordinator, and we took pride in producing Crabbfest. It was my favorite thing to choose talent, events, etc. Crabbfest had a 2.7 million dollar economic impact on the Owensboro, KY area. The state welcomed us, and the city of Owensboro rolled out the red carpet for the event. We got keys to the city, immense local publicity, and visitors from 40-plus states and a few foreign countries every year. It was an amazing event, with the midnight pajama parties, Crabb karaoke, hellfire-and-brimstone preaching in the mornings, a midnight buffet every evening, an 800-room hotel, and all of our friends gathered in one place for the better part of a week. We celebrated Jesus, His power to heal the broken, and His amazing power to take a blended family and make a sad story a testimony. We celebrated salvations, healings, babies being born, grace, and lots of mercy. We celebrated mercy with every note and every word, for we were the picture of mercy. This hillbilly family, who could have been labeled "Most Likely *Not* to Succeed," and with no righteousness of our own, had been blessed with *His* anointing. Yes, we were very blessed.

I was once told that the anointing wasn't on me, that I was just blessed to be near it. That stung me for years. I hope that man reads this book, and

I am CONFIDENT he will, for I have something to tell him: you, sir, know who you are. I was called before I was. My feet have always been ordered, and I am His. I have made many mistakes, and failure should have been my destiny. However, because of my faith, because He had placed an anointing on my life, I survived. I survived it all, and I am not living on someone else's anointing. Not now, not then. My kids are anointed, my grandbabies are anointed, and I claim that their seed will be anointed.

The narcissistic person who crushed me with this comment doesn't know what a favor he actually did for me that day, for I began to ask God: "Am I a backroom workhorse who has no purpose beyond managing details and creating marketing ideas?" It bothered me for years, but now I am over it, and *He* gave me my answer. God doesn't have an entitled class. Don't believe it if someone tells you He does. This walk is for all who believe, will pay the price, and live the life.

So, Sir, this is your response (about 9 or 10 years late). I am as qualified to be used as anyone, if I want it. You are not better than me. Actually—however, please know that you stirred up the anointing in my life. Thank you. Thank you for helping to make me stronger.

Whew, now I feel better!

13 DESTRUCTION

September 10, 2001. The new bus was shining. The kids had set up the booth, hugged necks, caught up with friends, and done a little shopping at Value City; the day finally came to a close on that first day of National Quartet Convention. They were here with enough number-one songs to do an entire set, a new bus, and a zeal for God that was still tender. Just six years earlier, these same kids had a yard sale to buy their singing clothes and set up an unnoticed booth. No one cared who they were in 1995. Well I cared, and our family and friends cared, but that was about it. However, this year, they were here with a six-booth set up, with people lining up to see them and get pictures and autographs. This was a mark of their blessing, their gifts from a generous God, Who had allowed the heavens and the earth to love them and bless them with favor; you know, that favor that the TV preachers always say "ain't fair." Well, it's true that favor "ain't fair," but it's often the result of butt-busting hard work and commitment to doing the same thing every day come rain or shine. Consistency brings favor. This favor was a lot of God, and a lot of work—and oh yeah, the singing wasn't too bad either. (Sorry to brag!)

The 2001 NQC was well underway, and the rows of buses were dark and quiet by the time I pulled into the parking lot at Freedom Hall in Louisville, Kentucky. It was after midnight, and this girl was tired. Kathy, the "over-committer" who always promises more than time will allow but somehow appeases the promised, was dead on her feet and needed a bed and a feather pillow. But we had agreed to a radio station fundraiser on the first day of NQC, one that was sold to 20 people who had paid a large amount of money to eat home-cooked food. It was advertised as a "home-cooked meal" at the Crabbs' house—not a catered meal, but a home-cooked meal. So this could only mean one thing. I wasn't going until late Monday night. Oh, but hey, that's okay. The radio station, WJCR in Upton, Kentucky, faithfully played our music, honored my every whim, and helped with Crabbfest marketing. That was how the career side of this entity was born, partnering with radio. So cooking dinner for 20 was no big thing. We owed these loyal supporters of the music, and we certainly had to lend our support to our friends Wanda and Gary Richardson at the station. That's totally how we rolled in those days; hence my late arrival to NQC.

The kids said that they had had a fun first night, but they were anxious for us to arrive. A late arrival and a new bus could only mean one thing: we would be crashing on the big bed in the back of the bus. I was too tired for the hotel check-in; dragging luggage for a half mile to those hotel rooms that were always on the back 40 wasn't how I would end this night. So the bus it was. I crawled under that leopard comforter in my newly-customized back bedroom. Sleep, on this night, was easy. There was a bit of eeriness in the air. I had just heard a song that was written earlier in the day. The first verse was:

"Satan has been raging like never before,
Destruction all around us, like a dark fatal storm.
We wonder what will happen, before this cloud passes on.
If we don't stand with Jesus, we must stand the test alone."
"Who Will Survive the Storm" (Crabb, 2001)

It clicked in my spirit, and for a minute on the drive back to Louisville, I became fearful. I am prone to short bouts of "hyper" or "manic" fear. It is a cousin to post-traumatic stress disorder, which I had as a result of being attacked and having my throat cut. Over the years, as I've matured and my faith has strengthened, I have learned to speak to those little waves of fear. I tell that fear, "I know the Word," and it usually runs. On this night the lyrics made me fearful for a brief moment. I had that feeling of impending doom. I can remember that "destruction all around us" line like it was yesterday. I immediately had images of an accident, a house fire, ambulances, and heartache. It made me uncomfortable, but I spoke to the fear. I quoted Scripture to the fear and the fear took a hike, gone from the gray matter of my brain, exterminated, at least for now. I was tired, and sleep happened.

For road people, 8:30 is pretty early. I lived in the Central time zone, so the two hours to Louisville created a lag for me, as 8:50 was really 7:50 in Beaver Dam. Louisville is on Eastern Standard Time. At about 7:50, my phone rang. I lived with the phone by my bed. I still do. That's what moms do. It was my sister Anneta, who was the Crabb Family administrator, the "one-stop" person who took care of us, our office staff, our everything. Between Anneta and Allison (Stinson), I could almost turn my brain off if needed to. They could think my thoughts. They were my soft landing when I fell down many "hills" of life. Anneta was my security. She never called that early, but on this day, she did.

Anneta quickly said, "Turn on the TV! Hurry! There's been a really bad accident." My memory rushed immediately to the "destruction all around us" line from the song! Dear Jesus. I didn't know what or where, but I knew it was bad. She continued to talk while I looked for the remote, "It's bad! It's the World Trade Center. Kathy! It's bad, really bad!"

I found the remote. I turned the TV on. I yelled at the family, who was on the bus, "Turn on your TV!"

I rapidly surfed all of the cable news channels to try to get the best video feed. Then it happened, right before the eyes of a hundred million people: we saw the second plane hit the World Trade Center. I knew. So did you. We were under attack. Once again the song invaded my mind, and the fear came back and brought a suitcase, for this time the evilness of people who want to harm and specifically want to harm with fear, these terrorists, had invaded our home. Terrorists know they can't kill *all* of us, but they want to kill our resolve, our peace, our pursuit of happiness, our ease and confidence that we are safe to go shopping, to fly, to attend large gatherings such as football games. They hate us. They hate us because we are Christians. Period. When you look in the face of these radical Muslims you are looking at evil. End of story.

We were all stunned, afraid, and I was screaming as I heard the airplanes overhead landing loudly. Freedom Hall is next door to Standiford Field, Louisville's commercial airport. I was screaming, "George W., stop reading that book and get the air traffic stopped!"

You know what happened next: the Pentagon, Flight 93 in the field, and yes, George W. and I were on the same page. In just 45 minutes, air traffic controllers had landed 25,000 planes, but there were still 1,500 in the air. The overhead noise grew quiet. Louisville had landed what seemed like 500 planes in those 45 minutes. The experience of being underneath the airspace with one after another after another landing was surreal. As fast as they could land them, they did. For some strange reason, I was in freak-out mode until they were all down. Who wasn't, right?

Anyone who remembers 9/11 can give you an in-depth description of their whereabouts, like the day that JFK was assassinated. I knew that it was important to remember the terrified faces of my kids, the vulnerable questions, the messy hair, the "no-makeup" faces, the mismatched clothing (which was the first clue that we got dressed quickly), and the hugs, all the group hugs. The vulnerable state of fear made everyone crave the familiar hand of a loved one. We were all looking for security. The babies even knew something was wrong. I saw the fear and tears of a 2-year-old Hope, with Kelly holding her tighter. We were watching groups gather in the parking lot, hugging and crying. I saw pilots and flight attendants coming into the hotel. We had driven the short distance to the hotel so that all of the family members who were in town could be together.

I stopped a flight attendant who was crying and said, "Were you on a flight from New York?" She quickly answered, "Yes." She had seen the smoke and the carnage of the first building from the air. She was visibly shaken. It was real.

I even remember the inappropriate woman who kept calling one of our cell phones. I was in the car alone; the phone was ringing and ringing, and I was a bit annoyed. I was trying to return calls and check on family members back in Beaver Dam. I remember thinking, *What could be this important? Go find your family and hug them. Stop calling!*

I don't answer other people's phones as a rule. I don't check other people's email or look at their mail. I am not nosy by nature. So the phone was ringing, and I didn't answer. It rang again. I didn't answer. Again; I didn't answer. It wasn't *my* phone. That West Virginia phone number wouldn't stop! I finally answered. The woman was hostile and immediately told me she wasn't calling me. I told her I didn't know of *any* reason she would call a dozen times in five minutes, on *this* day. She told me that her daughter was waiting to be prayed for at a hotel, and she expected the plan to be carried out. She told me I was not the person whom she expected to come pray for her. She didn't drive to Louisville to be stood up.

"*I* didn't make a plan with you," I said. "And furthermore, if you are making demands on a day like today you must not have a brain. I suspect that your agenda isn't prayer-driven!" and I was done. I have received hundreds of calls from people who are pushy, selfish, and a bit crazy. In the last 20 years, I have had calls from people demanding everything from an autographed picture to jobs, money, and a place to live. One woman even had a minister fill the baptistery and demanded that her husband be baptized during the intermission of our concert. She had even lied and told the pastor we had agreed to do it when we had not. We, in fact, had told him that we believed people should be baptized by their pastors, not gospel singers.

Once a girl broke into our house and stayed the night for several days while we were on the road. Her parents finally figured it out and notified us. I have gone to the bus and been shocked when a girl popped up in the front lounge with a suitcase and a pillow to try to convince me she was invited for the weekend by one of the kids. It was always a lie. Some people are obsessed and have no boundaries. They will offer anything, everything, to be close to or feel like they are a part of the family.

Believe me, some of the women were the worst, like the woman who wouldn't stop calling me. We had seen our share of preacher chasers and diesel sniffers. I had "been there, done that" and had the backbone to tell this one, and I did. However, strangely, this call, locked itself away in a memory bank, preserved with the images and sounds of the destruction, in an uncanny way. As I read my notes about that day, this call was highlighted.

On September 11, 2001, we were all staying together. The mother hen wanted her babies, and she wanted any ounce of security she could get. A pushy person was *not* going to dictate to *anyone* in my world, at least not on *this* day. For on this day, Kathy was calling the shots.

We as a country lost our innocence on 9/11. I was 45 years old. That day seems to have a weird parallel to my personal life. I never think of the loss of the innocence of our country without thinking of my own disappointment and pain during the fall of 2001.

We played to a somber crowd in Freedom Hall, because we were all Jesus people, right? We knew the answer. We knew how this story ends, but we were very human, and the sadness was like a cloud that rushed in the doors and hovered over all of us. The images of smoke, tearful people looking for their loved ones in the streets of Manhattan, and masked rescue workers carrying out the bodies became the images that we all saw 24/7. We cried; we wondered; we tried to imagine what would happen next. The joy and family-reunion atmosphere of the event turned into that of a wake. Other events canceled, but NQC thrived. For again I am reminded that we knew the peace speaker. We knew the one who had *all* of the answers. The powers that be decided that a cancellation was not in order. I concurred. That was the right call. The week is cemented into the halls of my mind, and I am sure I am not alone.

The week ended, and I had to return to running a business. What would this terror mean to our livelihood? After all, the kids had to be paid. All of our employees had to be paid. Would promoters get scared and cancel? Would there be an economic meltdown to match the Great Depression? Who knew? What would happen? I wasn't an economist, but I knew that when the psyche of 300 million people was being recalibrated, it would mean change.

So I assessed daily the temperature of church people, pastors, and promoters. The tide was turning. The church was pulling together. People who hadn't been to church in years were going. Ticket sales were up for concerts. Record sales were up. It seemed like a mini-revival had started when those evil men decided to murder Americans. Instead of shutting down, we decided to be unified. We didn't stay at home, and we looked to a president who was a Christian first, an American second, and a politician last.

This isn't a political book, so I will try and tamp the natural opinions I spew daily. However, make no mistake: I am a conservative who votes straight Republican. If an Independent had a snowball's chance in Hell, I would consider him or her. However, I want to win, and I want to restrain liberalism. I vote the Bible, and I vote to win. In my opinion, the Democratic platform is a disgrace to the written word of God. Period. I am sure there are Christians who are Democrats, but I sure wish they would read the party platform and then rethink their position. It's pretty clear.

Back to 9/11 ... George W. understood how evil these people were. He sacrificed his popularity to do what was right, to keep them at bay. He knew. He was subjected to horrific criticism daily from the media, Hollywood, and the liberal idiots of the world. However, W. stayed focused on keeping evil in check. He bought us time. The blood of our soldiers paid the price for all of us. They bought us a dozen or so years. What I would give to have another George W. today. He wasn't perfect, but he was a *real* person, a person who wasn't driven by polls, teleprompters, hip-hop moguls, or a terrorist agenda.

So, we all grieved as the death toll rose, the bodies were uncovered, and the buildings smoldered. Our lives in Beaver Dam, Kentucky, were unbelievably the same, but not. I went home and worked. We planned an event in Nashville aptly titled "Heal Our Land" at the Roy Acuff Theatre. It was slated for October 8, with the Martins, the Isaacs, and all of our family. A song was written with the same title. The event would go down in the history books as a glorious success, with only 2 1/2 weeks of planning. We raised over $100,000 for the children touched by this tragedy. I was busy coordinating and trying to relieve my natural instinct to feel guilty by doing something to help. We stayed busy and couldn't help but wonder how this era of our lives would end.

By the last weekend in September, I was mentally exhausted. I had to be in Nashville on the morning of October 1, so when the big red bus pulled into Beaver Dam on Sunday night, I was Nashville-bound. I checked in at my usual, the Baymont Inn at exit 97 (which is now a Holiday Inn Express), and settled in for the night. My friend Gerald Russell has accommodated the family with affordable rooms and generosity for many, many years. That night was no different. By midnight, I was asleep.

I awoke to the loud sound of what I thought was thunder, or gunshots, but was actually loud knocks on my door. My first thought was that the building was on fire. The knocks were aggressive and frequent. I answered. I stood there looking at 22 eyes staring at me. It was all six of the kids and five of the spouses. I immediately thought my mom was dead, and they were coming to bring me the news, but all of them?

I said, "Is anyone dead?"

The response was, "No, it's not anything like that. We need to come in. We need to talk."

The next two hours would change the way I viewed the world. Those protective kids, with their desire to uphold righteousness, to protect me, to follow their collective moral compass, which was on track, their fasting and praying about life, now all made sense. However, that visit ushered in a new era for me. I was numb.

Suddenly, I wanted to see New York City. I didn't want to fly, so we drove. The two of us rode in awkward, ear-deafening silence for most of this treacherous trip. Was this what prison feels like?

I wasn't sure how I should act. I hadn't seen the applicable rulebook for people with crushed hearts. What was the norm? My mind tried to process the potential roads that I should travel. My heart was broken. Could I hurt this much and actually survive? What was I to do? Scream? Cry? Slap someone? What was right? Which road would shield my kids and protect the integrity of my family? Suddenly, they were my concern. They were the innocent ministers of the Gospel. All they wanted was to follow Him. I was with them. We rode, and I quietly tried to imagine what the future looked like as I cried.

Twenty-four hours later the skyline of Manhattan was finally in sight. There it was. The emptiness of space wasn't something I had ever considered. The openness of that moment will forever be frozen in my mind. It is a timeless, never-to-be-forgotten snapshot. The missing towers took my breath away. That strong city of accomplishments and diversity, the Big Apple that we all knew and loved, looked sad. I wasn't sure she would ever be quite the same. I related. Time doesn't heal everything. It helps us cope, but it doesn't eradicate pain.

I smelled the smell. I wore the mask. I watched the debris being carried out, with a halt and silence when a body part was uncovered. I will certainly never forget the sadness over that city. I saw the flowers that were refreshed every day, the people who were looking for family members but knowing that there truly was no hope. I will always remember an Asian couple who came from their homeland and were asking every person they saw to look at a photo of their daughter, who was missing. I am sure they knew that their daughter was in that pile of smoldering rubble. However, these two hadn't accepted the horrible reality check that was looming.

There were hundreds of photos of the lost nailed to utility poles, bulletin boards, and anything that these desperate souls could get a nail through. The smiling faces of young people on most of these 8x10 paper fliers, with captions saying, "Have you seen me? Call _____ if you have info!" are still there when I close my eyes. I don't want to forget the sad eyes of those people, the smell of those smoldering buildings that contained my fellow Americans, Americans who were on the job, supporting their families, loving their neighbors, and living their lives.

It was a sad situation. I was sad. On October 7, as I crossed the bridge out of the city, the radio was interrupted to bring a speech from President George W. Bush. He said, "Good afternoon. On my orders, the United States military has begun strikes against Al Qaeda terrorist training camps and military installations of the Taliban regime in Afghanistan. These carefully-targeted actions are designed to disrupt the use of Afghanistan as a terrorist base of operations, and to attack the military capability of the Taliban regime."

And so it had begun. George W. was in survival mode to save his beloved country from a loss of freedom. So was I, because to be at the mercy of others is to be enslaved. I had figured this out. The ministry of my kids would be the center of my universe, for the success of this ministry brought freedom, both spiritually and emotionally. I would go home and recalibrate, then try to remember that the call of God trumped my pain. I would tell myself that personal pain was no big deal. Jesus was crucified. I hadn't been physically abused, and I certainly wasn't expecting a crucifixion. I could do this. For the next four years, I would feel like the sacrificial lamb. That may be a bit of a victim mentality, but that's how I felt. It's my story. I can say whatever I feel, right?

We crossed the bridge as I listened to George W. talk about terrorists and military strikes. I had a knot in my stomach. Life would never be quite the same—not in America, and not for me. I knew I had to be stronger if I was going to survive. I could no longer allow my heart to make the decisions. My head would have to take the lead in the decision-making from now on.

Broken hearts do not make good decision-makers, not until they are healed and stronger.

14 WHEN NOTHING BUT A MIRACLE WILL DO

I have always loved the song "When Nothing But a Miracle Will Do," written by my friend Aaron Wilburn and sung by those talented McRae sisters a few years ago. This song hits me every single time I hear it, for I have lived a couple of miracles. Actually, more than a couple. I have been dealt a measure of faith that is increased by using it. Boom: the crisis hits, it looks hopeless, Jesus steps on the scene, and everything resolves quickly. That's a faith-building exercise, muscle-building, much like Adam at Gold's Gym pumping iron. It's sort of like that. No crisis, no pain, no trusting: no gain.

Sometimes we don't get what we ask for. We don't get that miracle. Sometimes, God has other plans. However, the fact that God is still in the miracle-working business isn't discussed enough. The church is afraid of the subject, because after all, wouldn't it make one look like their faith is weak if they speak of miracles, ask for them, and they don't happen? Well, that is a common thought, and it's easy to become a traveler of that road of thinking. However, let me talk to you about some "I don't have time to worry about my pride or my perceived reputation as it relates to faith" kind of emergencies. These kinds of crisis situations are immediate and critical. If God doesn't show up, it's over.

March 27, 2005. Brooklyn, New York. I was leaving my hotel room when Kristi called. She said, "Can you come look at Hannah? She is really sick!"

We were on our way to Brooklyn Tabernacle, where the kids would be singing at the morning and afternoon Easter services. All six kids and all of the grandchildren were there. Adam had a new Versace suit I had bought him the day before at Century 21, the Manhattan clothing store, and it looked so good on him. I was excited to see him wear the suit (with pink pinstripes, I might add), but it wasn't to be. Well, at least it wasn't to be for the morning service, for they would be in an emergency room instead of church on that Easter morning.

Terah had been home a short five months, and she was reacclimating to singing and the road. I was *so* looking forward to this day. We had been through some stuff, and there was an intentional choice to redirect the career path to just the five kids. It was working. The memory of the group that included "the parents" was quickly becoming no more than just that: a memory. That was my goal. It was the proposed exit plan of the parents. It had to be. But on Easter Sunday in 2005, we were all there.

On Easter 2005, we were all there as a family. The city was beautiful, Jesus was my savior, and Pastor Cymbala was one of my favorites. Everyone loves and appreciates the amazing talent of Carol Cymbala and the choir. I was personally pumped about a good day, since I had spent 24 of the last 29 months away from one of my girls. Krystal had been gone for a year, and as soon as she came back, Terah had left. This is unrelated, and Lord knows there wasn't a problem between the two of them.

Truthfully, these kids never fought. They still don't. If they fought, they kept it a secret. There is much to be learned here. When we put them all together, I said, "We will treat you *all* the same; no favorites!" That, my friend, will take the ugly out of blended families. The trouble is usually rooted in adults who favor their own children. Most women control the household budgets. I controlled ours. I was fair. In my opinion, the "household communism" rule made the four Crabb kids trust me and know they could depend on me. My girls already trusted me. To this day, that is still true. When a problem arises, I am still the one who gets the call. When an honest opinion is needed, I get the question. I am not a cheerleader parent. They don't need a fan, they need a parent; they have fans already. They need a parent who loves them enough to tell them the truth. The path of least resistance is to be the "popular" mom, stepmom, or mother-in-law. I rarely take that route. I am honest, but they know I love them. They also know I *am* their biggest fan. They know I believed in them enough to risk it all. When I get the call, it's okay; I *should* get the call. That's what moms do. I am truly still on deck and hands on daily. That's what I choose. That's why I live, and breathe, and work. I love my kiddos, *all of them*.

Back to Brooklyn: Hannah had been a sick little girl from the time she was born, but it had been worse for the last couple of years. The doctor would give her antibiotics, but the infection would return quickly. It concerned me. She was sick more often than not, but she is such a spunky little thing. She was so much like Adam in that she rarely complained.

Adam doesn't complain. He deals with it. He hates conflict, and he is low-maintenance to a fault. If he was sick when he was a kid, he rarely told us. So Hannah's "push-through-it" nature is similar. Actually, Kristi is a bit like that, too. She isn't a big complainer either; well, unless it's cold. Then she complains. She is from Florida. She hates cold.

So poor little Hannah, on Easter Sunday 2005, was a very sick baby girl. Her little neck was so swollen that it was preventing her head from being aligned with her tiny shoulders. Her head was drawn to one side. Her neck was red and had that "angry" look that you immediately know is serious infection. We panicked. I always panic when it's a baby. She was so sick, she was lifeless.

This part is fuzzy to me, but I think they immediately took her to the emergency room. She was treated and released. Adam and Kristi came to the afternoon service at Brooklyn with a limp, sick, feverish baby girl.

A physician who went to Brooklyn Tabernacle sang in the choir. He looked at her and said, "She must get to a hospital, *now!* She has a high fever and her neck is so swollen that she can't turn her head!" That Godly young man, who had devoted his life to medicine and Jesus, interceded for our Hannah. He directed and instructed. He pro-actively made preparations and provisions as if she were his own child. I have no words to express the gratitude my heart feels. Words fail sometimes. They are lame and inadequate. If that young man hadn't been at church that day, if he hadn't taken the lead, our Hannah may not be here. When we look back at this sort of crisis from the other side of it, we see the outcome as it is, but we also see the outcome as it could have been if just one thing had been different. If Scott Pilgrim, the Brooklyn physician, had not been there, I don't know what would have happened. He was our difference-maker on March 27, 2005.

Dr. Scott, Adam, Kristi, and Hannah went immediately to Maimonides Medical Center, which is a teaching hospital where this born-again doctor had practicing privileges. They admitted her. We got the word back at the church that she had an infected lymph node in addition to her sinus infection and ear infection—hence the unbelievable amount of swelling in her little neck. Remember, she was 2 years old at the time. Her little bitty face was overwhelmed by this swelling. She looked so pitiful. I worried. I begged God to touch her. I remember thinking, *Why?* Yes, I am honest. She was so sick. She was so swollen that the swelling was cutting off her airway. Her blood count was triple the normal white count. She was in trouble, and the physicians were honest: she was one sick little girl.

Church was over. I was cordial but distracted. We did a quick photo op and then headed out to see Hannah. We needed a miracle. The family would head home, but I couldn't go. Adam and Kristi would stay with her, but I needed to be nearby. I had to be. So when the bus rolled and the flights left, Kelly and I stayed in the city with Adam and Kristi.

Hannah could only have two visitors at a time, and there was truly nowhere to stay at the hospital. However, knowing I was 20 minutes away in a hotel versus 15 hours was the best I could do. We took a cab over to see her. I will never forget how vulnerable she looked. We prayed, cried, and I promised God everything I would ever own if He would touch her, if He would heal her forever.

The doctors were good, and for that I was thankful. The hospital was very crowded. Many of the patients and staff were Jewish. There are over two million Jews in New York City, and Brooklyn has the highest concentration of Jews. We are country folks, and although I have studied the culture of these Orthodox Jews with their side curls, the modest clothing of the women (many with headscarves and all in skirts), and the men all in black, this was the current environment, not a picture in a book. To be immersed in their culture was surreal for me, and it felt Godly. We had a glimpse into the lives of these modest, brilliant people. They weren't enamored by Hollywood. They lived in a manner that reminded me that vanity is poison to people. They had no outward vanity, and their value system appeared to be intact. Certainly, I am sure there are exceptions, but I was intrigued with these people who wore the curls.

Hannah was very sick, and I suppose she was actually worse than when she arrived. On the fourth day, the doctors wanted to do surgery and cut into her neck to drain and remove the infection from the lymph node. I Googled this today as I was writing. I have no words. The procedure involved a large square incision, like a flap, on her neck. Not only did it look like it would leave a horrible scar, it appeared to be dangerous.

Kristi and Adam requested time to pray and ask other people to pray, which was an overnight wait. We needed a miracle quickly. We were bombarding Heaven and populating the need on our website. We weren't on social media at that time, but we were doing all we could to rally the saints who believed in healing.

Jesus stepped in. Not only did Hannah not have the surgery, but she was released and was well enough to travel by the fifth day! We got our miracle, and we got it fast. When it seems that we are down to the wire, hanging by the last thread, then God can do His thing. He gets the glory as our humanness becomes helplessness. He then becomes miraculous.

That big ole jet was bringing our baby girl home. We had our miracle. Mercy was in action. We had received a new, fresh bundle of mercy. I never think of Brooklyn, New York, without mental images of a sick, lifeless, blonde 2-year-old with blue eyes, Jewish men with side curls, and a small hospital room, where a young couple begged God for His indescribable mercy and it came.

Those two kids who chose to commit to each other and asked God for this child had been given a pass. Their baby was better. She wasn't brought home to be put in a little pink casket. She was in a little pink dress with a huge hair bow. She would wear many more pink dresses, for God had been *so* good, and He had spared her. God was merciful to this young couple.

They wouldn't walk through the death of a child together. They would walk through the drama of a teenager, the tears of a little girl who couldn't find her favorite toy, the normal stuff that we live and sometimes forget. It was that good road that God generously gave us, that good road that includes lots of laundry, many miles of being a taxi driver, hundreds upon hundreds of hours assisting with homework, an occasional spanking, and many hugs—the normal things we trod through on the good road that we walk while raising a child. She would live to sing and raise her hands to praise. She would live to memorize the Word of God. She would live to understand the power of God and feel the touch of His anointing. She would live! I am thankful that God was generous. He is still God, and He is still good, even when we get awful news and the outcome isn't a Hannah story. I am forever grateful for the mercy that God poured out on Adam, Kristi, and our entire family. I can't even imagine a life without Hannah.

That little girl is now a 12-year-old cheerleader, healthy, and full of life. As I write, I am once again tearfully thanking a sovereign God for His hand on her then as well as now. I am praying blessings and protection like never before over this child.

To make matters better, Adam and Kristi welcomed Charlee in 2006. This blue-eyed boy loves sports more than anything. He is disciplined, and he is called. There are no boundaries on his life. God has amazing things for both Hannah and Charlee!

Adam Crabb may be the gentlest spirit on this planet. He cries for the lost, he cries for the broken. That's who he is. This 35-year-old man has somehow managed to keep his 12-year-old heart. Granted, his heart has been broken, and granted, life has thrown him a curve or two, but the world through the eyes of Adam Crabb is always a beautiful place. I have watched him walk through the fire, I have watched him navigate situations that would have taken most of us down, and he stood. He was weak, and hurt, and tired, but he stood. He's God's kid. He's anointed. He was chosen before he was formed in his mother's womb. So was Aaron. That was a womb full of "chosen!" My love for this child is unconditional. He makes me smile with his innocence. And this granny is fulfilled and smiling just knowing that Adam and his little family are minutes from my front door. I love them!

15 THAT'S ALL, FOLKS. GOODNIGHT!

"I've been on the other side of the mountain, I've seen the night give way to day, delivered over and over, when it seemed there was no way. I've been rescued by mercy and lifted by love, I may not know much, but I know enough" (Smith, B., Henry, M. 2013). I love these lyrics. My friends wrote them.

As I sit on this rocker looking at Mt. LeConte on this November afternoon, I am watching the sun set. I can hear a child down in the "holler" playing and laughing as he or she runs and squeals in this mountain air. Sound travels differently in the mountains. Those sounds from the "holler" are amazingly loud on the mountaintop where I am sitting. They resonate loud and clear. If that child's joyous giggles were to turn to distress, I would know the difference, even way up here.

There is so much to be said for mountains. Songs, sermons, speeches, poems, essays, and thousands of quotes have been inspired by the majestic feeling that a mountain invokes in most of us. Today is typical. I am looking at the mountains, remembering, and wiping tears from this face that has more sunsets in my past than I do in my future. My makeup is long gone and my eyes are puffy. There is no fresh disaster, no "today drama," just me and God talking. I am thanking Him for always being faithful. I am thanking Him for always providing. I am thanking Him for hearing me scream down in the "holler" many times. I am thanking Him for wiping my tears, reminding me that life is worth living, and that the word is always the answer. The valleys have been real and frequent. So have the mountains. It's called life. There are many winners and losers. To be a winner you must pass the test.

April 14, 2005. *The USA Today* headline read, "Switchfoot, Crabb Family Top Dove Awards." The Dove Awards were held at The Grand Ole Opry House on April 13, 2005. In a world where Southern Gospel is often considered the music choice of grandparents and old school quartet fans, my kids had made a huge in-road. The music industry as a community loved them. The ticket buyers came to see them. The GMA members were on board. The Doves would be on our shelves this year. It wasn't our first award, but it was our most notable accomplishment on paper. The press was good, and the music was better. It's a given that we were about souls and ministry. God had specifically ordered us to give it all we had, step on the gas, and work as if our shirttails were on fire. We did. The career path to success had been shortened for us. We were blessed, and we knew it.

I quote the *USA Today* story:

"The Crabb family won four Dove Awards—for Southern Gospel Recorded Song ('He Came Looking for Me'), Country Recorded Song ('Forever'), Traditional Gospel Recorded Song ('Through the Fire'), and Southern Gospel Album ('Driven').

"'Our goal is to reach all ages,' Jason Crabb said. 'We want to reach from the oldest to the youngest, because they all need the message of Jesus Christ.'"

Yes, all of the press was good. It was a new season. I truly had no idea how quickly the seasons were going to change.

Terah had been home for six months. We moved her into a house on the same street as her sisters. She was back on the road. Krystal was doing pretty well. All of the other kids were thriving. Life was good, for the most part.

However, there was a scar on my heart, a scar that I nursed in my private time. Betrayal is a deep wound that doesn't respond well to dialogue, roses, cars, diamonds, new houses, or stuff in general. Betrayal has eyes that shift quickly to avoid seeing a reminder of the pain. I nursed my scar and spent all of my energy on work and family. Those kids and grandkids were my everything. They deserved my all, for they were dedicated ministers of the gospel, and they had been loyal to me. I was their caretaker, wasn't I? I was responsible for the public image of this ministry, wasn't I? The kids deserved to be protected at all costs, didn't they? After all, they lived what they preached.

I felt as if I were living on an out-of-control roller coaster in those days. My work, my family, and my self-worth were all knotted up in one huge ball. The ball was growing. I was loved, and I invested daily in adding layers to the ball and making it everything that it should or could be.

The scar was there too. I knew I had to keep that hidden. I knew that scar was too ugly for public dissection. I also knew that the scar made the kids upset. We didn't talk much about it. We quietly marched forward with the plan toward the branding of the touring entity as just a sibling group. The plan was going well. The scar? That was personal. I had to deal with it, but maybe it would heal. Maybe I could get through it. Maybe true repentance and forgiveness would be the easy ending to this "hidden" book. I wasn't sure. My instincts told me to always protect my kids, and that meant I had to stand still. I did. The road was a thing of the past; I now needed to stay home for many reasons. It wasn't my choice; it was my sentence. I stayed home, and I worked a lot.

I love houses. I always have. We moved to Tennessee and bought a house in Gallatin that I loved, but it was in a neighborhood that was under construction for the most part. We bought the home in July, and by December there were 80 homes under construction. I hated it, so we moved. Boom. That's how I roll. The hesitation was there when the new home was chosen, but the agreement finally happened. It was more expensive, and I insisted on a short-term loan. I was 48 years old, and I knew I wanted that thing paid off in short order. We did a 10-year loan instead of a 30-year loan. When I look back and think about the "fog brain" thing I had agreed to regarding this purchase, I am ashamed. The price was at the top of our affordability comfort zone, and we reduced the term so much that the payment doubled. I am totally embarrassed to acknowledge this, but I promised truth. So here it is:

Our payment was ridiculously high. However, with the writer's royalties being at their peak earning years, we could afford it. I didn't get a regular paycheck from the Crabb Family; however, I met many expenses and got some perks. Also, we owned the assets and certainly carried any and all of the debt. All of the kids, spouses, and employees got paid 52 weeks a year, whether a week was profitable or not. As with all small businesses, we had the final say in everything financial. We made many great choices. However, we made many not-so-great choices as well. Our kids were well-compensated, and they were amazing employees. They made me proud in those days. They learned their craft, and they learned the value of hard work. That has served them all well.

Back to Dove Awards week: our week was slammed. Totally, insanely slammed. Actually, as I look back, it's a blur. We had an out-of-town guest in our home, and the kids did at least 20 or so downtown events. The move to Tennessee made sense. The decision to make recordings with just the five kids had been the right thing. This overnight success story, truly the intense work of the last decade, was my world at that moment. It made me forget about the scar.

We basked in the acknowledgement of the music and the commitment of these selfless kids and their spouses, the committed band, and our entire team. This particular week would go down in the catalog of my mind as a glory week, a week when God was on display front and center. The music wasn't hard to interpret; it was in-your-face Jesus lyrics, and in-your-face passion about the Jesus lyrics. It was about unashamed performances without a single ounce of trying to be cool or being a Nashville hipster. They didn't try to be cool; they just *were*. The anointing drew the listener, and the five photogenic siblings certainly were a delight to watch and easy to love. Sorry to brag, truly.

The bus left for the road on Thursday night after all of the festivities ended. All of the kids with the exception of Krystal left. We stayed at home. Jason was slated to do a guest appearance on the new Brooklyn Tabernacle recording on the Sunday following the Dove Awards. I was pumped. I wanted to go, but it didn't seem to be a popular decision. Looking back, I think I know why. I will not elaborate.

Anyway, my friend Brian Hudson was going to go in my place, and I was comfortable with that. However, nothing can replace being there in person. Nothing. I regret to say that I stayed in Nashville. The vibe was strange, but I wasn't sure why. Our houseguest left. The vibe was even stranger after he left. I wasn't sure what was up, but I knew something was.

A good night's sleep should help. I went to bed and went to sleep.

The doorbell rang. I answered. An old man, who appeared to be in his late 80s, was on my porch. The columns seemed so tall beside this stooped, white-haired man. His nose was prominent. His eyes were the color of the water in Maui. He was thin and frail. He said, "Kathy, is that you?"

I replied, "Yes. Do I know you?"

He had a tear on his cheek. He said, "I am your dad. I had to go away when you were 13. I didn't die; I just had to disappear. I have watched your life, and I want you to know how proud I am of you!"

I screamed and grabbed him. "Daddy! Daddy, where were you? Why didn't you tell us? Who was that man in the coffin?"

He answered, "I can't tell you any of that, but always know you were loved. I have always feared that you felt unloved by me. Please know that I love you!"

My heart raced. Was I having a heart attack? The sobbing I was hearing was my own voice, but it seemed far away. Where am I? Where is my daddy? It's dark. He's gone. I was fighting for the consciousness to find him. I felt I must find him. I felt my pillow. It was wet. It was a bittersweet moment, a dream of what he would have looked like, the aged version of that young man who left me 35 years earlier. I saw him. I couldn't shake it. I couldn't find my reality. I went to the porch and turned on the light. I suppose I was praying to see a little white-haired man. He wasn't there. I cried and cried, and finally the sun rose. I had rarely dreamed of my dad. I rarely dreamed about anything. This meant something. The significance was great. I was sad all the way to my core. In my normal style, I tried to shake it off.

The solution, at least short term, was to go to the mall. In those days, I frequently shopped for matching outfits for the grandkids, which I am sure they hated, my friend Crystal and I decided a bit of shopping would be our Saturday. We went to the Old Hickory Hollow Mall. I truly am not sure why, but we did. All day long my phone kept ringing. The day was turning into a very strange unexplained series of events. The day ended with four of us at Monell's. Crystal and Krystal drove separately. We ate. It was strange.

What was it? Why? I had not shared the dream. Something was wrong. The mood was strange. We went home. Crystal and Krystal didn't go with us. We went alone. We drove to the lake. I told him about the dream about my dad. I wept like a baby. Then he told me. A 15-minute conversation at the boat ramp by my house changed the landscape of our family forever. He was leaving.

Now I was alone. I was in shock. I called the girls over: Kristi, Amanda, Crystal, Krystal, and Shellye. I told them everything. I burned the bridge so that it couldn't be crossed again. I knew my pride would be my boundary line, and I would no longer nurse the scar! The truth that we all possess down inside, my gut, had told me hundreds of times that this day would come. I ignored that voice. I told myself over and over that it was because I wanted to protect my family. Was that the real reason? Yes, but it was combined with a little girl who felt abandoned by so many. Death took my dad, my brother-in-law, and soon, my brother. Relationships? I was only valuable if I was a wage earner. I wasn't good enough, pretty enough, skinny enough, and I knew the truth. I allowed myself to be used over and over.

My future was a divorce, and except for Krystal, my kids were on the bus. I have been told that when they got the call, they weren't surprised. I've also been told they all went to their bunks. I am confident they cried. Jason was leaving the bus at 4 a.m. to fly to New York, and I was worried about him. How would this impact him for the Brooklyn video? He was a professional, no doubt, but this was so personal and painful. Me? I was replaying the dream over and over in my mind. The air was heavy. I was dizzy. The house felt so big. Why did we buy the big house? Had I known, I would have rented a one-bedroom apartment. Nothing made sense. Sleep wouldn't come. Could I elect to not exist anymore? How would I tell my family? How would I tell the world? The humiliation level for the kids would be high. I cried.

I went to my walk-in closet, made a bed on the floor with a quilt, and cried all night. The fear in the eyes of the girls was fresh. The tears on the face of Crystal, who wasn't privy to family matters, told me she was blindsided. I will never forget this night. Was it wrong to want to die? Where did this end? What about my grandbabies? What would I tell them? What about Edie? She had been like ours. We had nearly raised this child. She was attached to both of us. I could see an 11-year-old redhead in my mind's eye. I could see her crying and feeling abandoned. Little Edie, the inspiration for "Two Little Feet" and the child who had lived too much and seen too much in her 11 years, needed me. So did my six kids. Yes, I must fight, but not tonight. Tonight, I would cry in my closet, miss my daddy, and try to figure a way to tell my grandkids and my momma.

My mom wouldn't be surprised, but the grandkids would. Cameron and Hope were 4, Eden was 11, and Ashleigh, Kate, and Hannah were toddling.

Logan and Eli were less than a year old. Somewhere in all of this, I felt the Holy Ghost rise up and meet me in the dark of that closet, and, like every other time, I knew the devil wanted me to die in despair. However, the spirit of a true and living God showed up. There were no fireworks, no epiphany, no instant answers—just a desire to go on, a feeling of purpose in spite of everything. God whispered that He would decide when my destiny was finished, and He assured me that He was the only one who could.

Sunday came, the bridge was burned, and that was the end. No closure, no confrontations, nothing. My 15-year commitment, which had taken the best years of my life, was over. The toughest part? No closure for myself, and no closure for Edie. Call me stupid, but I didn't know it was coming. Yes, feel free to call me stupid. The show that had started so abruptly in the parking lot at Robert's Motors in Owensboro, KY, many years before was over just as quickly as it had started. The end.

You can't unscramble eggs.

16 LOVE IS STRONGER

April 17, 2005. The house wasn't empty; actually, it was anything *but* empty. People were milling in and out. I had been officially "alone" for less than 24 hours. Jason was in Brooklyn, and the report was heartbreaking. He sobbed and struggled, but in typical Jason fashion, he made it. The result was one of the highlights of his career, vocally and emotionally. On that day, the "professional" Jason was in the room singing with the award winning Brooklyn Tabernacle Choir, but the "little boy" Jason was disappointed and wanted to go hide from the world for a long time. I know him. I know what he suffered that day. However, true professionals have this extra battery pack on and they can flip the switch in a crisis. It gets them through the most difficult days. That extra charge pushes them to walk on a stage and exhort, sing, and share when the very heart that beats in their chest is broken. They often sing to their own soul and preach to their own broken heart. Talent isn't the defining characteristic of a music professional; learning to push through and be a pro on all days is the definition of a professional. Once again, please allow me to brag: all of these kids have that. It's more than a learned skill. It's a gift, a choice, and the Holy Ghost. The formula is complicated, but the result is silky-smooth comfort for an audience. The singer is in control, and a curve becomes no more than a detour to a great experience.

April 17 has significance for me. It was my mom's birthday, my first day "alone," and the day Jason recorded "I'm Amazed" with the Brooklyn Tabernacle Choir. Dates stick in my head. This one is tattooed.

I still hadn't slept. The day is foggy at best in my memory. When would I sleep? The kids were worried and called Dr. Rhear. He and Judy drove the three or so hours from Jackson. Doc had been taking care of our sniffles, earaches, and such for a mighty long time. He is a precious man of God, and his Judy is a saint. They are what I term the "good" givers. They give of themselves to bless others, not for a reciprocated gift. Kelly called them, and they came. I could see nothing but sadness on their faces. I cried, and they loved on me and encouraged. Others came and left. The house was quite busy with kids and friends coming and going. Dr. Rhear suggested something to help me sleep, and the girls agreed that I needed it. I was nearly delirious and could barely focus on anything. My brain actually hurt. I am a fixer. When I tried to assess the steps needed to *fix* this, to keep the ministry of The Crabb Family above the rocky waters of potential scandal, gossip, and the biased words of those who had an agenda—the perpetrators, if you will—I became overwhelmed. I was hyperventilating. My mind hadn't moved forward enough at this point to realize that I would cease to be a parent to Terah, Adam, Aaron, and Jason. The legal description of "stepmom" would be removed with the divorce.

The good doc had a prescription filled, and I took it. They sat by my bed and monitored my blood pressure. They loved me. They cared. By this point, I was on suicide watch. My family had never seen me like this. I was *always* strong; I always had a plan. Now I was crumbled like a broken China doll. I was in a million pieces. Those who loved me looked fearful. I don't remember how many people spent the night there, but it was several. The pills worked, and I slept. Monday came. I woke up refreshed, and for a moment I didn't understand why I was alone in my room and who all of the voices in the house were. Suddenly, I remembered. Once again, I ran to the closet, where I hid and cried until people found me and convinced me to come out.

That closet would be my safe place for many months. This may seem crazy, but it's the honest truth. I hid there. It was the safest place I could find. There were no questions in that closet, no one calling me fat, no one criticizing my managing style, no sharks trying to destroy our business, no one lying to me, and no one breaking my heart. It was my controlled "safe" place.

A day turned into a week. My caring friends insisted I hire an attorney. It appeared I would need one. The details of this divorce are immense. I won't share things that would embarrass anyone. However, in the end, I accepted all of the Crabb Family debt, and I retained control and ownership of all things Crabb Family the touring entity and Crabbfest. There were many factors involved in this. The main factor was my desire to keep the kids working.

It took nearly a year to agree on the terms of the divorce, and remember: I was the lucky recipient of a huge house payment that we began at the height of the housing bubble and had financed for 10 years instead of 30. Try getting a house refinanced while going through a divorce, especially if you're self-employed and also a business partner with your soon-to-be ex-husband. Yeah, try that sometime, just for a fun exercise. The last sticking point was a property we owned in Hendersonville in which we had a good amount of equity. Terah lived in the house. I was determined to retain this home for her, and I eventually deeded it to her a month later.

After all of these months, all of the anger, tears, and bitterness … with one sloppy signature from a judge, I was unattached. That moment is frozen in my mind. With my little fireball 5-foot-tall attorney, with her Greek heritage, her vocabulary that was peppered with descriptive four-letter words, and our frequent meetings, my marriage would be a thing of my past. Done.

The Crabb Family, which included the parents, was now in the history books. Those parents were divorced. Krystal went with me, but she was uncomfortable. It was like seeing a corpse. I looked at my oldest daughter in that courthouse and I saw her shock, anger, confusion, and her protective claws. She was there to protect her momma! She got me through the day. Thank God for love, real love. I drove home. I cried and then decided to go out to dinner. I had lost 50 pounds in those months. I rarely ate, but on this day, I feasted! A new era was around the corner.

It would be an understatement to say I was a bit down on men. Of course, not the boys, but middle-aged men who thought they were God's gift to women with their cool hats, gold chains, and an occasional motorcycle. Men made me sick. I had tried and failed miserably. My work would be enough, along with my "Golden Girls" and "Ya-Yas." They would get me through. The Ya-Yas are my childhood friends who still hang out and do slumber parties a couple of times a year. After my newly-found single status, I reconnected with these girls, and we started the now-famous Ya-Yas from Ohio County, Kentucky. We are an exclusive club, but may consider a new member or two! Linda, Dinah, Brenda, Portia, Debbie, and Ruth all swooped in like real friends and helped me stay sane. Women need women. Women understand women. And there's nothing more valuable than true friends, especially friends from your neck of the woods, friends who understand your dialect and *slightly* redneck thoughts. I love my Ya-Yas!

The Golden Girls were Crystal Burchette, my cousin Portia, and yours truly. Portia needed a place to live, and Crystal was still nervous about robberies in her neighborhood, so they stayed with me for a year. Actually, they saved me. We ate together, we cried together, but mostly we laughed together. We laughed at everything. Women are amazingly gifted at helping you feel better about *you*. They can get right in there with you. They can even add stories that they heard through an email or a friend. Goodness, they can build you right back up with things like, "Girl, you got this. You don't need a man to be happy! I mean, you're looking good, girl! You don't need him!" Girls talk with their hands, and they're so expressive when they are bashing men! We all learned it from our mommas! The big eyes, the hands waving, and the expressive phrases to describe the "culprit," whoever he may be, all let us know that we've got this!

My cousin Portia was also going through a divorce, and there was a fresh conversation about men and their choices daily. However, it was harmless. We didn't resort to anything to make God ashamed. We could have hacked email, but we didn't. We could have populated information about the scorned, we didn't. In the end, I knew that this chick needed God. I didn't care what other people did; I was going to walk in truth, and I wanted favor. No matter how broken I was, I needed Him. The only way to achieve favor is to be obedient and live right. I was in.

I was nearly 50 years old, and I had spent all of my energy on this family ministry since I had been 35 or 36. It was a labor of love. The music, the family, the ministry, and seeing God do what He said He would do were my life. They were the glory years; well, sort of. The mountains were so high, and the valleys were so low. The personal pain was killer, but the collective joy was indescribable. In my heart, I knew it must end soon. The pull of outside opinions weighed on all of the kids about different issues.

Once the divorce was final, it seemed the vultures moved in. I was damaged. The kids were damaged. Confusion was the norm, instead of abnormal. The questions were often; the answers were concealed. We said nothing. Silence. God knew, and that would have to be enough for me. The opinions of others were typically unimportant to me, but in this season, I found a new wave of insecurity. I felt that anything I decided in the old style of management, which had worked so well, would be picked apart by outsiders; not the kids, but forces that were currently not on the payroll. Too many opinions were trickling in.

In the old days, I would have forged ahead. However, my insecurities wrestled my common sense and became the "go-to" in my head. Common sense had never failed me as it related to Crabb Family business. I took very little advice and kept the business plan simple. We competed with ourselves. Each year the growth was measured against the previous year. We were *always* our own measuring stick. We didn't compare ourselves to other groups or other ministries. I knew we needed to be the best *we* could be. The Crabb Family was a "no-competition group." We didn't compete; we encouraged. We didn't have jealousy; we had security. When other people sang, we were the first ones to stand and encourage the crowd to respond. That is actually the game changer. That little thing called jealousy has no place in ministry. However, that's another book for another time. I will move on.

In terms of the business, I knew in my heart of hearts that 30-something adults with families of their own needed to fly, grow, and make their own musical choices. I also knew that it would be treacherous to get them to the "free agent" status they would need to move forward with their individual careers. God had lovingly shown me the future once again. He knew I was grieving. He knew I felt as if I were cutting my baby into six pieces. He knew that my whole life had been invested in branding the name Crabb and trying to make it synonymous with music and good. He knew that I had prioritized very little except the family. I had forgotten about me for those 15 years. I always needed my hair colored, clothes, and "me" time, but I didn't want to take away from what I was doing for others. I was on a mission. I was driven. I am not totally sure I knew who I was. I lived, breathed, and slept the Crabb Family. Now it was over.

The natives were restless. I could see that look a snake has right before it moves in on its prey. I saw that look a few times. A couple of lawsuits later, the kids were free agents. This actually took an entire year to transpire, but I don't think anyone wins when I talk about it. I get angry and want to eat cake, so I will move on. A year and $100,000 later my babies would be starting down the road to find their own voices. They would no longer be directed; they would now be *giving* directions of their own. This was the big-boy stuff, and the choices would be theirs. I don't think there's a single one of them that would say it was easy, and God knows they have all had bruises and bumps, but I declare this day that God was in it. He knew. They grew. They are still growing, and as old Frank Sinatra said, "They did it their way!"

Looking back in the frequently-used rearview mirror of life, I can truthfully say that the end of the Crabb Family was the most painful thing I have ever been through. The year that I was involved in the litigation, I was soon to be unemployed, and I had grown insecure about the Crabb siblings. Did they love me like I loved them? Would the end of the music dictate the end of our family? Where was the blueprint for this? I worried. I wanted to always be the granny and the loving parent to all of the kids. When I made the vow to always be there, I meant it. They were mine. Time would tell, but love would win.

On a hot July night, somewhere in South Carolina, Jason and I sat in the front lounge of the bus. We made a pact to approach the retirement of the traveling Crabb Family the following week, when we could talk in private with all of the family. I remember the blue couch, the outfit I was wearing, and the tears that wouldn't stop when I went to bed, but it had to happen. It was "the plan." I had to be willing to be selfless. They had to be willing to be brave. We could do this.

On Tuesday we gathered at my dining room table and made an exit plan. The Crabb Family would retire in a year. A year would give everyone the opportunity to recalibrate their income and put their individual dreams into a business plan. Grief is such an inadequate word for how I felt, but it's the best I can find. I nearly grieved myself to death. I knew it was God, but I was human. I knew He was faithful, but I was broken. I knew He owned the cattle on a thousand hills, but I was in debt; the group was in debt. The preceding year had not been a growth year. We were all distracted with pain, and the "profit and loss" statement reflected it. The buses could be sold, and the group could work hard to try to liquidate the rest of the debt. This debt included large lines of credit used to operate the Crabb Family during winter months and for special projects. However, it wouldn't be enough. We needed a plan.

We owned the master copies of our records. That was one of those "right" decisions. They had value. I decided to pitch them and bring an end to the financial crunch that the family would suffer in the next few months. Day one, I had a bidder. I was thinking this should work. It was a big Music Row company. We needed lawyers and contracts, but we had a deal. God was working all things out.

But Jason wanted to talk. He didn't want the Music Row company to own those records that we had worked so hard to accumulate. He offered to buy them. I remember thinking how wrong it felt to sell these records that he had poured himself into back to him. However, there were two issues. The cost to produce them was hundreds of thousands, and I needed to recoup that. Also, if I split them equally, it would be a bit of a logistics nightmare. Truly, I needed the money. I was 50 years old and soon to be unemployed for the first time in many years. I was scared. Jason manned up. It was impressive. He didn't want to be chosen as the recipient over his siblings. He wanted to buy them outright, fair and square.

Now remember, these masters weren't his future. He didn't really need them. If he borrowed hundreds of thousands of dollars, he would be forced to work for three or four years non-stop to pay them off. I immediately knew this was to save me. He was taking the bullet. Was it some sense of guilt, or just protection and appreciation? I am not sure which was stronger, but most likely it was all of the above. However, I am including this in my chapter to make this point: it's easy to be a hero on the stage when the people are cheering and you are feeling nothing but good things. However, the rubber meets the road when your ex-stepmother needs $300,000 and you man up and decide that you will not let her fall under the bus. You will love with the same measure that you have received. Friends and neighbors, that's the story of a "real" man. Jason Crabb privately pulled me from the clutches of financial disaster, and he didn't have to do it. It was his idea, not mine … and now you know the real story.

The end was hard, and the pitfalls were many, but we navigated it together, always supportive of each other. That's what families do. Don't misunderstand this. Of course, it was not a walk in the park. Lives were changed forever. Employees who were like family would be looking for jobs. Finances would be uncertain. Relationships would be tested. However, in the end, everyone won!

Today, Jason and Shellye live five minutes from me, and I am proud of everything God has brought them to and brought them through. I always said that he could sing the phone book and I would love it. He is the definition of charisma meeting talent. He is also the definition of anointing meeting talent. It's what the Nashville folks call "the package." I have been blessed to be there to watch him from the awkward days of bad haircuts and red ugly blazers. I am still here. We are family. Love is stronger.

For several years after the breakup, I struggled when I went to hear the kids. I cried and knew it was not in the best interest of my heart to torture myself. I knew no one wanted to see that ugly cry, so I stayed away. I did what I had to do. However, those days are behind me. I am the loudest, most annoying person in the room. Who is the biggest Jason Crabb fan on the planet? Well, I am pretty sure it's me. His accomplishments are *my* accomplishments. I smile and watch and tell people at the grocery that he's my boy. God has been good, but so has Jason.

Shellye and Jason have two very talented girls whom I love more than life. Ashleigh is almost 12, and Emma is 9. Jason's girls fill his life with sunshine, and that makes this granny happy.

Blood is thicker than water, but love is thicker than blood. Am I blessed? Yes. Am I stronger? Yes. Always remember, this story is a story of triumph, not tragedy! We won.

17 STEVE (PART 1)

Okay, friends, buckle up. This is going to get good.

It was February 2006. I turned 50 on the 11th. The judge signed my divorce papers on the 17th. February was like a punch in the face by a heavyweight boxer. The Crabb Family was still touring, but I knew it was short-lived. I had a huge house that I couldn't afford. The Golden Girls were living with me; actually, both of them worked for us. So we were together almost 24/7.

Crystal Burchette had celebrated her 30th birthday in October, and I was planning on finding her a feller. Portia was newly divorced and a little disgruntled right alongside me. We were truly a reality show that didn't happen. We counted calories, walked around the fountain (I always walked in a circle out front and they made fun of me), and entertained lots of stragglers who came to Nashville to visit. I personally love stragglers. I collect them. My best friends are stragglers; *I* am a straggler. At the drop of a hat, a straggler will pack a bag and go on a last minute trip. That's totally me, and it is many people I know. They visited and we talked, cried, and always asked for the nutritional menu at restaurants because we were determined to be skinny! Actually, I would have just been happy to have a BMI that wasn't considered morbidly obese, and I was finally there.

My friends circled the wagons. Troy and Katy (Peach) cleaned the garage and closets in an attempt to remove some of the memories. J.P. (Miller) pretended to be a shrink on bad days, and walked me through some truths. Valerie (Pearcey) accompanied me on out-of-town trips that would be an entire book if I told it all. You see, these folks were trying to keep me sane. They knew I had too much house, too much alone time, and they also knew that my kids were hurting. Not only were they hurting, but they were on tour, gone much of the time. So my friends did what friends do. They stepped in and stepped up. I depended on this "band" of carefree kids (well, they were kids to me). I remember calling Michael (Hahn) in the middle of the night and asking for ice cream. He brought it. These friends were a phone call or text away. So were my kids. But sometimes I didn't want the kids to see the blubber and tears. Sometimes it was too much. Heartbroken people need friends as much as they need oxygen.

I had spent the better part of the last year in that big house with which I had a love-hate relationship. The house had felt like a chain around my neck, but it was the place Terah brought Logan to when she came home from that awful year away, the house where we had parties for the grandkids every other week. Nevertheless, it was out of my budget now, and my list of "to-dos" included selling that thing as soon as spring arrived. Given all this, my 50th had come and gone without fanfare because Jon Penhollow's sweet momma had died unexpectedly, and we all headed to Delaware for the funeral. Jon was heartbroken, and I was overwhelmed at the fragility of plans and life. So in February 2006, Jane Penhollow went to be with Jesus, my divorce was signed off on by the judge, and I turned 50. Reality was settling in. I pondered life and death. I felt oddly alone, even in a room full of people.

One night I told Crystal, "You really need to find a great guy and build a life, a life that's about you. Friends are great. Friends are fun, but when the years are gone and you're looking back, I don't want you to be alone!"

She resisted, "I am fine. I don't need anyone!"

Portia and I continued to encourage her daily. Finally, the idea arose; I am not sure who gets the credit for this, but one of us Einsteins said, "Crystal! Online dating!"

Crystal replied, "*NO WAY!*"

I reminded her, "You don't go to bars; you work and go to dinner with us. Everyone we socialize with is like a brother to you. Where else are you going to meet Mr. Right?"

After a bit of arm-twisting, we started making her an online profile. She was hot and then she was cold. I won't tell you the rest of her story; she may want to write her own book someday. However, I will pick up with my story here. She insisted that Portia and I both make a profile too. If *she* had to make one, so did we. In typical "Kathy Big Mouth" style, I said, "I will. What do I have to be afraid of? I won't use my picture, my name, my real email, or my real birthday. Okay. I will post a fake profile. Done!" After all, we were the Tennessee version of the *Golden Girls*! I had cried for nearly a year. God knows I hadn't as much as talked to a man unless it was a family member, an employee, or a server in a restaurant!

Contrary to anything you may have been told, I didn't commit adultery or have moral failure. I was faithful to my husband. I was the least likely to flirt in any room. People call me "sharp" occasionally, but trust me, I am not sharp when it comes to men. I think my track record speaks for itself.

No arguments. I would never have believed that at 50 I would have two 15-year marriages that had failed, along with a string of other failures. I didn't know how to pick men. No offense to anyone; truth is truth.

So, with that said, know that the online thing was fodder. It was laughter and self-imposed degradation—or at least for me it was. I considered myself the poster child for relationship failure. I truly wanted Crystal, who was beautiful and had a spotless track record, to find a wonderful man. She wasn't stained like me. So we made the profiles. I left my photo blank. I didn't give up any real info. My birthday is February 11, but I said it was July 4 on my profile.

Crystal's and Portia's also had their birthdays as July 4. We chose different years, none of them correct. Beckie Simmons' birthday is July 4, and I always thought that was the coolest thing. So, I suggested we all use the "firecracker day" to easily remember. We did. We laughed.

Portia says she went to bed and that I totally built her profile and told her the password the next morning. She says I also let her know that I needed to help her manage it! Imagine that. For the next few hours, we looked at the profiles of Crystal's potential dates and laughed. Then we looked at the profiles of *my* potential dates and laughed even more!

I was a faceless, nameless, Republican woman from Hendersonville, and I was pretty sure that I wouldn't get much attention! I once heard someone say that no picture for a woman's profile meant that she would "field dress" at 400 pounds, and no picture for a man meant that he was a "baldy" or both bald and heavy-duty! So we did it, we laughed, we forgot it, and life went on.

The really good news was this: we were leaving to go on a cruise. The kids were singing, and I was blessed to take friends (Ya-Yas) and family with me. I was a single woman going on a cruise with all of her kids and grandkids. Yes, that's how I roll. After all, is there anything better in the entire world? Great music, my babies and their babies, food, and friends should cure anyone who's feeling rejected and down. Caribbean, here we come.

Dinah, Debbie, Linda, Portia, and Crystal joined me for the week. I'm not sure why Brenda and Ruth, the other two Ya-Yas, weren't there. I don't remember why. I just know they didn't go. I had a 50th birthday cake on the boat. On about Tuesday, we went to our fancy dinner. I had on a blue pantsuit. Think Hillary Clinton, and it was a size 10. *Jubilee!* I was smaller than I had been in years. For my height, I was still overweight, but hey, I was getting there. Anyway, I celebrated my 50th birthday with all of the kids singing, a foreign waiter from some Latin country that I can't remember playing the "role" when he served me, and such is life. We were looking for a new normal here. Could we find it?

The night was turning into a fun evening when in walked Kelly. She looked shaken, and they were late for dinner. She said, "Mom, we need to tell you something. Sit down. Don't freak out. I'm *pregnant!*"

I gasped, "*WHAT?* But you can't have more babies. You are on that five-year birth control, right? You said no more, right? Are you sure?"

Let me explain: I take childbirth decisions very seriously. I think babies are deserving of time, finances, and attention. Mike and Kelly were *so* busy. Mike had just started his own group, bought a bus, and his world was turned on a dime. The stress and responsibility was looming on him, so this was very strange timing. They assured me that it was an "oops" thing. Mike had bought Kelly three pregnancy tests in the Carnival gift shop, and they were all positive. The truth is that we all had suffered much stress the previous year. Kelly had suffered and grieved the "no closure" pain right alongside me. She often said that it was like grieving a death. That's what the "no closure" thing feels like. Death. Now she was pregnant. I swooned. I saw stars. In that blue pantsuit, in the middle of the Atlantic Ocean, I learned that there would be a Gracie. God knew we needed her humor! My mom always said those girls needed a third part. She was right. Somehow I think she knows.

So, let me assess February one more time. I celebrated my 50th, got a signed divorce decree, Jon's mom passed away suddenly and unexpectedly, and Kelly was pregnant again, *totally* by accident. Finally, let's not forget, the Golden Girls were all born on the Fourth of July, and they were *all* on a dating web site. While I was on a cruise ship being thrown around by the rough seas, learning about a new grandbaby, and eating my chocolate mousse birthday cake, I gained a fan. Stay tuned. Meanwhile in Hendersonville, a lonely realtor had decided to look for an online date.

In those days, cruise ships had internet lounges. You had to buy a package; granted, it was expensive, but that was the only game in town. Smartphones weren't perfected. Laptops didn't have wifi available in the rooms. The internet lounge still had dial-up, but my work dictated that I use it. So I did. When I play, I am still working. My mind never stops. I wish it did, but it doesn't, sadly.

This was a scary time for our business with the changes and gossip, and I couldn't drop my micro-managing personality. So my girl Cindy Goff was keeping me in the loop with Crabb Family updates, and of course, Beckie Simmons was communicating the necessary info on touring. Krystal, my daughter, was also at home manning the fort while the rest of us were cruising. Spam mail wasn't as bad in those days, so my normal email volume was mostly Crabb Family.

I didn't love email; I still don't. It's entirely too sanitized for me. I want to see the eyes, hear the tone in a voice, feel the intent when the words fail to express, but for this week, email was my only option, so the internet lounge was my home for a few hours every day. My Ya-Yas fussed at me.

They would say things like, "All work is not good for you. Relax!" Geez, I've never heard that before. Of course, I ignored them, and of course they knew I would. However, on about Wednesday, my inbox started filling up with messages from the dating site.

There were a few odd messages from various people. I deleted them. They were stupid. They went something like this: "I am a good-looking man who works out all the time and owns a Harley. I'm looking for a good Christian woman who likes weekends on a motorcycle." Delete. First of all, I ain't interested in anyone who works out all the time. That is too much to live up to. Second of all, I ain't going on no weekend trip on a Harley unless we are married and I get over my fear of motorcycles. Third of all, I bet you don't own a Harley, or a house, or a gym membership. I bet you are a pathetic married man trying to pick up women. So there you have it. Delete, delete, delete. Truly, it was nauseating. The gold necklace with an eagle, the perfectly-placed tattoo, and the standard do-rags with the Harley logo. No, it was not for me. I was planning to unsubscribe. Now remember, there was nothing to connect me. No photo, no employment info, nothing. There was a fake date of birth, no picture, and a paragraph that described my "take" on life. That's all.

But in the midst of all that deleting, I had a message from a guy who looked normal. I didn't respond. That night, I had another message. He seemed nice. He made it clear that he only wanted my email address. He wasn't requesting a phone number or a picture. He said something like this:

"My name is Steve Hannah, and I live in Hendersonville. I love the paragraph you wrote about life, and I love the fact that you seem to be, based on that paragraph, a conservative who believes what I believe. If you don't want to meet me, I understand, but could I just have an email address?"

These web sites don't disclose a real email; instead, they get the messages and forward them to the recipient. There is no way to interact with people unless you want to. It is safe if you have a brain and exercise sensible caution. So, this Mr. Hannah would get the old Google search from a computer on a cruise ship.

Results: Century 21 Sales, Madison, TN. Address: Hendersonville, TN.

It appeared he had been a realtor for many, many years. He had been divorced for almost three years, had blue eyes, and was tall and nice-looking. I quickly went to get the Ya-Yas and showed them my search. I decided to send him my email address. Then, after I had a friend back home drive by his house and send me a picture, I decided that I would send him my photo and name. He seemed nice. I felt safe. After all, I was a thousand miles away on a cruise ship. He didn't have my phone number, just my email.

We went to the beach, had a photo shoot, and did what cruisers do. We ate and ate! The captain's dinner was that night. Dinah had an acrylic toenail because her nail had been removed after an injury. We were getting primped up and dressed up when the phone rang. Dinah was frantic! She was putting a new acrylic nail on her toe, and the superglue got on her finger. She had her hand glued to her toe and couldn't get it loose! No, I am not kidding. We had us an emergency, and mind you, a hilarious emergency! So we got Dinah's hand/toe problem solved, went to dinner, and I shared my info about knowing where the realtor lived. He lived real close to all of the kids, off Walton Ferry Road. He had a pool, and he lived in a one-level house.

After dinner, I went to the internet lounge. Of course, he had sent me half a dozen emails. I was flattered. This girl who had suffered more than her share of rejection was flattered. The bad news was that many people ruin their lives because of a flattering email. I was blessed; no, I was God-protected. I also had common sense. I deleted the narcissistic womanizers on the site because I would never, ever, ever in a million years become involved with someone who wasn't like-minded. Here are the facts: for adults who don't go to bars, clubs, and also work so much they don't have time for groups and extra-curricular activities, well-managed, sensible online dating can work. I was in line to learn the ropes of this process.

The ship docked and we shuttled to the airport. The bus was taking the kids to do some concerts, but my Ya-Yas and I flew out and landed back in Nashville by early afternoon. It was back to reality, back to that big old house and my uncertain future. The cruise had been a nice diversion. The sun was welcomed. The news of Gracie had settled in, and I was excited, but I knew troubled waters were ahead.

That blueprint for blended families that were no longer family was still a bit blurry. We loved, but we faced constant battles from outside. However, we worked hard to be a family. We all wanted it. The opinion from all of the kids was that *we* didn't choose this. When we were little kids it was chosen for us. We were all told that we would be a family and love each other. I didn't get the memo that the family was disposable. We're not little kids anymore, and we will love whom we love! It's abnormal to walk away and throw people away. We worked, we loved, and we worked and we loved. All of us are good at these two things: working and loving.

I was back at home. My Ya-Ya girls left and went back to KY, all except Crystal and Portia. I was tired. I needed to unpack. Everyone crashed, but in my typical "no-sleep" world, I stayed up late, probably until 3 or 4 a.m.! I decided to work a bit. When I checked my email, I had the sweetest email from the realtor; he wanted us to meet! Butterflies! I was not ready for this. I hadn't been on a date in many years. What would I do? What would I say? Would I talk about my divorce the entire time? Note to self: Kathy, *don't* talk about your divorce the entire time. That would be a negative.

I counted at least a dozen emails from him. He was a persistent something! I went to bed. I slept, with the help of Ambien. I woke up very late and immediately decided my day was ruined. It was already 11 o'clock. Ugh! When I told the girls about the barrage of emails, they said, "Go meet him! We may go watch from the car. We want to see him." I checked my email again; there was another email! This one said, "Could I take you to a late lunch? Maybe Mexican?" He suggested a restaurant that I didn't frequent. It was an old Pizza Hut building that had been converted to a Mexican joint, and honestly it looked a bit undesirable. This should have been my first clue that he was unpretentious. But hey, it was really close to my house, so I agreed.

I was *nervous*! I almost felt like I was doing something wrong. I pulled out my divorce document. I did a walk back down the memory road. I felt the pain, and I actually had a bit of a meltdown. I didn't want to date. I didn't want to be divorced. I wanted my grandchildren to have both grandparents at Christmas, but they didn't. I knew you couldn't unscramble eggs. The damage was too deep. I had to move on.

So a chimichanga it would be. A chimichanga and a realtor were the next four hours of my life. I sat down at that sticky table that needed to be wiped down, and we both ordered a Diet Coke and a chimichanga—him chicken, me beef. I looked into the kindest blue eyes I had ever seen (with the exception of my daddy). However, soon I knew it. This man was kind. He was selfless.

The conversation began. I quickly learned that he had been married at 29 to a woman who was a bit older and already had three children. The oldest was a special needs child who was in a diaper and a wheelchair and was now an adult. He had been divorced for three years and didn't have a girlfriend at the moment. He had been handed a surprise divorce, in a similar situation to mine. They had been married for 13 years. He had no biological children, but he seemed to really care for the kids he helped raise. The children were still very much in his life. He showed me pictures, and they were beautiful.

I proceeded to show him pictures and explained that I had a passel of grandchildren. He seemed a bit overwhelmed when I explained just how many there were. However, he quickly recovered, and we continued to "interview" each other. He had been a realtor since 1986, and I could tell that he hated change. I could also tell that he had loved his ex-wife with everything in him. This teddy bear of a man had been handed his heart on a platter, in pieces. He was good. I could tell he was good.

We were now moving toward the Q-and-A part, where I would solidify that he was *not* a Gospel music fan. I was not interested if he was a "gurm," an overzealous fan who wanted to know my kids. Believe me, it happens. Believe me, *many* people fall for it. I was *not* going to be one of them. I had been used enough in my life. So my series of questions went something like this:

"Have you ever heard of Bill Gaither?" I asked.

"No," Steve replied.

"Have you ever heard of the Crabb Family?"

"No."

It was extremely clear that he hadn't Googled me, as I had him! He still had a tiny bit of trust, unlike me.

He asked, "What's a *Crabb Family*?"

"Never mind," I said. "All is well."

He passed the litmus test! I told him a little bit about my job, my life, and my family. He asked me if they had "real" jobs. I suppose he wanted to know if they *all* lived with me so they could go play their music jobs at night. He thought it was like a hobby. I explained that it was a *real* business. I explained that they had never had "real" jobs, and that in their genre they were at the top of their game. I tried to minimize the success, but I explained the personal financial independence. I don't think he got it at that moment, but he later told me that he Googled me when he got home and thought, *Wow!*

Finally, he said, "My dad is retiring from Channel 5. He used to know a guy named Jake Hess. Is your family something like Jake Hess?"

As I tried to conceal a giggle, I said, "Yes, I suppose so, but the boys still have hair; no rug yet!"

He didn't get it. Obviously he didn't realize that there are lots of toupees in Southern Gospel, but then, he had no clue what Southern Gospel was. I decided I liked this blue-eyed realtor who had taken a handicapped child to her caregiver every day for 13 years. I liked this man, who was noble and loyal and carried a wheelchair everywhere he went starting at age 29. I liked this man who talked about his ex-stepchildren and beamed about their importance in his life. How could this be? We had so much in common when it came to loyalty and kids. I was glad I had come, sticky table and all.

The last time I had been on a date, I had been in my early thirties and had a trusting heart. Now that girl was gone. She was nowhere to be found. She had been replaced by a strong woman with a broken heart. Would this Mr. Hannah, the realtor, pass the test? Would he teach her to trust again? Only time would tell.

18 MORE STEVE (PART 2)

Steve and I sat at that restaurant for four hours. The waitress was a bit "ill." We assured her that we would tip her well. I don't think she believed us. It was dark outside. We had met for lunch, but we were still there when the street lamps came on.

What was the deal? Was I starved for male attention? Maybe. I was living the "silly girls" life of my Golden Girls and occasionally the get-together of my Ya-Yas, but day-to-day was Portia and Crystal. The kids were supportive, but they were hurting too. I felt like my presence was a reminder of the fracture. I rarely went on the bus in those days. The moment I walked into a concert, the questions bombarded us. It was better to be out of sight, out of mind in the beginning. My face was the trigger at the product table, so I stayed hidden. I truly felt like an embarrassment, even though this wasn't my design. The kids didn't deserve these questions. Neither did I. I let the circumstances rob me of the next eight or nine years of enjoying the fruits of my labor, of *our* labor. I was beaten down. I heard the slurs, the nasty rumors. They hurt. They were lies. I cried and hid. I protected my heart. I probably attended only one or two concerts during that year. This life change, not hearing them sing, not feeling the music, was a dark, sad spot in my soul. I didn't talk about it. I didn't tell anyone. It hurt too much to talk about it. The insecurity was a full-blown part of my personality now. The rejection did a number on me. The details are private, but there's not a person reading this that would have come through it all unscarred. I am confident of that. So, the point is this: I soaked up the conversation of a man that night, a man who was interested in me.

This man wasn't impressed with my family, my work ethic, or my "go get 'em" personality. He just wanted to talk to the girl who wrote the profile. He wanted a girl like that. He wanted a girl who believed we should vote by the Bible, stand up to bullies, always love kids, eat cake, and go to the beach every chance we got. He wanted the girl who had blue eyes, a round face, and a strong manly nose. He wanted to talk to the girl who had criticized her own image in the mirror, tried to improve the result, and still felt ugly and unwanted. He wanted that little girl in the yellow dress who felt abandoned and alone, and that's who this realtor was talking to. He was oblivious to the folks who said I was "a force to be reckoned with" and a "workaholic." That Kathy wasn't there that day. He saw the insecure, broken version of me. The chips were gone, the chimichangas were long gone, and we left. This should have been my first clue that we were both foodies!

Steve suggested that he drive me by his house to give me comfort that he wasn't an axe murderer; that way I could see where he lived. I hadn't told him that I already knew where he lived and worked. I stayed mum and agreed to drive by his house. He awkwardly asked me to drive. I had an amazing "fun" car, so I was good with that. He was driving a "manly" F-250, and he said it was a bit tall. He would ride with me, since I was short and his truck was tall. I bought it. We did the "realtor" drive by while he explained why he had bought a house in that neighborhood. He explained that when he bought the house, many years earlier, he wanted to get into a good school district and his wife wanted a pool. I thought it odd that she had left and he had kept the house. However, he explained that she had moved out and he had had to assume all responsibilities for the mortgage and expenses. This sounded familiar. He now wanted to see where *I* lived. I hesitated, but he said, "You know I can go to tax records and find out if I want to." He laughed that jolly laugh, and I felt safe, so we did the next drive-by. He told me that he loved my neighborhood; it was his favorite in town.

So now we had exchanged phone numbers, done drive-bys, and confirmed that he was not an aspiring bass singer or songwriter. The day was a good one. I went home to answer a hundred questions. I was a bit giddy. I felt stupid, because 50 year olds don't date, do they? Privately, I smiled and crawled up in my king-sized bed to reflect. Sleep came easily.

Monday morning came with a vengeance. The prior week of cruising meant that I had a mountain of calls to return and a meeting or two to attend. My day was busy. However, something was bothering me. When I had taken Steve back to his truck the night before, he had made a comment that we were about the same age and then said he was 44. Whoops! I remembered the fake birthday on the profile and looked closer. We had my birth year as 1960, which would make me 46, not 50! Oh no. This conservative Christian with high standards had inadvertently lied! I had to tell him that it was all a joke in the beginning!

By midday, he called me. He wanted to have dinner. We agreed on the Black Eyed Pea. I was nervous about disclosing my age. Why, oh why, did I not remember that earlier? *Why?* I already liked him. What if he rejected me because of this?

When I walked in he was already seated at a booth in the back. He looked handsome, and he told me I looked pretty. I discounted the compliment, as always, and asked him about his day.

He said, "I bought a new car today!"

I responded, "Really? You should have told me. I was in the car business for years; I could have helped you beat them into submission on price!"

We laughed. I had to tell him about the lie. I couldn't stand this much longer. We ordered quickly, and then I told him that we must talk about "something." He looked panicked but said nothing.

I began with, "You know that profile you read? The birthday is wrong. I wasn't born on July 4; I was born on February 11. I wasn't born in 1960; I was born in 1956! It's a privacy thing, you know, and I guess we didn't think it through."

"Okay," he replied. It wasn't what I was expecting.

"Are you upset? Do you still want to eat with me?"

"Sure I do. I don't care about that, and I understand," he grinned.

I was *so* relieved. I repented and everything! (We Pentecostals repent every day, you know!)

"Now, I need to tell *you* something," Steve said.

"Oooookay? …"

Steve: You know that part of the profile where you check smoker or non-smoker?"

"Yes … "

"You would never date a smoker, right?"

"Right."

"Well, I lied: I smoke. I bought a new car today so you wouldn't smell smoke in my truck. I asked you to drive last night because of that. I will never ask you to ride in it, and I promise I will quit! Please don't be mad. I feel like such a bad person, but I bought a really cool car. I think you will enjoy it."

"Well, it better be really cool! And furthermore, I am allergic to cigarette smoke, so you're right, I will never ride in your truck."

At this point we were both laughing hysterically. I couldn't wait to tell the Golden Girls that he had already lied to me! We walked outside, and that shiny yellow Roush Mustang was screaming to be driven. So, we drove it. The report back to the girls could wait for a minute. Fast cars were my vice, one of my drugs of choice, along with sugar. It was a stick shift and it was bad, as in good. I was a bit flattered that he had bought a $50,000 car so that he could take me out. That was a good way to combat the cigarette info! Go Steve!

In later months, Steve got a speeding ticket in Kentucky in that yellow rocket, and the trooper clocked him at 110. That brimmed hat walked up to the window and said, "Sir, I need to see your driver's license. Do you own this car?"

Steve said, "Hey buddy, can you give me a break? This is going to kill my insurance rates!"

The trooper said, "I'm not taking you to jail; that *is* a break."

I was nervous too, but I knew people, and thought I could possibly make a call and get it handled. I was amused at the gutsy question. No dice. However, my sweet friend got it dismissed. (Don't ask who. I will never tell.) Actually, Steve is a serial offender as it relates to speeding tickets in Kentucky.

Now back to the Black Eyed Pea day: we had confessed our little nagging "untruths" and I had given my best "Elaine" sermon on cigarettes. He was still in the car, and he wasn't smoking. Don't you know he wanted to, though!

That night he followed me home and met the Golden Girls. I think they eavesdropped on us; no, I *know* they did. I have a house with an open floor plan, and privacy is tough unless you go to a bedroom, so eavesdropping was easy. We talked a lot, mostly about houses. I liked that. It reminded me of my sister and my brother. I understood the building process, and he liked that. We had common ground: houses, kids, and broken hearts that were mending. He was ahead of me, having been divorced for three years. He quickly encouraged me to forgive, starting immediately. He would say, "You are the person drinking the poison. Stop it." I didn't. There was a pattern forming.

He left, the girls approved, and I went to bed. I suppose I was trying to process the cigarette thing. I *hate* smoking. I get sick within minutes if I am exposed to cigarette smoke. This may not work. I was aware of the statistics on quitting, and I was aware that Steve had struggled with cigarettes and weight. His weight was in check for the most part, but the cigarettes weren't. He had suffered a heart attack when he was 40, and that made me worry even more. Who smokes after a heart attack? I will tell you: a man who lost his life as he knew it, a man who needed a crutch. It ain't rocket science. He was a big "teddy bear," and he was a hugger. Steve's hugs are the best. They are intentional, not an afterthought. When he hugs you, the world feels like a safe place. On that night he hugged me tight, and I liked it.

One more thing was lurking out there in the conversation: I learned that he had a dog! He had a poodle no less, a *white* poodle. Why did this "manly man" have a white poodle? *Why?* I giggled thinking about it. I had a mental picture of him putting bows and clothes on this poodle. It wasn't a good thing. I laughed and laughed.

I had never owned a dog. I am not an animal person. I think it's awesome that other people love animals, but me? I didn't understand them. I always had children to care for since I was 18, and I had always worked. I didn't have the time to babysit the needs of dogs, and I was highly allergic to cats. So the dog thing just made me laugh. Why a poodle? The Golden Girls hooted when I told them. They knew I was not an animal person, and we laughed and laughed and laughed. The poodle had a name, too: Diggy. Yes, he was Diggy. A boy poodle; maybe that was better, the boy thing. Time would tell.

A few days later, Steve picked me up in the yellow rocket, and we went to meet some of the family for dinner. He stopped at an unfamiliar strip mall on the corner of New Shackle and Main.

Steve isn't a great communicator at times; he doesn't explain *everything* like I do. He asks lots of questions, but he doesn't offer much information unless you ask him. I actually hate that, but it is the truth.

He pulled in and said, "I will be right back!" Okay, so I was going to sit there. He even took the keys. That is a habit that greatly annoys me; I couldn't even listen to the radio. However, no real worries. He bopped back within a few minutes with a dog in his arms. The famous Diggy was handed to me as if he were a Kleenex, or an ink pen, or any inanimate object. I crouched down in the seat. I raised my hands instinctively, as if to say *NO!* He plopped that dog in my lap. I shrieked!

At that moment, I realized I am a bit scared of dogs. I remembered a dog chasing me when I was about 5. I think that was the end for me. I never asked for a dog, and I was not comfortable with this white poodle in my lap. Goodness sakes, it looked like a dog that would belong to Paris Hilton or Anna Nicole Smith, not a manly man.

I asked Steve, "What do I do? He's licking me. Make him stop! Can we put him in one of those cases or something?"

Steve laughed until his entire body shook. That's how Steve laughs. He laughs from the inside out. It's something to be experienced! Anyway, he said, "Just pet him! Just love him!"

I said, "I don't understand how to do that. I think he has germs."

We rode with the dog in my lap and my hands raised to the ceiling, flat on the headliner. I didn't want this girly "boy" dog to lick me. Ewww! My last comment was, "We must discuss *why* you feel you need to own a white poodle. It weirds me out a bit!"

The backstory was this: the dog was his ex-wife's. He was hurt, so he wouldn't give it back. Diggy was like a hostage, but big old softie Steve had grown used to that little dog when he came home to the empty house at night. Steve sat in a recliner and was a potential recluse at times, so he has told me. The life change of divorce hit him square between the eyes. He had no clue. When it was over, he says it took 15 minutes. The shock of her decision devastated him. So when she wanted her dog back, he said no. It's actually almost funny, but it shows that we are all human, and we all need to be loved. So before Kathy, there was Diggy. However, Diggy's days were numbered.

19 TAX DAY

Steve had become a daily visitor at my house. My kids met him, and it went okay. The grandkids giggled at him. It was early, and they were still raw. Actually, we all were, but I am such a type-A personality that I have to keep moving. If I don't, I think too much, too deep, and the pity party sets in. My job was 24/7 in those days, and I was being actively courted by this realtor who also built a few houses now and then. I enjoyed his attention, and I loved his occupation. This was before the housing crisis, and it was before the tough times that we would both live to tell about. However, in April 2006, I was heavily courted by this quiet, big guy with that big laugh, khaki pants, and polo shirt (always a polo shirt). Steve shopped at Macy's. He would go into the men's department, choose a Ralph Lauren polo in every color, and he was finished shopping. He had seven shirts, just alike, in seven colors. That was his wardrobe. He was predictable. He hated shopping. You should have been in the room the first time he told me he bought clothes that were full price. I had a *meltdown!*

I said, "Have you *ever* heard of T.J. Maxx? Oh my goodness!" He was clueless about saving money on clothing. So, my khaki guy was hanging out, learning from me, and I was learning from him.

More than learning from him, I was drawing strength from him. He was solid. He was steady. He was not an attention seeker; he was the ultimate supportive person. If he had known how big the job would be, he probably would have run really fast, but he didn't. He stayed late, and he doted on me. He liked the music, but he didn't understand it. To me, that was a redeeming quality. I wanted to be wanted for me, not for my connection to the music. To him, I just had a job. He wasn't tremendously intrigued by my music life, and I liked that.

I made it perfectly clear that I only had sex with husbands. He made a funny comment, but he seemed to accept that. Daily I found myself running to him with the highs and lows of my day. He was calming. He understood my emotional roller coaster. He understood the struggles of a fractured family and the outside gossip and spitefulness that were hurled at us. He understood the dividers who would try to sow insecurity in each of us to destroy our unity. It was happening. It was clear to me that this was going to be challenging at best. The solid ground under our feet was shifting. Yes, we loved, but there was uncertainty at times. The fiery darts were flying, but we dodged them. However, every day seemed to bring more. The world wanted a dramatic story, a story that included all the sordid details. People tried to divide and conquer with gossip and rumors about a fight between the kids and me. It wasn't true, but the rumormongers continued to say that I was a witch with a "B" and the kids wanted to be away from me. It hurt. It was wearing me down. I was becoming so focused on defending our relationship and my motives that I could barely work.

I had a mole on my payroll; I knew it. He was a spy who constantly reported an enhanced version of my life based on bus conversations that he overheard. He needed to go. He was playing kiss-up to the family to secure his position, but I knew what was going on. People talk.

I was exhausted with being tough. I was exhausted with having a $30,000 weekly budget to float this ship so lovingly known as the Crabb Family. We had many employees. We had buses. We had a band. We had an office staff of four or five. We had huge marketing budgets, and we paid for our own recordings and comparable salaries. The kids were well provided for, and so was I, but that $30,000 a week budget wasn't always met in those days. I had had to borrow $100,000 just to meet budget the previous winter. The best description of the overall feeling came from Crystal Burchette, who said, "When assessing the split, the rumors fly. We know the truth, but people don't bother to stay long enough to figure it out. They do exactly what they do when someone tracks dog poop in a room and the room stinks. They don't stop to determine who is guilty, who brought it in on their shoes; they simply leave the room! They don't care who did it. They just know it stinks."

The rumors and mudslinging could diminish the brand. I was sad about that. I wanted the best for these kids. I knew there was no good to come of the slanderous comments. I also knew the perpetrators wouldn't shut up until the four kids were severed from me. I was sad, but I was tired. I was so tired that I began to look for a sensible exit plan. I asked God thousands of times, "Am I released from the prayer in that closet in Philpot? Am I out of Your will if I shut this down? Help me, God; I am so confused!"

Truly, the kids were sick of their lives being dominated with the drama, "he said, she said," and ugliness. No one deserves that. They had lived it twice, and they all buried themselves in their own little families. In the end, that's probably what saved them. For all six of those kids to be serving God today is nothing short of a miracle. They have all been scarred. So the love was solid, but change was in the air. I knew my life would soon take a sharp turn. I worried about employment, but that little dab of confidence that my daddy fostered would always rise up. It was there to assure me, and I quickly realized that I would make it. God would help me. He alone is faithful.

I took Steve to meet my mom. She liked him. Anneta liked him. Noble, my stepdad, asked him if he was building a front porch as he patted him on the belly. I died. Steve laughed. The front porch shook! We were inseparable. I had met Steve's family briefly at a birthday party for his niece. They seemed amazingly normal. They were nice. I feared that they were protective of him dating an older woman, and I said so. He assured me that they were thrilled to see him smile again, and more thrilled that I didn't drink, smoke, or chew, as they say in Kentucky! It appeared that the family had been worried about him, and I was a hit, or so Steve says.

My daughter Krystal got married, and I asked Steve to escort me to the wedding. He did. He was attentive, said all the right things, and genuinely liked my kids. It was still a bit soon for them, but he understood.

Steve took me to meet his kids as well. They were precious. His daughter was dating a Tennessee Titans player who is now her husband. However, Steve is so unpretentious that he didn't even tell me that Drew was a professional football player. I had no clue. I am a sports idiot. I know nothing except Kentucky basketball, but now *that* I do know. That is the extent of my sports knowledge.

Steve invited me to Maggioni's to have dinner with his daughter and her boyfriend. Heather was a talker, and her warm personality was bubbling. We were instant friends! She was saying, "Drew, her kids are a really big deal. They sing and they are famous!!"

I said, "No, not at all famous, but they are great kids. God has blessed them." All the while, I noticed that people were coming by the table and asking for a picture with Drew. They asked for autographs, and it confused me. Heather looked like a model, but Steve said she was an intern at CMT. So I was pretty sure she was a regular girl. Drew was … hmmm, I wasn't sure.

So I asked, "Drew, what do you do?"

He replied, "I'm a professional athlete."

I didn't get it. I was blank, very puzzled. What was a professional athlete? Oh, I struggled, but I finally asked, "So are you a trainer?"

He said, "No, I am a professional football player."

I thought, *Is he a coach, maybe at a school?*

I asked once again (yes, it was a dork moment), "Where do you play football?" (I told you I wasn't plugged into the sports thing.)

He said, "I play for the Titans."

Now I felt like an idiot. He was a local celebrity, hence the pictures and autographs. What's even better is that he is a great guy. The moral of the story is that Steve Hannah wasn't a name-dropper, an egotist, or a user. He was unpretentious, humble, and loyal. I was amazed that he hadn't told me, but more than anything, I was impressed. Steve was a keeper! He was a quality human being. Without realizing it, I was becoming dependent on this big guy. He was becoming my stability.

I was beginning to see clearly that the mountains were looming up ahead. And this time, I was too weak to climb them. I was tired of strife. The ministry that I loved, and the kids I had made my world, needed to make their own choices. They needed to leave the nest. The thorns were prickly for all of us. I had been climbing mountains for 37 years. I was ready for someone else to climb. I just wanted to take that road around the mountain. Maybe I would even rest in this valley, but I had to find rest and peace.

My outlook was changing. The control freak was becoming an "I don't care" freak. I dreamed of the day that I didn't have a payroll and bus problems. I longed for the day when I could be like other friends and just worry about my nails, hair, grandbabies, and what color I should paint my dining room. I needed to figure this out. Meanwhile, in the yellow Mustang, this guy was hanging out and hanging in.

I took Steve to the SGMA function at the Hilton in downtown Nashville. I left him to his own devices. I am not a babysitter. If you need an appendage to survive in this world, I am not your girl. I am independent, and I expect everyone else to be. Be nice. Don't cheat. However, don't live in the hem of my shirttail either. It won't work. I am a social butterfly. Well, I am a bit heavy to be a butterfly, but I suppose I am more like a little fat owl or a chicken. Whatever … however … I am very social, and I don't like to be weighed down.

That night was a true test for Steve. I dropped him at the door after a few introductions, then I tended to the Crabb Family issues at hand, listened to the performances, hugged necks, planned lunches, and visited with people I hadn't seen since the big split. I love my friends. I love a gathering. I love Nashville. The night was good. After a couple of hours I went to check on my date. Truly, it could have been the end for us. However, in normal Steve "steady Eddie" fashion, he was fine. He mingled, laughed, and held his own in a room full of people who had no significance to him. I was impressed.

When we left, he said, "This guy came up to me and asked if I was dating you. I told him we were friends. He proceeded to tell me that if I was going to be in your life, I better hang on for the ride!"

I laughed and asked who said that. He couldn't remember. He said a middle-aged guy in black pants. That really narrowed it down. Anyway, if you said that and you are reading this book, Steve wants you to turn yourself in for an award: the "prophesy" award! He tells that story once in a while and gets a look on his face that says, "Why didn't I listen?"

The kids were singing on the General Jackson on Easter Sunday. I planned to go and take Steve. I had also invited Steve's family, who had accepted the invitation. So our Easter Sunday was planned with my kids and grandkids and Steve's parents and siblings. We would all ride down the river, enjoy the sounds of the Crabb Family, and get acquainted. That sounds like a simple plan, but don't jump to conclusions just yet. There wasn't *anything* simple about that weekend.

It was Good Friday, and everyone was in shut-down mode. Steve dropped by the house where I was working and said, "Let's go get something to eat." I agreed, and we did. We were sitting in Demo's eating our salad like any other day, when he said the usual, "Marry me!" He had been saying this for a week or so. Now mind you, we had known each other for seven or eight weeks. The proposal was tempting. I knew he was a good man. I felt his heart and his loyalty. He hated the pain that he saw in others. He hated sin. He loved God. He was Baptist; I wasn't. I was actually a jaded, hurt, Pentecostal girl who struggled to sit through a sermon. My mind wondered. It always wondered. I was a damaged Christian, like many of you, and no one understood but God. No one.

However, I wasn't a Baptist. I thought this was a big deal, and I told him so. His church was awesome. I loved his pastor, but I knew that eventually, someday, I would long for my roots. I would long for prayer lines and people who shout at the drop of a hat. It's not better, just different. So much of my life was entrenched in church, and I knew a mistake in this area would be fatal. Once again, I told him so. I explained that I believed in the gifts of the spirit. I believed in the manifestation of the Holy Ghost. He looked at me with a blank stare and said something like, "Well, that's alright. I won't try and stop you from any of that."

I explained that I was no more saved than he was, but it was personal preference. I said my normal, "Once you buck and shout, you can't go back!" The truth is I don't buck and shout, but my doctrinal beliefs are straight up Church of God, and I will buck and shout if God's in it.

So we had this conversation about being a Baptist versus Pentecostal, and we left. Then Steve said, "Let's drive to Gallatin, and see if the courthouse is open, in case we want to get a marriage license!" We did, and it wasn't. I knew my kids would kill me, but I was tempted. He was a rock, and I was almost sure that God had sent him.

A friend of mine had visited me the week before. We had a mutual friend who died suddenly, and we sat by the pool and looked at the stars one night. As we looked up and I cried a bit, my friend said, "Kathy, life is short. You have lived in far too much pain. Let Steve make you happy. Let him take care of you. He loves you."

Did he love me? *Could* he love me? My head was spinning, and I think his was, too. He took me home, and he left. It was Easter weekend, and we would talk about this some other time. I decided to clean out a closet, so I put on old shorts and a cotton shirt. I hadn't spent the energy I should have on my clothes, and the clothes that were now too big needed to go. Summer was coming, and the fat clothes were going to Goodwill.

It couldn't have been more than 30 minutes later when the doorbell rang. I had left my phone in the kitchen and couldn't hear the dozen missed calls. Steve was at the door. He was in a panic of sorts. He said, "Why didn't you answer your phone? You have 15 minutes to pack. We have to go!"

I asked him where in the world we were going. I proceeded to tell him I was cleaning out my closet, hence the terrible outfit.

"Well, Gallatin Courthouse isn't open, but I found one that is. Our flight leaves in an hour and a half. We have to leave for the airport in 15 minutes!"

"You're kidding, right?"

"No, and I paid a small fortune for these tickets. I thought you meant that you would have gotten a license if Gallatin was open, right? Is that not what you meant?" Remember I told you that he assumes a lot, and doesn't communicate real well?

I had about 60 seconds to go for it. I knew the kids were going to be *so* mad. They were so protective of me and knew I was vulnerable. They didn't want me to look like the offender either. Remember, the details of the divorce weren't necessarily public. I insisted on privacy for the sake of the family.

I was *so* stressed. What to do, what to do? I asked him, "Where are we going?"

He answered, "Vegas!"

I remember thinking, *Oh my goodness! This will be fodder for the other team!*

Dad's advice from my childhood kicked in: make up your mind quick, and change it slow. That is truly who I am. I said, "Yes!"

I packed nothing but clean underclothes. Steve didn't have anything either. I took lip gloss and my sunglasses. With my underwear in my purse, I flew to Vegas to marry a man I had known for eight weeks. He said we would get married and fly straight back. We did. We arrived late, and I will admit he smoked. I told him this may not work. He refrained.

He called his momma and told her he was in Vegas. I could hear her end of the conversation. He said Mom, "I am getting married in a few hours. We are going to get a license, find a chapel, and then fly back to town by midday. We are still on for the General Jackson on Sunday though!"

I heard my soon to be mother-in-law say, "*What?* You're *where?! Who* are you marrying?"

At this point, I laughed. He said, "Kathy. The lady I brought to Logan's to meet you all."

I was with Joyce on this one. Were we crazy?!

Steve assured me that he loved me, and I loved him, but I had loved and lost. I knew how much it hurt. He reassured me that he would never hurt me. He hugged me, and then he said, "Let's go do this!" We took a cab to the courthouse, and we waited. Finally, we got our turn. I was feeling like a crazy woman in a nutty movie. The last hang-up was that our anniversary was going to be on April 15: tax day.

Meanwhile, back on the Crabb Family bus, the mole overheard my phone call to the kids. He overheard my honest confession of the choice I was making. I suppose he overheard the discussion after I hung up the phone. The kids weren't opposed, but knew there would be talk. They didn't want that and neither did I. I tried to explain my concerns to Steve, and he didn't understand. On the flight I told him, "I don't think you know what you're signing up for."

He said, "Oh, anything and everything will be alright. We are divorced adults who didn't know each other until we were both divorced. What's to say?"

He didn't understand the vulture nature of people. He doesn't have the vulture nature. He doesn't know many people with that nature, but let me tell you, I did! It was fresh meat for the buzzards. He continued to assure me that no one would be that mean. I disagreed in my heart. I wanted to believe him, but it turns out he was wrong.

We got the license, went to the "Little White Wedding Chapel," headed back to the airport, and flew back to Nashville. Unlike the rumors that would follow, there was no gambling, no illicit sex, and no alcohol; no nothing. There was just a courthouse that was open 365 days a year and that's it! Just 24 hours earlier we were having lunch and discussing the Baptist thing. Now we were married. I was in shock.

Steve said, "You know what this means? I get to stay with you now!"

Oh my, I guess it did mean that. We went to the General Jackson.

These days, the kids say they were pretty sure I had lost my mind. During my year of crying, pain, and hurt, they—along with David, Lorie, Micah, Zach, and Justin— had kept the bus rolling. They had said little and worked much. This crew was the dream team. They had undergirded the kids during that season of pain. I am confident that on that day at the General Jackson *all* of them thought I had lost my mind. Truly, what were they all supposed to think? Kelly and Krystal voiced their disdain a bit louder than the others, but their hearts were in the right place. It didn't make sense, like so much in my life hadn't made sense, but I sure wasn't blaming this on God. I wasn't positive it was God, but I was leaning toward it. People who blame God for their stupidity get on my last nerve, so I wasn't going there. If this was a disaster, *I* would own it.

When I woke up Monday, a link to our marriage license was already posted online. A press release had been sent, and radio stations had been informed that "Kathy Crabb Weds Realtor IN VEGAS!" The buzzards were feasting. It took me days to get all of the online threads removed and the links deactivated. It certainly ruined our first week of marriage. I still cry when I think about the ugliness that people have festering inside of them. In the meantime, our marriage license got thousands of hits, and my poor husband decided he had taken a one-way flight to Hell. I will not say who sent that press release, but many of you will know. It was inappropriate and truly reminds me of our president. It was an attempt to distract. It was spin. I am an open book. If I weren't, I wouldn't be writing this one. My stories can be collaborated by my family. This hurt me deeply.

I will make this paragraph short. In the end, I had the pleasure of firing the mole who was feeding the info.

Steve had gotten his initiation. He understood better the contempt and hatred in which I was living. I didn't deserve it. He was shocked; he still is. He often says I am the poster child for "what doesn't kill you makes you stronger." I am happy to report that all the kids love Steve Hannah with everything that they are, and he loves them just as much. A long courtship is for sissies anyway!

20 EVA MEANS LIFE

April 23, 2009. The Dove Awards were happening. Sound checks, pretty dresses, red carpet, and a night of music was on the agenda—but not for me. I had been there, done that, and truly was a bit bitter. I had no desire to go. There were reasons. The bitterness was not at the kids, but it was there. The roots had dug into my soul and planned to use the pain of rejection to survive. So when I was offered tickets, I declined. I couldn't go. It hurt. Instead, I offered to babysit.

That night I kept Jason's Ashleigh and Emma. I promised a trip to Build-A-Bear as soon as Steve got home. They did the normal, "How long will that be?" and looked sad. We went to the backyard, took the usual Granny pictures, and waited. Steve finally arrived to little girl giggles, and they were ready to go. We headed to Opry Mills. I am sorry to say that I can't remember parts of this night. I think I have a mental block, but here is what I remember:

Steve parked the car. He let us out at the mall entrance like I had taught him to do in only three short years. The girls and I hurried out and grabbed a table at Macaroni Grill. They were anxious for those bears. We ordered our food, all the while enjoying that amazing loaf of bread with olive oil and just the right amount of Italian spices. Yes, we were also coloring on the white paper tablecloth. Their "I love Granny" picture is still in my office to this day.

During that season of my life, I was a bit heavy with self-pity on days like this. After all, hadn't I given my best years? Hadn't I been faithful? Why did I have to walk away from this music I loved? Yes, it was my choice, but it was the only way I could survive, the only way I could protect my heart so that I may live and not die. I had left to survive, but I was *bitter*.

The music exit was still fresh, and it was a personal grief, a grief that wasn't apparent from my "I decided to leave the music, I decided to disband the Crabb Family" comments. The truth was it was the greatest pain my heart had known. My 15 years of labor, my "baby," whom I felt I had birthed, nurtured, spoon-fed, taught to walk, and finally run ... my baby was gone. It made me so sad at times that I could hardly breathe. I was still numb as it related to the music and the music pain, which was always a bit separate from the personal pain. The loss was greater to me. The music had provided a means to live the promise that God made to me to serve Him. It had provided for my kids and grandkids, but suddenly it didn't include me. I grieved. I used distractions to mask the pain from others. This was one of those nights.

However, that night at the Macaroni Grill, I had balm on my wounds in the form of Ash and Emma. They chattered at the same time, hugged me, and reminded me that Granny was still intact, even if Kathy, the Crabb Family matriarch, wasn't. I ate bread, laughed with these babies, and decided that I was blessed. I always do. My pity parties are always a one-woman show. They take place, typically, only in my mind, and no guests are invited. I pose questions and answers and end up ashamed, most of the time, after I realize I have never chosen a casket for a baby, or gone to a federal prison to visit one of my children. I slap myself, get over it, and move on, at least for a minute, until a reminder invades the safety zones of my mind.

So, our food was coming, the bread was extra good, and the girls were loving on me. I felt blessed. Suddenly, Crystal Burchette sent me a text that said, "Where are you?" I immediately thought that was odd. I knew she was at the Dove Awards working the press room; she would be back stage, and incredibly busy. It wasn't a time when "Hey what are you doing?" texts would be happening!

Her next text said, "Who is with you? You're not alone, are you?"

I responded, "Steve and the girls."

Before I could explain the weirdness of the texts to Steve, she called and said, "Hey, please don't panic, but there's been an accident. Aaron and Amanda need you to be calm. They need you to go to the Vanderbilt Children's Hospital now!"

I immediately cried out, " Oh, Jesus, what happened?"

I quickly did an inventory of my grandchildren. I had two with me. Kelly was out of town with three. I screamed, "Oh God. Who, Crystal, who?"

She replied, "It's Eva. She has fallen out of a second story window at the babysitter's apartment! They are bringing her by ambulance. That's all I know. *Please*, keep it together for Aaron's sake!"

The walk to our vehicle is a blur. I was babbling to Steve, crying and saying "*Jesus*, Jesus, *Jesus!*" repeatedly. People were staring. I remember grabbing the arms of the little girls and dragging them. I don't think we even paid for our food, which was ordered but not yet served. I was in a state of mild shock. The girls didn't understand, and they were fearful. I was fearful, and they were taking the lead from me. I cried; they cried. I screamed; they screamed. There is such a lesson here, but that's for another day. I remember saying at least a hundred times, "Steve, drive faster!" I prayed in the spirit, and I screamed in the flesh. I thought we would never arrive.

The first few minutes are still a blur, a bit of a mental block, I suppose. However, she was alive! Eva was alive! Her little body had survived the horrific fall. Relief rushed over me in a way you cannot understand until you live it. Momma always told us, "When there is life, there is hope!" Hope was my new best friend. I would cling to hope for the next few hours.

Aaron and Amanda were back in the trauma unit with her. The room was already full of a mix of people. There were music people who were at the Opry House with Amanda and Aaron when they got the call, some of the family, the tearful babysitter, and her supportive friends. The police and child services were there all night, interrogating, investigating, and reviewing testimony. The nanny was a great girl, and my heart hurt for her. It had been a freak accident. She was in a living Hell, at least for this night. Soon the entire event would be deemed an accident, and while she was not in fear of legal retribution, her self-imposed guilt was obvious. We prayed for Eva, and we gathered around the nanny and prayed for her as well.

Amanda had been fasting for weeks, and I asked her why. She would simply say, "God told me to! I don't have a specific reason." She was hungry and weak. Now I knew why, and so did Amanda. When they walked into the room and saw their 2-year-old baby girl with a neck brace, the doctors were still uncertain if there was a spinal cord injury. A six-inch laceration was prominent, starting at her hairline and going straight back. It was a bloody reminder of just how bad this might be. In fact, Eva had a mouth full of blood, and she looked like a child with a long road ahead of her. However, she was alive. Then, Aaron and Amanda could see the full picture. The skipped meals and the hunger became a small thing. God's hand of mercy was apparent. She was *alive.*

After a fight from a 2 year old that would rival a wrestler, they finally got a CT scan on the second try. The soft Mommy and Daddy voices stilled her fear and calmed that feisty temperament. Eva is a mini Amanda and would take nothing lying down. The CT scan proved to be clear, and we all praised and shouted. This was the big one; God had answered our prayers. The clear CT scan meant they could start stitching that awful laceration. Could it be that this child had fallen out of a window from 18 feet onto an air conditioner unit and sustained only an external laceration? Could it be that there was no internal bleeding or organ damage? As the information trickled to us in the lobby piece by piece, I was uncertain. It seemed impossible to me. How could she be okay? Soon we got news from trauma that her lip was detached from her jawbone. Surgery was needed, but the doctors assured us that it would be successful and that she would be fine. I also got the assurance that she was fine internally. We cried and praised. We turned that lobby at Vanderbilt into a tabernacle, and the praises flowed like rain!

Finally, I saw her. By this time, she was a bit more sedate. She melted my heart with the obvious. She had been traumatized, and they were poking, sticking, and prodding. She had busted that little head into an air conditioner unit. Her head must have hurt. She must have been in horrific pain. That was a long fall, and she was just a baby, a tiny little thing. She should have been dead, but she wasn't. My screams from a few hours before had melted into a soft whisper. I was whispering to this baby girl. Once again, God protected. Our baby would live. I was one happy Granny.

I debated on what to write as I wrote about Eva, this child who was named "Eva" because it meant life. This is the child who was in a vision her daddy had had years before she was born. The blond, long-haired 10 year old was playing basketball with Aaron in the driveway in the vision that would stay with him. The promise of the 10 year old in the vision convinced Aaron that this 2 year old would live and not die. This vivid vision that God gave him would be his strength in such a time as this. This vision that would keep him sane on that ride to the hospital would be the story of Eva, the child who would live.

Does God do this sort of thing? Sure He does. Was this a vision for the church, the people? Probably not at that time. It was for Aaron and Amanda then, but now it is a testimony. The trial became a pillar of their family faith story, their story that will live for many generations throughout their children and their children's children. It was our God who spares nothing when it comes to detail. It was God who would use this to prove that He alone knows the beginning before there is a beginning. He knows what we will walk through before we walk it. He allows our trials, our broken hearts, our six-inch lacerations, our rejection, our bus wrecks, our tragedies. He allows them to be the fabric that we use to weave our own stories of faith, sure-footed faith, the faith built on rocks rather than sand. He allows the devil to bring suffering and trauma, but when we seek Him, the pain is understood and oftentimes expected. Our spirit knows; hence Amanda's fast. We live in an existence of pain, a world where it rains on the just and the unjust alike, but *we,* the just, the saved, the believers in visions and prophecies, shall live by faith. If we exercise it, it grows.

Why did Eva fall out of that window? In my opinion, it was the devil trying to destroy the future of this young couple who would be a force to be reckoned with as they grew strong, as they decided to bravely embrace a faith walk. It was the devil trying to replace their prayer time with pain time. It was the devil's attempt to bring that cursed alcoholism to these young ministers of the gospel as a coping tool, an addiction. It was the evil one trying to create an environment that would be marinated in blame, pain, and sorrow. The devil was allowed to touch her, but he couldn't control God's protection of this child who would live and not die. The hand of God protected Eva and the destiny of her family. Tonight, I will go to church, and I will watch a soon-to-be 8 year old as she lifts her hands in worship. I will watch her participate with no boundaries, for somehow, she gets it. She knows that her life is purposeful and special. This child whom we call Eva belongs to Him. She always has.

21 THE DAY BEFORE

June 30, 2010. On this day, life in Hendersonville, Tennessee, was busy as usual. Today marked the middle of my real estate year, and I was excited about the volume. God had surely blessed me. After the Crabb Family retired, I was forced to find something to do. Steve and I were married, and the real estate market was shifting, though not in a positive way. That "bubble" that had been long predicted, and the predictions long ignored, was destined to be. We collectively announced the Crabb Family's retirement at the end of July 2006, and sent out a press release that the family would tour until July 31, 2007. August 1, 2007 came, and I was officially unemployed. Steve saw the writing on the wall, and he was scared, as was I. I was unemployed, and I was scared.

We had lived our first 15 months of marriage fighting demons. Let's just say I had haters. Opportunistic people are everywhere, and Christian music is no exception. The church is no exception, and those who need to make you look bad so they will look better are no exception. The Crabb Family brand was valuable. The vultures were circling. I felt as if the thief had come in the night and stolen my life's work, the thief being the circumstances of this mess. So it was finished, I was out, and I was bitter. The circumstances weren't created by my choices, but, through all of the building of this new normal, the family had survived.

The kids had grown to trust Steve. They were beginning to realize that he wasn't the kind to pick up and leave. If you know him, you understand this sentence. He's loyal to a fault. If you stomped him into the pavement, he would defend himself, but he would assist you in getting a cast on the foot you broke stomping him. When he says he's in for life, he's in for life, not just until the next thing comes along. So this new family dynamic was living on love.

I had some royalty money coming in from publishing, and I had a little income here and there. I flirted with downsizing and retiring. If you know me well, you know that was a day that I was hallucinating. I will never retire. If I quit, I will die. Anyway, for a minute I considered it. Steve's work was taking a hit. The decline had started. The next six years of our lives would be spent trying to tread water.

This mortgage crisis didn't have to happen, but it did happen. The loose practices on which liberal politicians insisted caused the crisis. After all, we couldn't discriminate; *everyone* has to own a home, right? We couldn't make little things like having a job and assets a requirement. That would discriminate against minorities. While we're making sure the playing field is level, let's allow the builder to pay the down payment; or no, wait, let's just do 0 down, no doc loans. Yes, let's do that. Well, they did, and they didn't pay. Some people bought three or four houses at a time with a 580 credit score. One was for Momma, one for their favorite Auntie, one for the best friend, and on and on. Many of these deals closed, and the buyers didn't make the first payment. The bank had to go through the foreclosure process, which was starting to take years. With the volume of foreclosures ticking upward, it was becoming increasingly normal for it to take two or three years. Property values dropped on the average of 30%, so that meant that people who were transferring, retiring, or moving for any given reason couldn't sell. They were what we term "underwater" and stuck. This put our country in a tailspin, and hence the recession was escalated

I could write pages upon pages about the housing crisis, but I won't. That's another book sometime. The point is this: I saw the stress on Steve's face. His life was drastically changing. I was unemployed. On a Friday in September, I called a real estate school and enrolled. I started the following week. Three weeks later, I had my license. I went to work. Agents were getting out of real estate by the droves, but I was getting in. They had benefitted from the loose lending, and many had gotten rich. The fat lady was fixing to sing, and these folks were finding the exit. I told folks in passing that I had just gotten my real estate license, and they looked at me like I had two heads and both were ugly. It was challenging. I didn't have a clientele; I didn't even know that many people in Tennessee. I had as many friends in North Carolina as I did in Tennessee. The nature of the music business was such that my friends were sprinkled everywhere. For a successful real estate career, that just wouldn't work.

It took me about three days to realize that we were in crisis mode. Like the superhero that Steve Hannah is, he had refinanced my mortgage in 2006, shortly after we were married. He relieved the original purchasers of all obligations, I was one of those people. I think you can figure out who the other one is. It was entirely too generous, and he shouldn't have done it, but he did anyway. The payment was less, but it was still more than I could afford, and he was living in fear of the coming wave of unsellable properties that were under water, the knee-jerk reaction of the lenders, and the government intrusion that would limit lending by enforcing an overabundance of regulations.

The whole "over-regulating" thing is depicted something like this: if you allow your 13-year-old daughter to date a 25 year old with a Corvette and pretend that this is a common-sense choice, don't be shocked when she gets pregnant or injured in a car accident. The answer to that stupidity would *not* be to enforce a law that doesn't allow women to date until they're 40. Liberal agendas are always extreme and are never built on common-sense solutions.

Anyway, back to 2007. It was October, and I didn't have the first clue how to find a buyer or a seller. Steve isn't the most communicative person on the planet, and he taught me nothing. Once I started selling, he cleaned up my clerical mistakes and helped me learn the document protocol, but with the people side of the business, he was no help. I started calling agents and asking if I could Craigslist their listings. If they agreed, I did it. Then we stumbled onto an owner-financed listing, and the agent agreed for us to advertise. She was the builder's daughter-in-law and was happy for the help. We sold it.

An investor called after seeing the owner-financed ad, and I sold them a house. By January, I was rolling. The deals were small, but I was getting my sea legs. The market was in turmoil. Successful agents were closing offices and leaving the industry, but somehow God was helping me. We had a system starting. I would catch them, and Steve would clean them. He was a great problem solver, and I was a negotiator and deal-maker. He worked through the inspections, repairs, and the occasional restructuring of a loan. I had a background in finance from the car business and working at a bank in my 20s. I loved to make a deal. Getting a contract signed made me do an internal "woohoo!" I looked all cool and professional, but on the inside, I was doing cartwheels.

In 2008, we discovered two things that would keep us alive. We did a few foreclosure bus tours. We used an entertainer coach, much like the ones I had owned, but these coaches were compliments of my friend Olan. We advertised these foreclosure bus tours in the *Tennesseean*. The folks who came out to view the foreclosures were often qualified buyers. It worked. I now had some clientele. We were surviving, at least for now.

The other things falling into my lap were owner-financed properties. I sold three properties for an investor, and he noticed me. He noticed that I was working. In those days, almost no one was working. Realtors were shell-shocked. They were looking for jobs elsewhere, anywhere. I didn't know what a good market looked like. My short year in the business had been grueling hard work, but what were we to do? The choices weren't there. We had to hang in and hang on.

This investor, who had deep pockets and bankrolled projects that were bigger numbers than I had ever seen, called me one night. I had never spoken to him and didn't know his name. I just knew the company name. I got a random call on a Saturday night while I was eating at Monell's with Steve, Linda, and Gale. Monell's does not allow phone calls in the dining room of their family-style restaurant. I answered anyway and stepped outside into the February air. It was cold. A voice on the line said, "This is _____, and I need you to sell some houses for me."

I grabbed a napkin and a pen and said, "Sure, I would love to." He sounded elderly, and he was matter-of-fact and in an obvious hurry. He quickly started rambling different subdivision names to me. I had never heard of any of them. I had written down his name, and I was trying to jot down these subdivision names.

I asked for addresses, and he said, "I don't know the addresses; I own thousands of properties. I gave you the subdivision name. Find the addresses on tax records. They're all in my name! There are about six or seven houses I am going to give you. I own a real estate office down on West End, but I will give you these listings on the north side of Nashville. And one more thing: I will owner-finance these houses. They're all new and nice. Bring me the contracts Monday. My office is on West End!"

I was stunned. A three-minute call was destined to change the next six years of my life. I had just experienced favor. God had done the provisional work to allow this momma to take care of her babies when the time came. The little detour that night, answering the "right" call, grabbing that napkin to write on, pretending I understood when I didn't but knowing I could "fake it 'til I made it" was part of the Word. God orders our footsteps. A sovereign God who knew the needs of the Bowling family would require nearly a year of my life and put me, a lowly rookie realtor, on the mind of a wealthy octogenarian. He did this so that when the storm came, we wouldn't be begging for bread. For I wasn't forsaken. I was hurt, and I fought a daily dose of bitterness, but I was not forsaken. I often said, "Nothing is God's fault. I have no problems with God."

I went back into the restaurant, had my pan-fried chicken, and couldn't wait to get back to my computer to see what I had just listed. Remember the mortgage crisis had destroyed lending. Loans were hard to get. These houses, the first of many that he would give me to sell, were nice. We sold them, and he paid us. We thrived. I was an owner finance expert within a year. 80% of my business was owner-financed properties. I had found myself at the top of the Century 21 regional sales numbers. God was faithful, and I was working. Awards don't make me work, but competition does. These awards were fair, unlike many popularity contests. They were based on numbers and truth. I competed. I won. The work was demanding, the hours were long, but I knew God had given me an inroad when most people were barely surviving.

One day I came home and asked Steve if we could talk. Of course he said yes. I told him that God had instructed me to help Mike and Kelly. They were the one entity to spring from the Crabb Family that didn't benefit from all of the Crabb branding. No one makes better records, and no group is loved more, but the start had been rough. They were faithful, but times weren't easy. I am a giver. I help all of my kids when they need me, and what's mine is theirs. However, I don't support any of them. I try to support their ministries, but I firmly believe that people should be self-sufficient. Mike was working at the hospital as a respiratory therapist, and Kelly was caring for those three little girls and dragging luggage on and off a bus every week. They were exhausted, and they needed some relief.

So, on this day, I asked Steve, "My average monthly income is _____. Would you be opposed to me giving Mike and Kelly anything that I make next month in excess of my average, just as a simple offering?"

He said, "Of course, I wouldn't care. You didn't have to ask me that. It's your money!"

The next 30 days were ridiculous. I sold property after property. Owner-financed properties can close in three days. God was in it. He opened up the windows of Heaven. If you have ever been blessed by a song on *Shine*, this will make you appreciate it even more. The kids needed money to make an album. They needed some transportation problems resolved. Just 30 days later, I donated $40,000 to their ministry. God provided it. He owns the cattle on a thousand hills, and he also directed a few buyers to a house in Brentwood and two in Greenbrier. I hope this is building your faith, not your opinion of me. It is meant to glorify God, not me. Within myself, I can do nothing. My righteousness is as filthy rags, and my ability is no more than a blundering fool without the Lord. However, be prepared to step up when you promise God. Be careful what you pray for. He's listening.

We celebrated, and they made a record. God continued to provide, and that big old house I was still trapped in was now worth $250,000 less than what was paid for it back when the Crabb Family moved to Tennessee. Poor Steve was on the hook for the mortgage. I worried, but I trusted God, and I worked like a mule every day. So did Steve.

Steve was loyal to me. He had held my hand through the unraveling of the Crabb Family, the year of lawsuits to free the kids from contracts, and had wiped my tears and hugged me often. We were learning to lean on each other. This marriage was birthed in pain, but the fire had proven him to be gold. I held him as we buried his sweet daddy. I watched the grieving process get suppressed so that he could babysit our life struggles. His most redeeming quality is loyalty. *My* most redeeming quality is loyalty. We were building a world on the honor of undying faithfulness, and I realized that I had married up; at least in my opinion I had. I also realized that he loved me more than I had ever been loved. I was learning about security. I was learning to trust. It was a process, but we worked hard. We didn't know what else to do.

We had great family times. Christmases and birthdays overwhelmed Steve. His eyes had fear in them when all 14 grand kids would run through the house, up the stairs, outside, inside, back outside, and so on. I made it clear to him early on that my family traditions were non-negotiable. I am a "go big or go home" Granny. I spoil, and I overdo most things. My motto is this: "I want to be so generous in my life that I will be terribly missed in my death." I want my grandchildren to remember me as the over-the-top, no-mountain-is-too-high, the-bigger-the-better Granny. Part of that legacy includes big parties, presents, cake, and cousin love. These are *my* wishes. My family doesn't require it of me; it's self-imposed. I want to go the extra mile to make sure the mashed potatoes have whipping cream in them. I want the Christmas presents to be chosen by me, not a gift card. I want my funeral to be full of comments about effort, determination, and going the extra mile; you know, the "go big or go home" statement. So my kids and grandkids didn't suffer the loss of Granny's Christmases or Granny's parties. I wanted those memories to be the ones that built them.

The only thing different was that Steve was now in the grandpa role. He was happy to be, but he didn't demand a title and was happy to be Steve. Time would tell. No one wanted any additional confusion for the grandchildren; they'd had enough already. So he started out as Steve. Granny and Steve became a stabilizing force to a room full of kids and young adults. Our home was still a safe place. They were loved. The family was intact. Love had prevailed.

The short version of a long story is this: Brian taught Sophie to say "Poppa Steve." Brian was raised by a man who wasn't his biological father. He has never met his biological father. He respects the parent who chooses to take the load when they're not required to. He taught Sophie to call Steve "Poppa Steve," and it stuck. The younger kids with no memory of days without him called him Poppa Steve as well. The older ones didn't, but that was okay. Things should be natural and feel right. A title does not define a relationship. I of all people understand that. However, a standing ovation would be appropriate for a man who married a woman with 6 kids, 6 in-law kids, and what was soon to be 14 grandchildren. When he got me, he got the entire tribe. And guess what: he's still here!

On June 30, 2010, I was going out with the Bowlings for the weekend. They were struggling to decide on a personnel change, and extra eyes and an opinion were requested. I agreed to go. We got to the bus at midnight, I think, and Melissa, a family friend, was there too. I remember saying, "I didn't know you were coming! But I am glad."

She said she had arranged the details with Terah, and we all loaded our stuff and did the usual visiting and laughing for the typical 30 minutes before the bus left. They were loading product and getting the kids settled into their bunks. I think the kids were already asleep. I noticed that everyone looked tired, and they started to trickle to bunks as soon as we pulled onto I-65. By the time we had gone a mile or two, the bus lost power. The engine wasn't allowing the speed to be over 20 or 30 miles an hour. The driver said it was a safety device to protect the engine, and he was going back to Prevost to get a mechanic to look at it.

I was not happy. I hate buses. Remember, I was the in-charge manager mom who had traveled a couple million miles on one, slept on a front couch, and jumped up every time the driver hit a rumble strip, slammed on the brakes, or drove too fast. I have been on buses when they hit cars, blew engines, lost transmissions, burned out brakes on mountains, broke down on a busy interstate, had blowouts, and everything else you can imagine. Les Beasley always said that buses had a sticker on the bottom that said "Made in Hell!" He is right. So this wasn't the way I pictured this busy holiday weekend starting.

The driver got off on Old Hickory Boulevard and got back on the northbound ramp of I-65 to head back to Prevost. He had flashers on, and though the creeping speed of 20 or so seemed dangerous, we made it to the exit. As we turned into the long lane that led to Prevost, the bus came to a screeching halt. It was as if the brakes were pushed all the way to the floor. Everyone else was in bed or sitting down. I was in the back, and the sudden stop threw me into the door facing the back bathroom before I did a somersault down the middle aisle between the bunks. I was hurt. My ribs and leg took the hit. I pulled up my pants leg, and I could see the screw in my leg coming through the skin. I had had leg surgery in 2001 after I broke my leg, and thus have a screw in my knee. Seeing the screw was too much; I was dizzy. I started to lose consciousness.

Mike wrapped it, but it bled. My ribs were hurting, and I was sure they were broken. I couldn't breathe, but I didn't need to slow the bus down. The Bowlings had to be in Indian Trail, NC to tape a show for INSP the next day; well, actually the same day, for it was now after one in the morning. The bus was being pulled into the bay at Prevost.

Bus repairs are never quick unless Jeff Easter is there. Time was starting to be a concern. My leg and breathing were of concern as well. Kelly insisted I go to the hospital. For about 30 minutes, Kelly, Mike, and Terah encouraged me to call Steve. But I am stubborn, and I didn't want to. I wanted to go to the taping. I wanted to see Kim White, an old friend who produced videos and was producing the show, and hang out with the girls for the weekend. I had scheduled my weekend around these plans, and I didn't want to change anything. I felt that I was needed, but the pain was increasing.

Finally I called Steve. I offered to take the Bowling girls home with me. Kelly said, "Mom, you're not able to take care of kids in that condition. I would never do that to you!" So I promised the kids I would go to the hospital. Instead, I went home and worried. I wasn't worried about me; I was worried about that doggone bus. I promised Steve that I would go to my doctor after I slept a few hours. I didn't want to sit in the ER all night. I wrapped my leg and put an Ace bandage on it to slow the bleeding. I propped myself on pillows to help with the breathing and pain from the ribs. I was a mess. My nerves were shot, and I felt like I had been in a car wreck. My bones hurt, my teeth felt like they were loose, my head hurt, and those ribs hurt like no one's business! Sleep didn't come. I stayed awake all night, touching base with Mike and the driver every hour or so.

At 8 a.m., they had the part and finally had the bus repaired. It was a simple hose, but they had to wait until a parts store was open to get one. Then a runner rushed it to Prevost and they quickly got it installed. However, the bus had sat idle all night waiting on a $40 hose. The kids had slept a bit, but not much. At 8:15, Mike called and said, "We're rolling. Should we cancel? We won't make our sound check time. There's a studio audience, but there's no way for us to be there at report time."

I was so troubled. As momma used to say, I was uneasy! However, I had a screw showing through a big gash in my leg, broken ribs, and no sleep. I chalked it up to all of this.

Mike was asking me for direction, which isn't unusual. I told Mike, "Let me call them. You can't make it on time, agreed. I will call you right back."

I made the call, and the graciousness was there. They left it up to us. However, they assured me that they would wait and accommodate. Truly Kim and this network were the best. I relayed the info to a sleepy and exhausted Mike. He pondered; I pondered. What to do? Well, in typical family tradition, they went. Their commitment to the ministry was stronger than their exhaustion. The honor to be included outweighed the inconvenience of the late sound check. The bus rolled, and I went back to prop my leg in my big comfy bed. I had to keep it elevated to slow down the bleeding. Steve once again made me promise to call when I was ready to go to the doctor. I agreed and he went to work. My memory is fuzzy on this detail, but I think Edie came to stay with me because of the injuries. Maybe she was already there; I am unsure. However, somehow, on that day, Edie was with me. I was troubled and checked on the bus every hour or so. That fall had left me unnerved and feeling like the younger version of my momma the worrywart.

I tried to sleep but was never successful. I told myself that I would be able to relax as soon as the bus arrived safely at the Indian Trail stop. It was not to be. At about 4, I tried to call Mike but got no answer. I called Kelly; no answer. I called Terah; no answer. They had stopped for food and fuel.

With traffic, it was impossible that they were already there. Maybe they were in a bad cell service area. I waited and tried again. No success. At about 4:15 or 4:20, Kim called. She was producing the show and wanted to know if I could reach them. She told me she hadn't been able to get them for the last few minutes. She said she talked to them an hour before and they were close. I panicked. Kim calmed me. She told me to let her know as soon as I heard from Mike. I promised I would.

22 I-85

I called and called. No answer. I was freaking out, but I kept trying. Finally, Terah answered her phone. She was breathing heavily. I could hear wailing, carnage, and high-pitched crying. I knew. Way down in my stomach, I knew that the long dread fear of a bus wreck was no longer on my dread list. It was on my reality list. They had been in a wreck.

The sounds were indescribable. Terah's voice still rings in my head. She said, "Are you alone?" I told her Edie was there with me. She said, "Go in the room with Edie. Sit down. Please stay calm. We need you to be calm. We've had an awful wreck. The bus slammed into a semi. The front of the bus is gone. I think Kelly is okay, but Mike ... Kathy, he looks like he may not make it. I think he may be ... well, he's bad. Be prepared, and please keep it together for Kelly. Kate-Kate is bleeding really bad. Her face is cut, and she's pouring blood! Come now, but please be careful!"

I heard enough to understand that Katelanne was bleeding out. My 6-year-old baby girl, who was named for my momma, was in the balance, and Mike, the loyal son-in-law who had more talent in his little toe than most people have in their body, dead? Could he be dead? *No!*

I fell to the floor. I have no words to describe what I felt. This was a living nightmare. We had traveled a couple of million miles on buses. Those babies had gone to sleep on pillows with tractor-trailer trucks passing 18 inches from them as they slept. I knew the risk, but now it was real ... it was Terah's voice and the carnage noises. My mind couldn't take it. I felt like I was going to pass out. Edie overheard. She knew. I began to scream like only a mother or grandmother can when they know a family member is dying and an immediate miracle is the only answer.

I screamed, "*No! Not* today! Not this day! Katelanne *will not* die today. She will live. Mike will live. He has babies to raise. *They will live!*"

I think Edie called Steve, and within minutes Jon and Steve were at the door. Kim White says I called her back as I promised I would. She says I was screaming, and it was nearly impossible to understand what I was saying as I sobbed. I have no memory of calling her, but that's to be expected, I suppose.

We got in our car and left. Edie asked Krystal if she could go. Krystal told her no, but she went anyway. We drove. I asked them not to tell me anything while we were in the car. I couldn't handle it. If I was going to learn that Katelanne was dead, it couldn't be in that car. I was so uncertain of how I would physically respond to the news, and I knew that if I was in that car I might go insane; that "snapping" point might happen. I didn't want my 15-year-old granddaughter to be subjected to what I knew I was capable of. Since the attack when I was 17, the attack that left me with 43 stitches in my throat, the devil had repeatedly told me that I would lose my mind, go insane. That thought reared its ugly head on this day. My instincts told me to protect my mind; hence the no information while in the car. I wanted to freeze my mind and protect it. It couldn't take anymore, not yet. I heard bits and pieces of the hushed conversations registering through the fog of my mind. I kept reminding them that I couldn't get bad news and to please stop talking.

Apparently Terah was fine, a bump or bruise, except she had seen it all. Hope had as well. Terah and Hope were fine physically, but mentally they would carry scars. Terah still struggles with the memories and the visuals of the impact, the glass, the metal against metal, the bodies flying, the smell of rubber, blood, and the wails of Gracie and Katelanne. She remembers the wet sticky blood pouring from Mike and Katelanne's injuries onto everything, and the realization that Kelly was counting her kids to see if any of them had been thrown out onto the interstate. Terah would be left with a catalog of memories in living color. I now realize that the level-headed 21-year-old sound man who immediately turned to Mike and tried to keep him alive until someone could help most likely saved his life. Somehow I know that God knew Kris was needed, and he was there, on that bus, for such a time as this. They say that he was unbelievably calm and knew exactly what to do to assist the injured.

Kelly has told me how she gathered her kids, with Katelanne bleeding profusely, and tried to keep them from seeing their dad because she thought he was dying. She didn't want their last memory to be the unrecognizable man who lay bleeding in the front of that bus lounge. On impact his head instantly enlarged, his eyes swelled together, and he didn't resemble their dad.

So, while we drove in that white BMW, Charlotte, North Carolina was experiencing a big traffic problem on I-85. A blue bus carrying a family of singers, a family who loved God and had been faithful, a family who could have easily given up when times were lean, on this day, was strewn out onto the pavement of I-85, on the bridge over Catawba River, awaiting ambulances and helicopters. Traffic was backed up, and the area was swarming with news vans. However, God was still good, and it rains on the just and the unjust alike. Bad people have wrecks, and good people have wrecks. Such is life.

Later, I learned that while we drove, Mike was in critical condition with an obvious head injury. A helicopter was spotted. They were clearing a place to land it. Mike went by air. His blood pressure had dropped to 60/40. It didn't look good. The ambulance driver said for everyone to prepare for a fatality.

Kelly says she realized that she may not see Mike alive again. She knew she was injured. She feared that her back was broken, but she thought she would live, and she knew that she may be left alone to raise her girls. She tells often how in that moment she knew that God was all she had. I was far away. She didn't know if we had been told yet, and certainly we couldn't have been nearby. It was down to her and God. She says as she watched the helicopter take Mike away, she felt God's peace. She wasn't convinced that God would spare Mike, but she knew that either way, He was sovereign. He would be her rock. Lying flat on the pavement on I-85 at approximately 5:30 on July 1, Kelly fully understood faith, the faith she had been singing about since she was a kid. The Jesus whom she so readily told others to trust; would she trust Him? Now it was her life, her tragedy. Would she believe? The spiritual rubber had met the road. She chose peace. She said peace rushed over her like nothing she had ever experienced. That's God. That's how He rolls.

As I rode in that car, the information began to be uttered between Steve and Jon. I absorbed that Gracie was being held by Melissa, our friend who had randomly decided to go out that weekend. I later learned that she saved her life. Gracie was only 3, was walking in the front, and would surely have flown though the broken windshield. God prepared a fish for Jonah, and God sent Melissa to hold Gracie that day.

I knew Steve and Jon were seeing the image of the bus. The slight gasps told me it was bad. I was aware that the other kids were also en route to Charlotte. I took three calls while in that car; the rest I didn't answer. I couldn't process it. I answered Aaron, Jason, and Kevin McManus. Aaron was looking for a flight and calmly assured me that God would not fail us. Kevin was offering to fly us to Charlotte. Jason was angry about something on Facebook, and I told him not to tell me anything bad. I couldn't handle it. He didn't. I knew Krystal was in touch through Edie, and Adam was following us a few miles back.

If you don't believe we love each other, come hang out when one of us is facing a disaster. Remember the love-is-thicker-than-blood thing I always say? It's true. It may not make everyone happy, but it makes no difference.

It can't be changed, and no one wants it to change. Our security is in each other. This fractured family grew back stronger than before and is a mighty force to be reckoned with. Keeping the family together is one of the greatest testimonies of my life.

On July 1, 2010, the family was manifested. As always in time of struggle, we came together as a family. The brothers and sisters and the prayer warriors all around the world were praying. The images of a blue Prevost that had smashed into the rear of a stopped tractor trailer were everywhere. This terrible wreck was caused by a faulty sign at a weigh station, a sign that was out of order because an employee dropped the ball on the Thursday before this holiday weekend due to a relaxed protocol. However, people were praying. They stopped in parking lots, grocery stores, concerts, and movie theaters and fell on their knees. The corporate body of Christ bombarded Heaven for my family. I love them, but you all loved them, too.

This weigh station problem had caused accidents in the past, we would later learn. During these times, the weigh station would become congested, and they would fail to turn the light off. The trucks would then stop on the bridge. Oncoming traffic would top the hill on the interstate and enter the bridge, approaching stopped traffic with nowhere to go and no time to stop. On this day, the driver had to make a choice in a split second. He could veer to the concrete wall and possibly crash through the wall with the 30-ton bus into the Catawba River; he could go to the other lane, where he immediately saw a mini-van with several people in it; or he could take the hit and most likely sacrifice his own life but maybe save others. He chose the latter. He took the hit.

What happened next was nothing short of a miracle. The result defied physics, but that's how God works. He's not restricted to the laws of gravity, physics, or man, for that matter. The driver was spared with minor injuries. The piano player was in the buddy seat in the front passenger side of the bus. The bus crashed into the back of the tractor trailer at 60 miles an hour. The law of physics tells us that that is a forward-projected injury. The persons in the front, especially without seat belts, should be thrown into the windshield, which in this case was totally gone. That means they should have been ejected from the bus and flown through the air to land on the pavement or slammed into the truck. That didn't happen. The passenger buddy seat was ejected backwards. It broke off, and the person in the seat was propelled to the back of the front lounge. He landed on Hope. The driver was exposed and appeared to be in a death seat. However, somehow, as if he were wrapped in a miracle, he walked off the bus with minor injuries. Yes, it was a miracle. We had injuries, but the multiple fatality predictions made by first responders over the radio were not to be.

I was in shock, and the world was reaching out. Unknown to me, the news helicopters were flashing images to a world that is always interested in a bus wreck, a train wreck, or any other disaster. The footage was graphic, and the pictures were shocking. Social media was buzzing with info and updates. I didn't do social media at that time. I had a Facebook account, and possibly a Twitter account, but they were dormant. I probably had less than 50 friends and didn't like the intrusion of my privacy. It wasn't my thing. However, Edie, or possibly Jon, quickly accessed info on Facebook. I heard them whispering. I was trapped in this car. Would we ever get there? I later learned that Facebook was reporting two fatalities. The whole family was reading about it. Jason and Shellye were calling the hospital and texting Jon. Krystal was texting Edie. Info was sketchy and unconfirmed. When we were going through the gorge in North Carolina, Edie said, "Granny, Katelanne is definitely in surgery. Someone has just talked to the hospital. If she is in surgery, that means she survived to get to the hospital. I hope that relieves you. They are going to make it!"

I clung to her words. I took that little glimmer of good news and comforted myself. I was beginning to find my strength. My leg hurt, and my breathing was shallow. My leg had bled through my bandage, but it would be a very long time before I would have a chance to change it.

While we had been driving, they had put everyone except Mike in an ambulance. Mike was in the helicopter. Kelly was in an ambulance with Katelanne. Suddenly, Katelanne's blood pressure dropped. They quickly got a chopper to come get her. She would be taken from her momma, and once again Kelly was left with doubt about the survival of her 6 year old. The bleeding had depleted Katelanne's blood supply.

Katelanne would later tell the story, "Momma was in the helicopter with me! She held my hand!"

Kelly would tell her, "Baby girl, I wasn't with you. I stayed in the other ambulance. Mommy had a broken back."

Katelanne would argue, "No, you were there. I saw you. You held my hand the whole time. I promise."

I believe that God allowed her to think that. She had no fear. She still talks about that ride with no fear. There are no rules to limit what God can do, and the security of a child is certainly important to God, so what's not to believe?

Everyone was treated and released except Kelly, Mike, Katelanne, and the piano player, Spencer. Spencer had a broken foot. Kelly had a broken back and a broken foot. Katelanne had facial lacerations and a broken clavicle. Mike had a fractured skull. There was a visible fracture in Mike's forehead. He also had a broken arm and bleeding in the brain. Terah promised Kelly that she would stay with her kids. Kelly couldn't walk, and they had no clue at this point how bad her injuries were. It would prove to be many days before she could walk. Terah kept her promise. She stayed with those babies for days. She wouldn't leave them.

We were almost there. Kelly still had not seen Mike, but she knew he was alive and somewhere in the same hospital. This was relayed through a friend who was with her and had called Steve's phone. Katelanne was in surgery. We were so close that my no-information rule was finally lifted. I was getting my game face on. The lead was forming in my backbone. That strength that only comes from Jesus was well on the way.

We pulled into the emergency room door. It was a level-one trauma center, and my family was truly blessed to be near this facility. They took us to Katelanne first. Terah was with her. They were all covered in blood; it seems that they didn't even have shoes on. Katelanne was crying and afraid. She had just come out of surgery. The sight of her made me sob. That pretty face now had a large stitched laceration over her left eye. The doctor assured me that time would make it better. An additional surgery might be needed, but surgeons would fix it and make it normal. I didn't believe him. She was bruised across her chest and had on a sling. I asked about internal injuries, and they assured me the bruising was not an indication of internal problems. Despite this, she didn't look fine. She had blood in her hair. She was upset and in pain, but she would live. God had spared her. I was grateful beyond words. Tears streamed.

The lobby was full of friends from the area. Many had seen the news and came. Friends were there whom I hadn't seen in years. Other artists came, though in my state of mind I cannot recall who all was there. The love poured in. The phone messages were unmanageable. I was fully aware that we were loved. I was fully aware that we were blessed. Even on these kinds of days, I felt God. He was there.

I wanted to see Kelly and Mike. Hope and Gracie were okay. Gracie had a golf ball-sized knot on her cheek, but they said she would be fine and released her. Hope complained about pain in her back, but the scans were clear, so she was released. Terah was released, too. All of the others were released, except Kelly and Mike.

Kelly had been taken to a trauma unit. She was in trouble. Her back was broken. They needed to do an MRI to understand the spinal cord situation and to see the severity of the injury. But she couldn't tolerate the pain to be moved into the MRI tunnel, and the X-ray had been nearly impossible, according to the nurse. Now I was there. I saw her. She was alive. No matter what the result, we still had her. I believed God for a recovery, but either way, we still had her.

Now to find Mike. I wanted to see him. At this point we had been in the building maybe 30 minutes. First I had to see if the kids were cared for, then on to Mike and Kelly. Kelly was safe and sedated somewhat, but she wanted me to find Mike. She was not sure that he was going to make it. Neither was I.

They took me to his room. By this time, he was in a room on the trauma floor on the opposite wing from Kelly's room. Nothing prepared me for what I saw. I spotted his family in the room, but my first reaction was why were they in *that* room? Then I realized it was Mike. *Oh, God! That can't be Mike!* There was no resemblance between the guy I was looking at and Mike Bowling. Truly, it was like a horror movie. I was unable to process what my eyes saw. I knew I had to tell him it was going to be okay. But in that moment, I didn't believe it. I prioritized. Mike needed a miracle. Kelly was stable; Mike needed the bleeding to stop. He was in danger. Brain bleeds are unpredictable, and they have horrific endings so often.

Mike had told me that he never wanted to be on life support or in a nursing home. He had faced lots of death. His dad had died at 50, and his uncles had died young, so we had discussed death and health issues. Mike, being a respiratory therapist, had seen his fair share of people who had survived injuries with no quality of life. I feared, but I spoke life. He was conscious and needed reassuring. We all reassured him, but if he had seen what we were seeing, it would have been really bad. His family sat with him, and God came on the scene. The bleeding stopped. He was turning a corner.

Kelly was still in horrible pain, but they couldn't increase the meds. She was so anxious, and the anxiety worsened her back pain. I slept in that room for the next five nights. We got her to the MRI on day 2, late in the day. She was a mess. Her panic was in hyper mode. While they did the MRI, they let me stand at the head of the machine and touch her head. She hadn't seen Mike since the wreck had happened that first day, and I don't think she knew if he was going to recover. He was still in danger, but he was stable.

Kelly's MRI lasted for an hour and 45 minutes total. After 10 or so minutes, she panicked. They told me to go to the end of the machine and keep my hand on her head. I was still in the same clothes I had left my house in the day before. The bandage on my leg was dried and dirty, and I looked rather pathetic. As I held her head and spent an hour and a half standing there, constantly reassuring her that she was okay, I realized that my body hurt and I needed a clean bandage. Isn't it amazing how small our pains become when our babies get hurt? A mom with a broken arm will manage to take care of her baby's scraped knee. A mom with broken ribs and a screw busted through her knee will press through when her child has a bus wreck.

The messages were coming in from everywhere. As Kelly and I watched the news, I saw the footage of the helicopter airlifting Mike and then Katelanne. I saw the bus, the river, the interstate traffic backed up, the report that Mike and Kelly were in the hospital, and that Mike was listed in critical condition, with Kelly in stable. It was starting to sink in. I was in Charlotte. My daughter wasn't going to walk for a very long time. Mike?

Who knew? If he was going to be back to normal, it would be a long road. Meanwhile, the INSP folks had rented a block of hotel rooms for our families and the crew. People fed and cared for those injured and their visiting families. That's what God's people do.

Terah held the girls close. They were sleepless and struggling. Shellye and Kristi came to mother them. I kept vigil with Kelly, and Mike's family stayed with him. Mike and Kelly were suffering, but they were blessed. They had family; they had friends. They were soon to find out just how many friends they had.

I was planning for their transfer back to Nashville, and there didn't seem to be a good answer. Olan Witt and David Roberts were each offering to come get them in a bus. Olan owned Coach Quarters, and he was a great friend of ours. David and Gary Roberts owned Robert's Brothers Coach, and David was a good friend of the family. We were truly blessed. The Roberts Brothers sent a bus to take Terah, Jon, and the rest of the family home. I don't remember who stayed with the girls at the hotel, but I think Kim Bowling did.

On day three, they wheeled Mike to Kelly's room, and for the first time since we had been there, I think she believed he was going to be okay. He still looked awful, but he was in a wheelchair, and he was joking and saying he was happy that he didn't get his teeth knocked out. Mike was improving quickly, and suddenly, on day five, they released him. He went to the hotel.

The result of Kelly's MRI showed a burst fracture. Her L1 had exploded on impact. The fragments of bone were disbursed into the tissue, and a large sliver had narrowed her spinal cord, but she could move her legs. The doctors disagreed about whether or not to do surgery. Finally they decided to contact a neurological team in Nashville, as well as an orthopedic team to, prepare Kelly to be released to make the trip home on an air ambulance or a bus. They would make the long journey back to Nashville and then see a doctor the following Monday.

I had my work cut out for me. I am not sure how this happened, or why it happened, but Jason and Shellye came back on the bus that picked us up. They came to help me get Mike, Kelly, and the girls home. I was unaware how much I would need their help.

The word "bus" was met with angst, nausea, and horrible anxiety from both Mike and Kelly. They both said they couldn't do it. They didn't want the girls on a bus either. We discussed this for 24 hours or more. There was no other answer. Kelly couldn't ride in a car. She was fitted in a hard-shell vest that she had to wear while flat on her back for the next several months. An ambulance and a bus were the choices to get her home, and that was it. The truth was that a bus, given its size, was safer than a car. The executive decision was made to take the bus. We would sedate Kelly and Mike as much as possible to get through it. The last thing they told Mike when we were trying to load them from the emergency exit was "Do *not* throw up! You are still in a danger zone if there is sudden pressure to your head. Don't throw up. Don't sing. Don't scream. Don't lift. Don't do anything. Stay in a dark room, if possible, and rest. Your brain is injured. It will take months, maybe years, to get you better, and you are a candidate for a stroke."

The verdict on Kelly was months of recovery and a probable surgery.

"What will we do?" they asked. "Where will we go?"

I answered, "You will go home with me. You will stay in my downstairs bedroom until you are well enough to go back home."

We all knew we were talking months, not weeks.

Remember the investor whom I spoke about who had the owner-financed properties? During the first half of 2010, I had been busy selling for him. Sometimes I agreed to get paid out in monthly commissions as the new owners paid him. This isn't standard fare in the real estate world, but we had agreed on this when necessary. As of July 1, 2010, I had accrued a receivable from him of almost $100,000. God knew. My income was already made and would be waiting for me for the next several months. I realized that we would make it.

We loaded Kelly on that bus that Olan so graciously sent for us, and she screamed with pain. We put her in the back full size bed, but she was hurting. The transition and getting her up the steps and into the bus was a challenge. Every move and every bounce was excruciating for her. It was a nightmare.

The first thing Mike did when he got on the bus was throw up. The emotion overtook him. Truly, this was awful.

The girls were a wreck, terrified. Shellye oversaw them. Jason and I went back and forth, checking on Mike and Kelly. It was the longest ride in the history of rides. We requested a very slow speed, which the driver respected, so that made the trip take longer. Finally, on a late night in July, a star coach pulled up to the cul-de-sac in front of my house, and we slowly took Kelly inside with the aid of a wheelchair that had been sent by a sweet friend. We had so many people trying to help; the sight was unbelievable. We walked into that house, which had been empty for a week, and brought all of them home.

Ultimately, we didn't have to choose a casket. We didn't lose a grandchild or a son-in-law. Steve and I would have moved Heaven and Earth to help them. Thank God all we had to do was manage a nursing home and a childcare center for the next few months. God was good. The spot where I fell on the floor screaming a week earlier was now the spot where Gracie was playing. Somehow, I was changed. Life would be trying. The days would be long, and the nights would be longer. It would take an army to care for them, but they were alive. The sun was brighter. The flowers were prettier. The songs were sweeter, and I held all of them tighter.

For weeks upon weeks the house was full of visitors. They all brought food. Heather Boles, whom I'd hired to work for the Crabb Family in 2003, moved in with me. She had been with us since Katelanne was born. She was Logan's nanny in 2010, but with the "shut down" of the Bowlings, Terah wouldn't need a nanny. She would be at home, patiently waiting for them to heal. So Heather, the beloved second mom to these girls, moved in to help me.

The family pitched in. The sisters and sisters-in-law helped me bathe Kelly. It was a two-person job in the beginning. She had to be placed in a reclining lawn chair in the shower. Thank goodness I have a huge shower. Four people can easily get in it. Her body had to be covered with a garbage bag, with a hole in the top, but her legs could get wet. She would lie on that lawn chair as we washed her hair. Actually, we had to wash everything. Her pride was gone from day one. It was humbling for her. She cried. She had to use a bedpan. She was in a hospital bed. Mike was in my bed next to her. He had pain and headaches around the clock.

The girls were restless and wanted normal, but they wouldn't be getting normal for a while. Gracie would cry for Kelly to hold her. She was 3. She didn't totally understand. However, they prayed together, watched movies together, and Mike and Kelly tried to hang on.

We did the doctor's appointments, and I watched with uncertainty regarding Kelly's injuries. The jury was still out. The curvature of her back was 30%, which, according to the surgeon, required surgery. The standard for avoiding surgery was 25%. We prayed.

I didn't go back to my office the entire year. My desk had the notes scribbled on the note pad from June 30. No one else disturbed it. It was like a shrine, pre-bus wreck, frozen in time and space. The job of seeing them through was my priority. I spent 24/7 caring for them and the girls.

I had spent the least amount of time with Gracie. She was born just before Kelly went on the road with Mike and they formed the Bowling Family. They were gone a lot, and Gracie wasn't with me all that much. I was working real estate and trying to survive this "great recession." I truly hadn't spent much time with her at all. Boy, did that change! I spanked her little bottom up and down the steps daily. She was strong willed, and she was a screamer. I would say, "Gracie, if you scream, I will spank you!" She screamed; I spanked her. We repeated this scenario often. However, somewhere between spankings and cuddling, we bonded. I realized she was my mini-me. She was what I would have been had I been allowed to be. My parents were subdued, and the opportunity to be a mess just wasn't there. This child was a mess, and she was from my gene pool. Our togetherness during that year is obvious in her personality now. Sorry, Gracie.

Mike and Kelly were determined to keep their people paid, and it appeared they hoped to sing again. I was opposed. I didn't want those kids on a bus again, ever. They made a special appearance at NQC that year. It took a village to get them there. Again, Robert's Brothers sent a bus. We had Kelly in a wheelchair, and they hadn't sung a note since the wreck. Mike was scared to sing, but he wanted to. It was nearly three months after the accident. They were still like nursing home patients, but they desired to have a platform to thank the people.

Their peers had given, and given, and given. Jason and Bill Gaither had hosted a fundraiser at TBN and raised a substantial amount of money for the expenses they would need to keep the group payroll made. Their co-pays on medical insurance were mounting up, and they had all of the normal household expenses. They weren't living in their home, but they had one, and a mortgage. They weren't driving their cars, but they still owned them and had to pay for them. The Gospel Music Trust Fund gave generously. The Opry Trust Fund gave generously. MusiCares, a foundation of the National Academy of Recording Arts and Sciences, gave generously. The troops had rallied, and they took care of their own soldiers. It was impressive.

The wreck had created a need for me to update people, and I decided that Facebook would be the tool to do that. The response was overwhelming. Some gave $5, some gave $5,000, but their needs were met. Mike and Kelly wanted to go to Freedom Hall and thank the people who gave of their money, their prayers, and their love. On that September night in Louisville, the sweetest sound to ever ring through that building was the first note of a song that Mike began to randomly sing, with Kelly and Terah's help. It went like this:

"Too many miles behind me, too many trials are through,

There's been too many tears that helped me to remember,

I've got too much to gain to lose" (the Rambos, 1970).

With their friends and family surrounding them, that girl in the turtle shell stood for the first time without a walker and sang to the people she loved. The next song was about miracles. We watched and cried, for we were looking at our miracle.

One last thing before we finalize this chapter: the day of the wreck, Beckie Simmons got a call from a lady who had a message for Mike and Kelly. Melinda took the call and wrote down the message. They get lots of calls and can't stop on a dime and convey every message with a phone call. We all understand that. However, after the wreck, news filtered back to the agency. Melinda and Beckie called and said, "We must read you this message!" Now remember, this is the day of the accident. We were already at the hospital, so we were privy to a glimpse of the ending of this story. However, this last paragraph is to remind us all to pray for those whom

God lays on our hearts.

A lady form Florida had called the Bowlings' booking agency, attempting to reach them around lunchtime on July 1. Melinda told her that they were on the road and the lady would need to call back, or she could leave a message. She left the message. Here it is:

"God told me to pray for them, the entire family. He said for me to tell them that the devil is going to try and destroy them, but God will only allow him to touch them, but He can't kill them!"

Well, right now is where you all can shout! Mike and Kelly Bowling will never be the same. What the devil meant for harm is now the core of their ministry. The test brought a testimony. They don't look at the Catawba Bridge on I-85 quite the same. However, they bought another bus, they made another record, and they tell about that bridge, and that peace, and that miracle on the bridge every day. Real ministry happens when the story is bigger than the person. Mission accomplished. They are truly stronger.

23 JANUARY 2013

I am sitting in this chair, looking at these mountains, and thinking about Momma again. This time not the young Elaine, but the frail octogenarian Elaine who was my little Momma in 2012.

That was the year Momma got worse. She had been sick since the spring of 2011. Up until that time, she was self sufficient and lived alone on Main Street in Beaver Dam, Kentucky. She and my stepdad, Noble Stewart, lived a sweet existence in that little house. He was a mandolin player from Rosine, Bill Monroe's hometown, which was only six or seven miles up the road. Noble was on the beginning wave of the creation of bluegrass music as a genre. He toured a bit, and he was actually a great player.

I had known of him all of my life. He and his kids sang around the area when I was young. Mom always claimed that she met him in the produce section of the grocery. I am sure she was buying carrots and lettuce, skinny little thing that she was. He asked her to go out and eat. She agreed, and the rest is history.

Momma married Noble when she was 60, I think. Wow, I thought she was really old. I am speeding toward that number, and I sure don't feel quite the same about 60 as I did then. So, Momma was married to Noble for 20-plus years. In that 20 years, he taught her to pick bluegrass guitar. They sang at the nursing home approximately 1,000 times. They would go every week. Noble would say, "Those poor *old* people. They love music!" The funny part was that they were older than many of those "old" people!

After he passed away, she decided to stay in her little house. She loved her independence. Well, after a broken pelvic bone, a broken rib here, and a broken rib there, she started to struggle a bit. By the end of 2011, we knew we had a problem. She was going down fast.

By the end of 2012, she was bedridden, couldn't feed herself, walk, or swallow, and she could barely talk. There was never a real answer as to the why. We still don't know. However, she was 88 years old and had lived a healthy life, so we knew she had been blessed! This healthy woman who had helped raise most of her grandchildren, including mine, and who could work circles around me on her 80th birthday, now couldn't wipe her own mouth. Clearly, old age is cruel, and I know it has no respecter of persons. It will be waiting for all of us if we don't die young.

My annual appointment rolled around, and I wanted to cancel. Momma was in the nursing home in Gallatin; I was slammed at work; and I didn't have the extra time to fight Nashville traffic or fight for parking in that parking garage at Baptist Hospital! However, Steve insisted I go. Steve's mom is a nurse who always insists that people keep their appointments, so Steve was channeling Joyce. I went.

Dr. Smith walked in and said, "How are you?"

I responded, "I am fine, I'm in a hurry, and I'm not sick. I guess I am here for labs and for you to see how much I weigh so you can tell me to go on a diet!"

He smiled and said his usual, "I need to go on that diet with you. Okay, get on the table. Let me listen to your heart and lungs, and we will get you out of here!"

I responded with a nod. I jumped up on the table … well not actually jumped. I dragged myself, because I was tired. I was so fatigued. I had been for a while. I had also gained about 15 pounds in a year. I thought the weight was the problem. Well, it is always somewhat of a problem, but it wasn't the *only* problem. I had no artery disease, no blockages, good cholesterol, and good sugar levels. I had some pretty good genes, as it relates to plaque and blockages. I have always eaten like a teenager, and the last 20 years I have been overweight more years than not. However, I never smoked, and that's a big plus.

So, I was on the table. My lungs were good; heart … hmmmmm.

Dr. Smith said, "Have you had anyone listen to your heart since the last time you were here a year ago?"

I told him I didn't think so.

He said, "You have a pronounced murmur. I want to get you into a cardiologist as soon as possible. Your sister had two valve replacements, and your dad died from heart failure at age 50. Don't panic, but take this seriously. We are going to make you an appointment before you leave today. It may be nothing, but it's probably a valve. It may not need surgery, but you need an echocardiogram."

They made the appointment, and I went the following week. The echo showed severe regurgitation. I needed surgery. Soon.

The cardiologist was nice and informed, but I wasn't going to pretend to take his advice on a surgeon. He was not a Vanderbilt doctor. I knew he would be referring me to a surgeon who had privileges at the same hospital where he was affiliated, and that would make sense. However, that wasn't going to happen. We had researched and asked the experts where I should go. Hands down, the answer was Vanderbilt. Hands down, Michael Petracek was my man. He is the chair of the cardiac surgery department at

Vanderbilt. He is the most successful valve surgeon in the south. I wanted him. He teaches the great doctors. I wanted the master heart repairman to work on my heart.

I told my cardiologist that I wanted to go to a different hospital, and I wanted to choose my doctor. The reason I am addressing this is simple. If you are passive and don't have the aggression to speak up, that's not in your best interest. They don't care about you like *you* care about you. Stand up. Be heard when it comes to your health care.

Anyway, I got an appointment. The doctor was very busy, and it took me a month to get in. I had to go home, prepare, and have my family Christmas; I had to shop, cook, and tend to the demands I impose on myself for my family. All of this while I was on "house rest" and warned not to push my heart. My poor little heart was struggling. When I stayed busy, I didn't think about my fate as much, so I stayed as busy as my health would allow. I had to pace myself. I would Christmas shop for an hour every day, instead of three days all day, which was my norm.

All the while, Mom was slipping fast. Her health was bad. She was constantly getting pneumonia because she aspirated food into her lungs so often. She couldn't swallow. We kept trying to get her to agree to a feeding tube, but she said no. She started to tell me what she wanted for her funeral. She wanted to be buried in Elizabethtown by my dad. She wanted the grandkids to sing at her funeral. This was real. She was dying. It was also real that I had a bad heart valve. I was waiting on a surgery date.

Christmas came. We enjoyed all the kids and their babies. Momma had lots of visitors, and she knew. December was filled with visits from her grandchildren. Mom's first granddaughter, Donna, visited with *her* first grandchild. I took a picture of Mom and her new great-great-grandson, Sylar. It was a special picture. I cried. I always cry. She knew it was her last Christmas, and probably her first and last visit with baby Sylar. We all cried. She knew, and we knew.

Donna loved her in such a special way, and Mom loved Donna in such a special way. Mom had been Jesus to Donna, as she was to both of my girls. They would tell you today that they grew up believing that Momma had a direct line to God, probably like a "bat phone" or something.

Time marches on, and my momma was dying. I suddenly felt like I had walked through the door to full-blown adulthood. Was I late getting there? Wasn't I a bit old to still feel like I was a kid? *Does anyone else feel this way?* I wondered. But I committed to accepting my age gracefully. There's something about being the baby in a family; you never quite feel like the authoritarian. I have always been the go-to person for my kids, and I am a fixer by nature, but in the family order of Jean and Elaine Coppage's kids, I was the baby, the afterthought, the kid sister of three very bright individuals. I was well aware that they were bright, and I didn't pretend to rival their intellect. However, I wouldn't take a backseat on the social skills. I was always a people person. Go big or go home, invite everyone you know, every day, everywhere. I lived my life like that; I still do.

Having lost my brother in 2006 to cancer, I was left to be colorful, for my sweet Danny was gone. Danny was my funny older brother who had a struggle with alcohol he didn't conceal. The gallon of Kentucky Tavern in his car was a pretty sure giveaway. His go to line in a crowd was, "People ask me if I smoke, and I say no, I hate cigarettes. I only smoke when I drink, and I will admit I'm up to three packs a day!" Then he would laugh to give *you* permission to laugh. He was often a mess, because he was an alcoholic. However, he loved people. He was generous. He always said, "Put all of this on one check, I've got it!" I thought this was how it *should* be. I did the same thing for many, many years. If you went to dinner with me, you knew I would be buying. That's how my family did it. My dad, my brother, and my sister Anneta were all generous to a fault. It was easy to take advantage of them, and many did. I have the gene as well.

My dad died when Danny was 21. He was spoiled rotten by Dad. He had a Corvette, an airplane, and anything else his little heart desired. When Dad died, a piece of Danny died, too. He would spend the next 35 years depending on his friend Kentucky Tavern to help him deal with it. He wasn't a saint, he was a sinner, but he was a sinner who found Jesus. That's all that matters in the end. Truly, he was entertaining.

I was the tame little sister whom he never allowed to be around his rowdy lifestyle. He planned for me to travel a different road, and I was always happy about that. I felt respected by him. He knew I was different than the party girls he preferred, but he was proud of that.

When I was a little girl, about 6, my dad would give me a quarter to play "Mansion Over The Hilltop" on the piano, and my brother would give me a quarter to stop. He was 14. I got on his nerves. He was into the Beach Boys, not annoying hymns pecked out by a 6 year old. But the joke was on him: I was the one making 50 cents every afternoon. It was a bit of a ritual. I had learned to make a profit, and that would serve me well!

Now, fast forward to 1996, when the Crabb Family upstart was a whirlwind in the state of Kentucky. Danny was on board! He was one proud brother and uncle. I miss him every day. When he needed a reminder that Jesus and Kathy loved him, I got the call. When he got sick, I got the call. As he regressed, he talked about how much he missed Dad, how easy it was to believe in Heaven, and how much he loved his girls.

So my family was shrinking. Dad was gone. Danny was gone. Momma was next. The Coppage family of six would soon be three. Seasons had come and gone. The circle of life was truly more than a saying on a tattered quilt. It was God's plan. On this cold January day, 2013, my momma started to decline. She had a high fever and seemed delirious. My sweet niece

Shelly, my brother's youngest, was traveling from Delaware to see her one last time. My nieces and nephews trailed through that day, giving that last hug, wiping those salty tears. I "ugly cried" the entire day and blubbered. My girls sobbed when I told them it was almost the end.

Anneta's sweet family came: Kara, Steven, and Ryan, all of whom were so special to Momma. Krystal and family came to hug her tightly. Kelly had said her goodbyes and sobbed all the way to a tour bus, which I had insisted she get on and go "do what you do" as Mom would have wanted. Mom's sweet little Randy, her speech therapist, was checking on her frequently, as was the staff. They were so comforting. They also knew it was the end. Aunt Net and her big loving family said their goodbyes.

As Aunt Net bent over Mom to kiss her, Mom was trying to tell her something. You could see her lips form "I ... love ... you" to this little sister who had shared her world for 80-plus years, thousands of meals, and mountains of dishes they had washed in an old metal washtub as kids, daughters from a family that boasted 10 siblings but had nothing else in the world except each other. They had lived in a coal camp with a daddy who was an underground coal miner and a momma who was 4'9" and bore all 10 children at home. They slept six and seven to a bed, sharing shoes and clothes, taking baths on Saturday outside in a washtub. These little pigtailed girls had become gray-haired octogenarians. Decades had passed like a film on fast forward. Their youth was a distant memory. The hard times were well remembered, but the edges of the pain had softened with time. They grew up with little, but on this January day in Gallatin, TN, these two matronly sisters had much. They had the memories of helping raise each other's children, through thick and thin, good and bad. They had each other's back. Always.

Mom had known Jeanette longer than any other person who remained on this earth on this day. They said goodbye. I cried some more, and I knew that I would frame that scene in my head forever. I knew that Aunt Net had just given her blessing for Momma to go and cross the river, leave us, and go see those who had already crossed. We *all* believed. Heaven is real to us. That scene of the oldest members of a family standing in unison, knowing that Aunt Net would soon have one sibling left, my sweet Uncle Bill, would be the last one of the 10 Morris kids she could visit in the flesh.

They left, one by one: Mary Lou, Mom's beloved lifetime friend; Bruce, her faithful nephew; Portia, the niece who always took time for her; Jimmy and short little Shelta, who reminds all of us that our grandmother was short; and family member after family member. They all filed in to see Mom's sweet little face, with that gray hair pulled up in a top knot.

I remember Edie coming in, and I wanted a picture. I knew this would be the last opportunity to freeze a memory of the first woman to love me and the little redhead who owned me. I treasure that picture. The great grandkids, especially the younger ones, were a bit uncomfortable, but they came and did what the adults insisted they do. I realized in that moment that the small kids would know her through me. They would learn of her quirks and her commitment to Christ through my stories, my bridge between the past and the future. It became abundantly clear to me that they would be nurtured through the knowledge of knowing who they were. Hence the writing of this book.

On the evening of January 19, Shelly, my niece, and I stayed with Mom for an extended time. We babied her, talked to her, and I decided to tell her it was okay to go, tell her what a good momma she was, and convince her that I would make it just fine through the heart surgery, which she was worried about. Back in November, I told her I would be having it as soon as we could get a date and all of the plans in place, and that day she cried like a baby. She dreaded it for me. Mom had lived a healthy life, free of the disease that most of us face in later years. She had rarely taken medicine and had avoided aspirin and Tylenol, even now, because she didn't want to damage her kidneys. Here she was, in a nursing home, unable to walk and barely able to whisper, and she was worried about her kidneys. I would say, "Mom, your kidneys are going to last longer than the rest of you. You're 88. Take the Tylenol and have some pain relief!"

So Shelly sat over her and loved her, and I told her that we wanted her to go see Daddy and Danny and Jesus, whom she had talked about for 80-plus years. I said, "Momma, you either believe this gospel, or you don't. I know you do, so this is it. What you've waited for, the grand prize. I hope you have a really nice mansion, and please don't wake everyone up at 4 a.m. like you have done to us all of our lives."

She was a tiny bit responsive, but not much. A hand squeeze was all we got. My sister Linda, who is a retired nurse, suctioned her and kept check on her comfort and meds. Linda confirmed that she was almost there. She explained about the medical aspects of the next few hours, or days, whichever it may be. She told us about the shallow breathing. I remembered the shallow breathing far too well. My brother died and we were all there to witness firsthand those final breaths. How well I remembered.

I knew Momma was scared. Who wouldn't be? But after the talk she seemed better, calmer. Shelly and I left when Anneta arrived. She was determined to stay the night. We went to get food, and I had to go to the drugstore and get meds. We returned later and decided to call the singers in. My kids were on the road, all but Mike, who was at home on vocal rest due to a vocal cord issue. In December, Aaron and Amanda had visited, and their singing had seemed to make Momma so happy. I believe in singing people home. I believe music is salve to a wound, hope to the hopeless, and an escort for the dying. Music is what most people would choose while dying, if they got to choose. So I decided it was time.

Mike hadn't sung for two months, doctor's orders. I called him. He was at his momma's house, eating some of that awesome food for which she is famous. His brother Jeff and wife Kim were in town visiting. I said in typical bossy Kathy voice, "Get over here, now. I want Momma to have some singing."

In a flash, they were there. The singing ensued. It was beautiful. They sang "The holy hills of Heaven call me, to mansions bright, across the sea, where loved ones wait, and crowns are given, but the hills of home, keep calling me. This house of clay is but a prison, bars of bone hold my soul, but the doors of clay are gonna burst wide open, when the angel sets my spirit free. I'll take my flight like a mighty eagle, when the hills of home start calling me..." (the Rambos, 1968).

Lord knows we cried. I felt the Holy Ghost, and Momma was so calm. She was possibly in a state of semi-consciousness, I am not sure. However, I would bet you a farm in Texas that when Mike Bowling opened his mouth and started singing, she heard him.

Anneta stayed. I went home and started to think about what needed to happen next. I was exhausted; my heart wasn't efficient. I knew it. Kara and Steven were staying with me, and I wanted to visit for a minute with Shelly, too. So, we went to my house and loved on each other a while.

I love my nieces. I love my nephews, too, but we are a family of strong-willed women. My nieces and nephews are all bright and have chosen career paths that are admirable. We have a CPA, a dentist, a psychologist, and a realtor, just among the girls. In addition, they are all beautiful and confident. Momma was proud, as she should have been. The guys are pretty awesome, too, but there is something pretty amazing about the gene pool that the Coppage gene gave us girls. We are determined little somethings. Anyway, I was enjoying my nieces until I started imagining what it was going to feel like to see them open up the earth and lower Momma's frail little body into the freezing, cold ground. I felt like an orphan. I was soon to be one.

My selfless sister Anneta, who was struggling with big health issues, wouldn't leave her. She was so faithful to Momma. She is faithful to everyone. If there was ever a saint, it's her. She always thinks of others, but consequently, she wins, because that makes her the most loved person in the room, always. Anneta insisted that I go home and rest. She was worried about my heart, and truly, we should have been *more* worried about her. I took a sleeping pill and finally went to sleep. In the wee hours of the morning, maybe 3:00 or so, the phone rang. I answered. I knew. It was Anneta. She was gone. Momma was gone. Anneta was calling the funeral director. We cried a lot.

I woke Steve. He did his typical "I'm so sorry, baby" and held me tight, like only Steve can do. You feel like a big teddy bear has just decided to shield you from the world when Steve hugs you. This time I was ready for a big dose of his hugs. I was an orphan, officially. I envisioned Daddy meeting Momma at the entrance, and I envisioned them both young and happy. I had no memories of my dad except as a young man, so that was easy. The Steve hug and the memory felt good in a weird way, but I needed to go and I needed a driver because of the pill. I had to see her one more time. I was dizzy, but I needed to go.

We arrived before they got there to get Momma. Her tiny body was cold. Her hair was so white. She looked so much like her mother at that moment. I kissed her and rubbed her and told her that I was a bit jealous. Truly, death had no sting for her, just triumph.

Anneta was sad but fulfilled. She had been there. She stayed, and she was glad. Anneta the faithful, the best daughter a mom could have, had been there with Momma. In that moment, I realized that the stuff Anneta was made of was as precious as gold.

As for the funeral, my cousin Marty opened, my cousins sang, and then Mom's grandchildren spoke. Mom loved her grandchildren. They also sang. Mom thought her grandchildren could out-sing *your* grandchildren! Her last request was that the great-granddaughters sing. Mike taught them the requested song the day Mom died. Gracie, Cameron, Hope, and Katelanne sang "What a Day That Will Be" in three-part harmony, with a bonus on one of the parts. Her sweet great-granddaughter Colby sang as well.

Kelly brought the message. Mom would have loved that, for truly deep inside, Mom was a bit of a feminist in her own little way. She had unresolved issues with trust, and we all felt it. She wasn't perfect. I have a trace of a "man issue" as well. There are reasons. However, it was a beautiful funeral for a life well lived. Momma would have loved it.

Now, my mind began to wonder what open-heart surgery looked like. Soon Google would answer that question. I had four weeks to go. I was starting to feel the nerves.

One last thing about Momma: she had her first baby when she was 17. She said he was the cutest baby ever. Suddenly, when he was a month old, she found him dead. That was many years ago, and there wasn't much medical knowledge, but they told her he had a heart problem. So, Momma actually had two little boys waiting on her that cold January day.

24 HEARTS, STRAIGHT TALK, AND CAKE

February 11, 2013. My birthday was here. I was officially 58. We decided to wait to celebrate until all of the kids were home. I had cake anyway. I am sure I had lots of cake, now that I think about it. I was eight days out from my open-heart surgery. I deserved cake. I would have been drinking, if I were a drinker. I am kidding, of course. I knew that God was God. I knew that either way, I win. However, I would be lying like a politician if I didn't admit I was nervous. I stayed busy and counted down the days. The 18th arrived. That day we were having the late birthday, and the next, I would get my heart overhauled. Thanks, Dad.

My BFF, Linda Beth, arrived from Kentucky. We have been friends for nearly 50 years. I told her not to worry about me, that Steve would keep her posted, but she came anyway. She's cool like that. Anyway, we met all of the family at the Hendersonville Black Eyed Pea and had my birthday a week late. Their hugs were a bit tighter. The nerves were apparent in their gestures. Their eyes had fear. They were scared for me. I recognized it. When I saw their fear, I was calm. I mean, isn't that what we do, we who are in the "Fraternity of Moms"? Don't we speak to our kids' fears? Don't we assure them that all is well? I remember lots of "I am going to be fine" and "This doctor is a genius" in a rambling, disjointed, never-ending babble that night.

I had a spinach salad and a piece of cornbread. Shellye and Jason brought a bakery cake, a *good* one at that. It was pink and decorated with Minnie Mouse, which caused me to squeal a bit. Heaven; I was in Heaven. I was soaking up my youngins, just in case this was to be my last meal with them. I hugged them all goodbye, hugged my mother-in-law, and went home with Steve and Linda Beth to prep myself with the meds and sterilizing shower junk they give you. The kids asked for us to text when we were leaving the house the next morning. They all met me at the hospital.

I arrived, did all of the stuff they make you do, and finally, Dr. Petracek came in. He was calm. I was in a big room with curtains separating me from 8 or 10 other patients being prepped. I heard a small commotion. The nurse told a doctor, somewhere behind a curtain, that a heart was coming and a patient was being flown in to receive it. The heart was from a 20 year old. I heard all of this, of course no names, but I had an immediate mental image of an accident, some momma losing her baby, her 20 year old. Yet their generosity was going to provide hope for another family that I was also imagining. Life is so fragile. This was where people lived or died. This was Vanderbilt, a level-one trauma unit, and *the* heart hospital in the south. People either made it here or they didn't. I had decided months ago that they knew their stuff, and the rest of it was up to God. Sticks in the arm and an IV brought me back to reality.

My doc came back to talk to me. He said, "I plan to repair, if possible, but that's not extremely likely."

We discussed that I preferred the minimally-invasive procedure, even though they would most likely have to break my ribs to get in. They also had to collapse my lungs and stop my heart. The first week is more painful with the minimally invasive, but after that, recovery is speedier. That's what I needed: speedier. So I told him I was certain I wanted him to try the minimally invasive procedure. I also decided on a mechanical valve rather than a pig or cow one. They last longer, but now, I do like bacon and steak. No offense toward pigs and cows or anything. Another perk to the minimally invasive is there isn't a chest scar. The scar is under the arm, around to underneath the breast. All of the muscles are cut under the right arm, but this seemed like a more acceptable torture than having my rib cage sawed open. It's a bit like choosing between hominy and liver for dinner. I chose hominy.

He told me next that 95% of the people who go in wake up. However, 5% don't. My math is decent. Immediately, I realized that's a 1 in 20 chance. I didn't like that. I told him. He explained that his statistic includes all of the people who are extremely elderly and extremely sick with other health issues. He said I was a great candidate and would be fine. I accepted that. He left.

Steve was rubbing my hair. He wanted to cry. I remember the look on his face. He was scared. I realized how much he loved me. His eyes told it all. Once again, I comforted him. They made him leave.

Then, it was just me and God. I was sleepy from the Valium they had given me earlier, but I wasn't too sleepy to make it clear to God that I wanted to see my grandchildren grow up. I felt that all of the kids would need me, and I wanted to stay and be there for *all* of them. Lord knows, kids need love and support. I know my place. I know I am security for many. I wanted God to allow me to stay for a while. I told Him so, in no uncertain terms. I told Him I didn't want to leave Steve without a helper. I knew the devil wanted me dead. I've been fully aware of that since I was a young girl. He couldn't have my soul, but he wanted to distract and bring grief on the ministries of my kids. He wanted to derail the church that Aaron and Amanda would start. He wanted to break Krystal's heart. He wanted to blindside Mike and Kelly. He wanted to bring grief to Adam and Jason's ministries. He wanted to take Terah's security away. He wanted Edie to be stricken with loss. He wanted my grandchildren to feel deprived. He wanted to distract the destiny of all of them. I rebuked him and told God I wanted my years back. I knew that the lobby was packed full of a praying bunch of kids who knew how to go to war. As they told me to count backwards and I knew sleep was coming, I trusted those kids to pray me through this one.

I woke up with a ventilator down my throat and in the worst pain I had ever felt. I looked up and saw Philip Morris. I was thinking, *I must be alive; I know him.* Then I heard familiar voices, and oh, the pain. I struggled with that vent, and my recovery wasn't seamless, but I survived. I detest it when people dwell on sickness, so I won't. Within an hour, I was giving orders by writing on a dry-erase board. I was going to live.

The doctor confirmed that I had a repair, not a replacement, which meant no blood thinners long-term, but it was not an easy surgery. He almost had to go through my chest. After he opened my side and cut in, deflated my lungs, and stopped my heart, he realized how close it was. He said it was so hard to work in that little short space. He also said I needed to lose weight. He said, "You were meant to be a small woman. Your frame is small. Your lungs are the size of a child's lungs. You need to lose some weight."

He confirmed what Steve had already told me: they couldn't get my heart to start back. Steve said that the doctor was soaking with perspiration after the surgery. He said it was a tough one. So now we have determined that I am petite, and I am fat. Is that an oxymoron?

I hate recliners. They're ugly. I don't allow ugly furniture in my house. My name is Kathy, and I am a furniture snob. Anyway, I wouldn't agree to buy a recliner because of the ugliness factor. On the seventh day after my surgery, I finally got dismissed from the hospital. Poor Steve hadn't left the hospital for a week. He is the most loyal man in Tennessee, and I would say I don't deserve him, but we *all* know I do. So on the seventh day, we were being set free from "heart surgery jail," and I was *so* ready to be home. We went home.

Now I was starting to wonder, *Can I sleep in my big tall bed?* They recommended that recliner for a reason. Jason tried to tell me. Steve tried to tell me. They all threw their hands up. Remember, the furniture thingy. Momma don't allow no ugly furniture around here. So now I was home, but

I was miserable! Yes, I shouted that: *MISERABLE!*

For some reason Jason was at home, most weekends he's on the road. The next thing I know, Steve and Jason went to B.F. Myers, my furniture store of choice, and got the biggest, ugliest recliner I had ever seen. For six weeks, it would be my home. I was over it. Snob be gone! This chick evaluated comfort over prettiness, and I chose comfort. (Somehow, I am leaning more and more in that direction these days. I still won't do Crocs, but I sure do want some Clarks!)

When I went back to the bed six weeks later, Steve slept in the chair. I am not certain why, but he did. It was comfy, and it was in the middle of the bedroom, right in front of our armoire and flat screen. So the experience was a bit like being at a movie in one of those new theaters with the recliner: great TV-watching spot.

Eventually, we gave it to my nephew. In this family, we pass furniture around. Every relative abides by this unspoken rule. When we give you furniture, you are allowed to keep it as long as you want, but when you are finished, you can't give it away without asking the furniture czars, which are usually Anneta or I. If you sell it, we take you out of the will. The protocol is to take it to the furniture cemetery, otherwise known as my garage. There it is prayed for, brought back to life, and redistributed to another family member. There is also a 90% chance that Aaron will paint it.

Seven weeks post-op, I got a horrific phone call. Anneta had been airlifted from Kentucky following a horrible single-car accident. She had been en route to Nashville after a few days in Kentucky when she had run off the road, overcorrected, hit a guardrail, flipped her car, and gotten trapped. They used the Jaws of Life to cut her out. A Vanderbilt life flight helicopter landed on the William Natcher Parkway and whisked her away to the Vanderbilt trauma unit.

Bless her heart, she was alone. No one knew! Her grandchildren knew she was unaccounted for that afternoon. I didn't know she was coming back to Tennessee that day, so I didn't know to miss her when she didn't show up. They hadn't been able to reach her. They called and we talked, but I decided that she had probably gone to see a friend. They called, but she wasn't there. They called me back with much concern. Kara, her granddaughter, told me that she was going to call the Kentucky State Police in Bowling Green.

Within five minutes she called back, frantic. Anneta was at Vanderbilt alone, and we didn't know her injuries. The eyewitness said the wreck was bad. I wasn't allowed to drive yet. I was in panic mode. I cried, prayed, and begged God to let her be alive when we got there.

We called the family. They came. She was unrecognizable. She was critical. She had head trauma and a broken arm, and she was on life support. I was winded and exhausted. I felt like I couldn't take much more.

She was so pitiful with the tubes and that machine breathing for her. My momma had died only three months before. I had had open heart seven weeks before, and now this? My sweet Anneta, who loved me unconditionally, the sister who would walk to Texas to avoid hurting someone, was suffering a living hell. Why? Soon I would stop the whys, and I would repent.

I will never forget the 16-year-old girl in the bed next to her in the trauma unit. The unit was open for quick access to patients. These were the most critical patients in the hospital. Many would die. This teenager beside Anneta had suffered a similar accident in Kentucky. However, the helicopter couldn't land near the car due to it being a wooded area. They had to put her in an ambulance first and then move her to a helicopter. Time mattered. She lay there in a comatose state, with no brain function. Her family said goodbye. They cried. They were young parents, and this was their oldest child. I watched this process over a couple of days. They kept her alive no more than 10 feet from Anneta's bed. They harvested her organs, then unplugged her, and she died. We wept with the family, we wept *for* this family, and we prayed. My 72-year-old sister lived. I stopped asking why, and started thanking God that she was alive. She was on life support for two months, but she lived.

Anneta had another open-heart surgery later that year, her third valve replacement, but once again, she lived. When God says it's over, it will be over. Until He says so, it isn't. Anneta survived a horrific experience and a horrible year, but she is still celebrating life. I am proud to say that God sustained us both through 2013. Let it be known that 2013 was a tough year for me and Anneta, my friend, my cake-eating buddy, my unconditional love, my sister. Yes, it was a very tough year! But we are all stronger.

25 TROPHIES

I have worked on many projects that were award-winning. Most people don't care. If they *do* care, be nervous. The many gospel music awards that were presented to us no longer reside in my home. My real estate awards are in the closet. Truly, awards are nice. They uniformly put hard work into a metal seven-inch statue, and they allow us to be reminded that labor is a good thing, a God thing. Labor will be faithful when the world isn't. The plaques remind us that staying late and giving of your time and energy is the right choice. That's cool.

However, when asked what my greatest accomplishment is, or my proudest single moment, I can't find a real estate closing or even an award show that would qualify. The sweetest times were the altar services in those little country churches, the one-on-one prayers while wiping tears of a drug addict pleading with Jesus or wiping the tears of a child who had been abused by an adult they had trusted. Award shows are often about the "feel-good" of our own egos. I worked hard for those Doves, but not one of them now resides in my house, and I'm okay with that.

Now, let me take you to the heart of the matter. I don't need to be reminded by a statue on a shelf that I have value. I don't need to be reminded by a plaque on a wall that I am needed. I am secure. My ego is fed, I suppose. My daddy made the decision to instill confidence in me as a child. He told me to speak up, that my opinion may be the best opinion in the room. I have always felt validated intellectually. There have been many times I was too confident, too capable of changing the minds of others. Sometimes I would have been ahead of the game if I'd left well enough alone.

When life happened and the dust settled, I had no awards on shelves, but I had my family. My trophies have names. They have eyes, and smiles, and occasionally, they have chocolate on their faces. They have peed in my pool, wiped ketchup on my white rug, and seen me cry. They have seen me in tattered gowns and watched me throw together many last-minute meals. You see, *these* trophies are the only things that I will leave when I am gone. They are the reason I was born. They know me as "Granny" and don't truly understand the term "biological." My trophies have names: Eden Nicole, Cameron Faith, Loryn Hope, Hannah Grace, Ashleigh Taylor, Katelanne Elaine, Logan Nathaniel, Elijah David, Emmaleigh Love, Charlee Jaxon, Gracelynn Kelly, Eva Lyn, Sophie Caroline, and Ean William. Those are the names of my trophies, and no one can take these trophies away from me. We are bound together by an undying love.

Today, Eden Nicole is 20 and has her granny's feet and eyes. She's a rare beauty who causes heads to turn and eyes to stare. The brilliant red hair and beautiful blue eyes are stunning. She has Krystal's booty and smile, and enough life stories to write her own book. She loves deviled eggs and Kentucky hot browns. She also loves fashion and God. The tear-streaked face of an 11 year old is immediately retrieved from my visual images, and that little girl with the broken heart is still the 20 year old who wants to prove her own value. She will make it. I pray life is kinder, people are more loyal, and she finds out just how incredibly valuable she is. God put His hand on her life when her momma was huge with child. I remember the day, and I can take you to the place where someone laid hands on Krystal and prayed an old-fashioned prayer that got God's attention. Words can't describe the bond I have with Eden. She is the one who needed me the most. I have 20 years invested in loving her, and I hope I live long enough to have at least 20 more. In the end, she will listen to God, and together they will figure it out. They probably don't need me to help. She is my first trophy, and she will forever be my little redheaded girl.

Cameron Faith is 15 and is my passive grandchild. She is more like Kelly than Krystal, and I often say she is a perfect mix of her momma, her aunts, Sonya, Becky, Kelly, and Terah. She looks like her mom and Sonya. She acts like Kelly, Terah, and Becky. She is the child who always hangs to the back, willing to help with the needs of others. She is the little girl with those huge blue eyes, my Mam-Mam. She is currently the tallest of all of the grandchildren, but what would one expect? The offspring of Ben Isaacs is destined to be a tall drink of water. The fact that she is tall actually makes me happy. After all, my paternal grandfather was 4'7" and my maternal grandmother was about 4'10". So this tall blonde child is the exception. Cameron has talent, a heart for God, and will be a witness to many. I know that God has big things for her. So when you see a pretty blonde with a guitar singing her way into your heart, know that she is more than a pretty face. She is a story. Her story is a mixture of two families who love her more than life itself. She has my heart. She, too, is a trophy.

Loryn Hope is now 15, but she was a hot mess as a little girl. She slowly outgrew her willingness to do anything for a laugh. She was a "bus baby" who spent endless hours with adults and learned to read people while other children were learning to read *The Cat in the Hat*. There are many stories about this child. She is the one who inherited my facial structure, strong nose, and over-the-top sarcasm. I know what she's thinking without her telling me. I know her motives, and I know her weaknesses. When I watch her, I watch me. God called her before she was born, and He ordained her steps. She is overwhelmed with insecurity, but she is bathed in beauty and ability. Her weaknesses will be her strengths. She doesn't know who she is yet, but the devil does. When she opens her mouth and sings, the devil gets nervous. He knows. God gifted her with much; He has entrusted her with a mighty big thing, and my money's on her. She will pass the test, and she will lead many to the cross. God assured me of this. She is a much prettier version of me, and I love her. Hope is also a trophy.

Hannah Grace is 12 and is still a little bitty thing. She has always prioritized fun over food. She didn't get that from her granny! This little blonde is beautiful and was born to serve the Lord. She walks in a room and lights it up. To know Hannah is to love Hannah. She, too, is a mixture of her parents, but at first glance, she is a mini Kristi with her blonde hair, blue eyes, and thin frame. However, make no mistake, there's some Crabb in there, too. Like her momma, she always has a plan, an agenda, and is always in the middle of the work and the fun. There will never be grass growing under Hannah's feet. She is movement. But that's okay. I like movement. Ultimately, this granny knows something about movement. That movement will be bridled in later years, and it will be the foundation of her giving. She will have a work ethic that is unparalleled. That little girl who was called of God before she was born, the baby who we gave back to God as we dedicated her and then watched as He healed her and gave her back to us in Brooklyn, will be a force to be reckoned with. I know God is going to use her. I am not 100% sure what God has for her, but I know it's big. To know Hannah is to love her. She is one of my trophies.

Ashleigh Taylor is 12 and was born on a cold February day in 2003. She was the answer to many prayers, and she was the ultimate gift to a young couple who wanted nothing more than to have a child. She was loved. She, too, is tall. Her Aunt Leslie and her dad's height are the dominant factor, it appears. There is much I could say, and much you may already know. My Ashleigh story is this: she is soft. She is kind. She is often at the back of the line. Her personality is somewhere between her mom's and dad's, Jason being the outgoing big personality, coupled with Shellye's shyness. She doesn't seek attention; it seeks her. She is content with the back row but often gets the front. I have seen this before with her daddy. God has a plan, and it develops. We watch it, we enjoy, we take pictures, and we freeze it. Ashleigh is a child with a roadmap stretched out for her steps. She is mostly unaware, but occasionally, when I look in those eyes, I see that look that tells me she knows. Only God knows how big this plan is, but I know it's going to be awesome. She embodies beauty and goodness and has talent that simply amazes me. This granny treasures her. She, too, is a trophy.

Katelanne Elaine is now 11 and is a typical middle child, having been booted out of her position as the baby when her mom and dad had the last "oops" child. She was her momma's girl, and she still is. She has a different look and a different vibe than her sisters. Her beautiful lips and hair are stunning. She appears to be soft and sweet, but don't be fooled by this little innocent thing. Underneath that softness is a brilliant mind and a sharp wit. The difference in Katelanne and her sisters is she typically keeps her thoughts to herself. She appears to be reserved, but she will someday find her voice. When God was passing out talent, He gave her the gifts of many. Truly, she amazes me. Occasionally, we see a child who doesn't realize her potential and her lack of limitations. Yes, that's Katelanne. She is tough, beautiful, and thinks the scar on her eye is cool. She recently told me it was her reminder that God has a plan for her life. I have no words to explain my gratitude for God sparing her and allowing me to watch her life as it unfolds along the path that God orchestrated when she was in the womb. God has huge things for this beautiful talent. She is another trophy.

Logan Nathaniel is 10 and was born in the great state of Georgia. On a warm day in May, he decided to meet his mommy and daddy a few weeks early. He was the wonderful part of an otherwise trying year for his mom and dad. Logan too is tall, and when you see him, you see Jon Penhollow. He is going to be able to take care of his momma, granny, and any other person who needs defending. This child is capable of tough, but his heart is anything but rough and tough. He was the 1 year old who threw a bottle at me when I gave him milk because he wanted apple juice. He is the "bus baby" who would jump off the couch and bust anyone or anything that was in his way. He embodied the description "all boy!" However, the heart of Logan is something to be experienced. He is the first child to run and hug you when you walk into a room. His "I love you, Granny" melts me. That little boy who would climb walls and throw bottles became a loving 10 year old. When asked if he sings, Logan quickly says, "Nope, it's not my thing." I am not so sure, but here's the good news: he is happy to shine in his own right and has this huge heart for God without being in the spotlight. We need more Logans in the world. He doesn't have to be anything. He just brings his worship with him, no matter where he goes. This handsome little guy will be a soldier of the cross, no matter where he is. He will probably be a professional athlete who wins thousands with his witness. He, too, is my trophy.

Elijah David is also 10 and was the first child born to a young couple who would follow the call of God. This baby would be born with a huge family waiting and a passel of girl cousins to annoy him. He, too, is all boy. With those chubby cheeks and big blue eyes, he looked like a baby food commercial baby. We spoiled him. He played drums onstage when he was 2 or 3. He played church. He preached. He knew who he was before he could communicate. He doesn't aspire to sing like his mom and dad, at least not yet. However, what he does aspire to do with his life is this: he wants to be a youth pastor. He loves church. It's in his genes, his blood. He knows the sacrifice that only the child of a minister can know. He knows the late nights, the irregular hours that are his regular hours. It is his life. He is curious and very interested in the lives of others. Sometimes that's a good thing; sometimes not so much. However, as he becomes an adult, these are the things that he will build on. The nosy child becomes the concerned adult. The "roll with it" life is boot camp for those in ministry. Eli is being prepared. He is called, and he is God's. I knew the day he was born that he was called. This little fellow was given much when God gave out the good genes and gifts. He is incredibly handsome and has tremendous gifts. This granny is happy to be on the front row to watch God use him. He, too, is a trophy.

Emmaleigh Love is 9 and was born soon after I found out I would be getting a divorce. She was such a wonderful announcement that life goes on; at least that's what her birth felt like to me. I had been sad for many days, and the day she made her grand entrance to her huge family and the rest of the world is fondly remembered as a "marker" day. It was a day I realized that babies would be born, flowers would bloom, tides would rise, and I would live again. Emma is a mommy's girl, no doubt. Shellye was determined to be that mommy who always puts her girls first. Emma knew; she loves her daddy, but wants her mommy. She craves her daddy's attention, but she wants her mommy's hand. That's our Emma. She is Jason's little mini-me but Shellye's little shadow. The puppy dog eyes and her sweet little voice would melt the coldest heart on the planet. She is a vision of sweetness. Truly Emma is the most innocent child I have ever known and is a gift from God. If you are having a rough day, go talk to Emma Crabb. She will make you realize what's important in life. God is going to use this little girl in everything she touches. She is beautiful on the outside, but what's inside will leave you speechless. She is called and chosen, and another one of Granny's trophies.

Charlee Jaxon is only 8 but he is a little Adam Crabb. He favors his mom, too, but to know Adam is to know Charlee. First, let me say that his athletic abilities are fierce. He can do it all. He never gives up and isn't scared of any challenge. Like his dad and mom, he has the heart of an athlete. He likes to compete. He likes to push himself. However, don't color Charlee in the locker room just yet. As much as his mom envisions him as a quarterback, I envision him a singer. I envision him walking in the legacy of the gospel, winning the lost. Not to say that Kristi wouldn't be happy about this decision, but she knows he never gives up, and in sports, that's the missing element for most talents. They have talent and no heart, or heart and no talent. However, Charlee has both. His parents know. It's undeniable, but my prophesy goes something like this: the little boy who demands nothing, the child who eats only if every other child has something first, the "don't worry about me" Adam Crabb clone, will someday storm the gates of Hell to reach people. Charlee doesn't see class, or color, or disability; he only sees people. God has big things for this little trophy. I just know it!

Gracie (Gracelynn Kelly) is 8 going on 20. What can I say about Gracie? Her reputation precedes her most likely. When Gracie was 3, her parents had the bus accident. They moved in with me. I had not spent a lot of time with this child. Her mommy and daddy had been on the road singing since she was born, building a new group. I was 51 years old, trying to start a new career. I was busy. They were gone. Then, out of nowhere, I was the caregiver for this precocious 3 year old. She wanted her mommy, but her mommy couldn't hold her. I soon learned to entertain her. I talked, and she listened. I told her stories, and she asked questions. I explained things, commonly using my hands and giving her the entertaining version of myself. She soaked it in. The result? She became the grandchild who speaks like me, acts like me, and is definitely from the Coppage gene pool. She looks like her daddy, but she has our eyes, and she uses them. Her personality is driven by her eyes and her hands. This girl may have the biggest personality in the family, and believe me, there are some big personalities for competition. She has a huge life waiting on her; actually, she's already living it. God has big things for the beautiful Gracie Bowling. I love her, and she is one of my trophies!

Eva Lyn is only 7, but she is a little Amanda Crabb. She is a natural beauty like Amanda, and she has Amanda's personality. She puts that hand on her hip and lines out any room that needs it. She is amazingly independent and marches to the beat of her own drum. I like that. The story of Eva is well known. The night she fell from a second story window was certainly the night the enemy planned to destroy the peace and dreams of Aaron and Amanda. God knew what the future was, and He knew before this child was conceived that she would be the main player in the faith story of this couple! Her story became a cornerstone for the story of Aaron and Amanda Crabb, the young couple who learned early on that their family had purpose, their children had purpose, and there was a plan! The child whose very name means "life" has faced death, head-on and dramatically. However, that big hand of God, that hand that knew her before she was, was there. He softened the injury. God knew. He knows her future, and I think I do, too. She is a worshipper. She innately knows what God has done for her. We don't talk about it much, but she knows. It's in her soul. She was born for the purpose of the miracle. She is ours, but she is also His. We know that. Her future is solidified and planned. He will use her. She is also my trophy.

Sophie Caroline is 7, but she is as opinionated as an adult. She is the youngest granddaughter and is Krystal's youngest child. She is her paternal grandmother's mini-me, in my opinion. Brian is an only child, and Sophie is his only child, so I suppose that's fair. If you only get one grandbaby, I guess God decided that this would be the fair thing to do. So the other Kathy, the other grandma, got to claim the gene pool for this one. That's okay. She got my spunk. (Yes, both of her grandmas are named Kathy.) Like her mom, she is fiercely independent and doesn't really care what the crowd is doing. This little girl already knows God and has committed her little soul to the Lord. She is tiny like her momma, and has the "tomboy" gene, just like Krystal did. Krystal played with tractors and trucks; so does Sophie. I recently went to her school to eat lunch with her, and she told me she always sits with boys and plays with boys. I asked her why and she said, "The girls always pretend they're allergic to peanuts, so they sit at the allergy table. They're not allergic to anything. They're pretending, and I don't like that, so I sit with the boys!" This is Sophie: just tell it like it is. I suppose this could be a bit of genetics. But in the end, the combination of beauty, bluntness, and a heart for God will take her far in life. I know. The road is already paved for this sweet girl, and all she has to do is walk it. She is my trophy, and I love her heart.

Ean William, who is 4, is our baby who was born in the great state of Texas. He was born the same month as the bus wreck, so I was absent for his birth. Granny was back in Tennessee running a nursing home for Aunt Kelly and Uncle Mike. The thing I remember the most was this: Amanda and Aaron were in the greatest transition of their life. They were leaving their family and friends behind, moving across the country to work at Cornerstone for Pastor John Hagee. They were dissolving the road ministry, transitioning to a day job, moving, and selling their home. All of this was happening at once when suddenly, oops, Amanda was pregnant. They were in shock. We all were. The fanfare before this little boy was born was minimal. They were in Texas, and we were in Tennessee; the Bowlings had the horrible bus wreck three weeks before, and the distance to Texas was not our friend in those days. However, I will never ever forget standing in my kitchen on that hot July day that Amanda was in labor. I was waiting. Then, there it was. The picture of that sweet face came across my screen with a text. It said, "He's here!" I was in love. The smile says it all. This little boy is sheer joy to his parents and everyone around him. He's the baby, the caboose. Edie was the engine; he's the red caboose. We like him around here. He owns my heart, and yes, he is a trophy. Ean is my Texas trophy.

STRONGER

26 FINDING MY VOICE

November 4, 2014. As Steve and I were sitting in our matching recliners watching Fox News, I told him I needed to chat about something. I said, "I want to take at least eight weeks off from real estate. Will you handle all of my business?"

He looked at me over his reading glasses. They had moved down the bridge of his nose, and he looked at me as if he was my third grade teacher and I was in trouble. In the normal Steve tone he said, "What did you say?"

I repeated my question and followed up with, "God told me to go write a book. I have to do this. I can't write here. There's too much activity in this house."

Our home is big, and it would seem that I could find a writing room upstairs suitable for this challenge. However, I knew what I was supposed to do.

He said, "A book? About what?"

I said, "I don't know. I just know I am getting online to book a cabin, and I plan to go to a mountain and write. God said to do it. I'm doing it."

Steve learned early on that when I bring God into a conversation, the right answer is simply, "Okay, Kathy!"

He said, "Okay, I will do whatever I need to do."

I booked the cabin. I wrote this book on a mountain while my husband was at home working tirelessly. The truth is it felt like I was eating an elephant. I would take a bite, and the story got bigger. I felt I was incapable of conveying the big things God had done. I felt incapable of doing justice to the vocabulary and "mind painting" that "good writers" manage. I felt like Moses. I argued with God, as usual. However, I said "uncle" really quick. I am a wimp. God has my number.

However, my strength is faith. I know what He can do. I know who He is. I know He does what He says He will do. So once again, I obeyed that voice that directs me to some random endeavor, which sometimes brings raised eyebrows and smirks when shared with others. That same girl who moved her kids to the back of an abandoned church decided to go to a mountain in the middle of the winter to write this book.

Why now, 2014? I am not sure. He is.

The rewrites, editing, and all of the work took much more than 10 days, but the book itself was written in exactly 10 days. Two trips to that Gatlinburg cabin perched on a cliff with a glorious view of Mt. LeConte, and this book was birthed.

I felt as if I was giving birth to a 12-pound baby. I cried the entire 10 days. I am the first to admit that it was therapeutic. I wrote 90% of it sitting on a porch in temperatures that were in the 40s and 50s. I was cold, but I needed to see God. Gazing at the smoke-covered mountain as I wrote was like having a seat beside the Creator. He was with me. He revisited my life with me. He gave me truths and insights. He reminded me of ugly shoes I had worn, ugly things I had said, and ugly things I had done. He assured me that no matter how bad I was hurt, trusting is still right. He made me feel the love that we so readily talk about but too often fail to see when we look in the mirror. I reminded Him how hard the road had been with all of the snares and an occasional trap. He reminded me that He knew all about that road because He had walked it with me, every step and every mile.

I did an inventory with Him while writing this book. We talked about blood, and love, and right and wrong. We talked about loyalty, roads, and choices. I reminded Him how hard I had worked, and He reminded me how faithful He had been. In the end, we built a stronger relationship.

I told Him how sorry I was if my selfishness had overridden my common sense regarding my choices. He assured me that imperfect choices avail big blessings. I concurred. I inventoried the apologies that I had made in my life, and I asked Him to remind me of any that I had neglected. I needed peace. I needed Him. I wasn't backsliding or acting out. I needed His blessing in a *big* way. A decade of bitterness was enough. I needed Him to apply the salve to my wounds. I had to forgive without an apology. I had to let God be God. He is. He will deal with it. I am free, and I am at peace.

The real miracle of this story is this: all six of these adult children kept walking. They were bruised and beaten. They staggered, they slowed, and at times I was scared. Their disappointment was obvious, but they kept walking. Their trust had been battered, but they kept walking. They walked. They held hands. They avoided bullets of gossip, darts thrown by jealous haters, and they kept walking. The ground was shifting, the mud was up to their ankles, but they kept walking. This family of siblings who were bound by tears and love held hands and made it to the finish line. They chose love. Because they chose love, God smiled. They won and God won. The truth was validated and honor remained. The family survived. We are the exception, not the rule. The ultimate divisive act, which was meant to divide the six kids and certainly destroy the family, didn't. Truly, blood is thicker than water, but love is thicker than blood.

27 BETTER, NOT BITTER

Many people at various times in my life have encouraged me to speak and write. I have always said no. For the last decade, I have lived behind a wall of anger, bitterness, and distrust. It's hard for God to use that. He can love you through that all day long, but He can't use it, at least not in an honest way. I could put on the robe of hypocrisy and pretend, but that's not who I am.

I was vocal and outspoken of my distrust. I remember when I met Robb and Shanda Tripp, pastors of Fireplace Fellowship in Hendersonville, Tennessee, through a real estate transaction. Robb and I started comparing "war stories." I immediately said, "Just for the record, I don't trust preachers." I know that had to be an endearing moment for him. I didn't. I knew who God was, and I knew He wasn't the culprit. I often said, "I don't have problems with God. It's just people I don't like." Yes, this was a favorite quote of mine during the "bitter" years.

However, it finally happened. A pastor who was in the "people business" reached out. Robb and Shanda Tripp, pastors who were in the "God mends broken hearts" business, working in unison, loved on me. They both spoke life to this story I had lived. God used them. Like so many random phone calls that you answer, you never know when God will put someone smack dab in the middle of your life who will help mold your future into the version of you that God wants you to be.

As I try to draw this season to a close on this sabbatical that looked at my life in the rearview mirror, I am struck by an overwhelming urge to give advice to you, my unknown reader. Those of you who have braved this literary journey with me, this first attempt to convey a story, I can see you in my mind.

Some of you are thin, some not so much. There are big blue eyes, green eyes, pretty brown eyes, wrinkled foreheads, an occasional pair of reading glasses, an even more occasional youthful haircut, but always the kind smile of a friend. Yes, you have all been my friends. When life brought the drought, thank God, you weren't fair-weather friends. When times were bad, you stayed. When times got worse, you prayed. My life has been richer because of you. Some of you I have known since I was a child; others I will meet for the first time through the words on these pages. However, we are all bonded by the fragility of our lives, the insecurity of our imperfection, and the love that we share as believers in happy endings, for truly, *this* is a happy ending.

We are all the same. Yes, I am, in many ways, just like you. I may get angry today; I may feel blessed tomorrow; I may possibly be a tiny bit bitter the next day. However, the thread that weaves through every thought that this hyperactive brain churns out is this: God is faithful.

He is good, even when life is bad. He is faithful, even when people are not. He walks with us through divorce, death, poverty, addiction, and an occasional wayward child. He is all that we need when He is all that we have. He dwells on mountains and valleys. He doesn't have superstars, just children. You matter just as much as the most famous televangelist in the world.

No matter what you have been told, you are good enough, pretty enough, skinny enough, and smart enough. You are His. You already know He loves you, but here's a newsflash: He likes you, too. He thinks you're funny. He is amused that lime green is your favorite color. He smiles when you order extra sour cream on your potato. He likes your big feet. He delights in you, the human being, the imperfect son or daughter. He laughs at your attempt at humor and marvels at your talent and intellect, for you are *His* creation. He is proud. He desperately wants you to love Him in your flawed state of humanity, just as you are.

That advice I was talking about? Get to know Him, if you don't. Taste Him and know that He is good. He will make you stronger!

KATHY JO COPPAGE, 2 YEARS OLD, 1958

THE SONGBIRDS, 1963

SIXTEEN YEARS OLD, 1972

THREE WEEKS BEFORE MY THROAT WAS CUT, 1973

THE DAY I WAS RELEASED FROM THE HOSPITAL
WITH 43 STITCHES IN MY THROAT

THE LAST KNOWN PHOTO OF MY DAD, 1969

MOMMA, 1970

KRYSTAL, MY MIRACLE BABY, AT 4 WEEKS OLD

GRACE CHAPEL, 1993

OUR FIRST CHRISTMAS AS A BLENDED FAMILY

THE FAMOUS FIRST DISNEY TRIP
AS A BLENDED FAMILY

THE FIRST CRABB FAMILY ALBUM

THE BUS I BOUGHT WITH MY RETIREMENT MONEY.
IT WAS *REALLY* NICE.

THE FIRST VERSION OF THE TOURING CRABB FAMILY

THE HOUSE MY DAD HAD BUILT FOR US
WHEN I WAS 5 YEARS OLD

THE FAMOUS RICKY SKAGGS BUS

THE CRABB FAMILY HOMECOMING, WHICH WE
LATER REBRANDED "CRABBFEST"

THE KIDS WITH RICKY SKAGGS

MY BABIES, 2005

THE KIDS ON THE RED CARPET
AT THE GRAMMYS

ACCEPTING OUR VERY FIRST DOVE AWARD AS THE CRABB FAMILY FOR THE SONG "DON'T YOU WANNA GO", WHICH MIKE PRODUCED, 2003

CRABB FAMILY BUS LIFE WITH THE BAND, ZACH, MIKE, KELLY, MICAH, LORIE, AND TERAH, 2005

TERAH REJOINS HER SIBLINGS ONSTAGE THE MORNING AFTER HER RETURN TO THE FAMILY

MY 49TH BIRTHDAY WITH MY MOM

DOVE AWARDS, 2005

NO DESCRIPTION NEEDED, 2006

OUR FIRST VACATION, 2006

THE CAR STEVE BOUGHT THE DAY AFTER
WE MET

CELEBRATING MY 50TH BIRTHDAY
A FEW DAYS LATE

ADAM & AARON'S 30TH BIRTHDAY PARTY

THE NIGHT TERAH CAME HOME

THE NIGHT BEFORE MY OPEN-HEART
SURGERY

OPEN-HEART RECOVERY

MY 57TH BIRTHDAY

THE YA-YAS, 2007

THE GOLDEN GIRLS

SINGING NEWS PHOTO SHOOT, GRANDKIDS, 2003

WITH MY BROTHER 3 MONTHS BEFORE
HE PASSED AWAY

WITH MY SISTERS THE DAY OF
MY BROTHER'S FUNERAL

GRANDCHILDREN, 2008

KRYSTAL, EDEN, CAMERON, AND SOPHIE

WITH MY GRANDCHILDREN, CHRISTMAS, 2010

ALASKAN CRUISE

ME AND MY GIRLS

THE GRANDKIDS, 2012

WITH MY "TEDDY BEAR", STEVE

ON THE STREETS OF MOROCCO, WITH STEVE
AND CRYSTAL BURCHETTE-JOHNSON

A GRAVELY ILL 2 YEAR-OLD HANNAH
IN A HOSPITAL IN BROOKLYN, NY

EVA, THE DAY AFTER HER FALL

THE BOWLING BUS WRECK

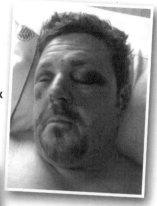

MIKE BOWLING, 24 HOURS AFTER THE WRECK

THE BOWLINGS DURING THEIR MONTHS OF
RECOVERY AT MY HOME

TERAH, KELLY, AND MIKE PERFORMING WHILE
KELLY WAS STILL IN HER BACK BRACE

AUNT NET AND MOMMA A FEW WEEKS BEFORE
MOMMA PASSED AWAY

MY BFF, LINDA BETH

MIKE

BRIAN AND JONATHAN

THE BOYS

THE SISTERHOOD

EVERYONE, CHRISTMAS 2010

ME WITH MY OLDEST DAUGHTER, KRYSTAL, AND
HER OLDEST DAUGHTER, EDEN

ME AND GRANDCHILD #13, SOPHIE

ME WITH CAMERON AND HOPE, #2 AND #3

ME AND #11, GRACIE

ME AND KATELANNE, #6

ME, EMMA, AND ASHLEIGH, #5 AND #9

MY FAVORITE PHOTO OF ME AND HANNAH, #4

ME AND CHARLEE, #10

ME AND ELI, #8, AT DISNEY

ME AND EVA, #12

ME AND EAN "THE CABOOSE", #14

ME AND LOGAN, #7

ME AND THE KIDS, CHRISTMAS, 2014

THE TRIBE, CHRISTMAS 2014

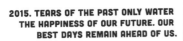

2015. TEARS OF THE PAST ONLY WATER
THE HAPPINESS OF OUR FUTURE. OUR
BEST DAYS REMAIN AHEAD OF US.

CREDITS

Too Much To Gain To Lose
(1968)
Writer: Dottie Rambo
Publisher:
DESIGNER MUSIC

Who Will Survive The Storm
(2001)
Writer: Gerald Crabb
Publisher:
BRAVO AND ENCORE MUSIC
CHRISTIAN TAYLOR MUSIC

I Know Enough
(2010)
Writer: Marcia Henry
Writer: Belinda Smith
Publishers:
CHRISTIAN TAYLOR MUSIC
SEVENTH   ROW   MUSIC

ABOUT THE AUTHOR

Kathy Crabb Hannah is the matriarch of the musical Crabb Family. She founded and managed the business of this blended family for the entire 15 years that this award-winning group toured. Kathy was the behind-the-scenes force behind the group's rise to prominence. She is a daily advocate for blended families. Kathy lives in Hendersonville, Tennessee with her husband Steve. All of her 6 adult children and 14 grandchildren also live in Hendersonville.